Ella's Song

& Other Tall Tales From The Distance

Gordon James Cook

Contents

Prologue..1

ACT 1

Living The Dream....................................7

Living The Nightmare 21

Surviving The Living 31

Fallen Angel 43

Little Pond, Big Fish............................59

Becoming Undone 77

Something New.....................................81

Manipulating Person............................85

ACT 2

Unfinished Sympathy 111

In Bloom...117

The Distance 125

Union..133

Sid 139

Near Death Experience.......................151

Back To Life 173

ACT 3

Living In The Distance 179

Let There Be Light 191

Gangles Manor 197

The Hungry Dragon 211

Dragons & Monkeys 215

The One That Got Away 219

The Friendly Wasp 227

Meanwhile at Gangle Manor 235

Prince Albert 241

Ultimate Corporate BS Success 247

Sting In The Tale 261

The Assassination Of Bon Lemon 275

An Angel's Ascent 277

Battle Of Beehive 285

Weeping Angel 289

The Awakening 295

The Lone Shark 297

Meanwhile At Gangle Manor................ 305

Father Thomas McKenzie..................... 313

The Richest Person In The Graveyard 319

Shark Face.. 335

Amortizon.. 341

Fishy Campaigning 349

Assault at Amortizon............................353

Falling Tree...................................365

The Awakening.................................367

The Crooked Vulture...........................369

Meanwhile At Gangle Manor..............371

Laissez-Faire..................................381

For The Birds..................................393

Try Not To Die................................405

First Blood....................................409

The Club House...............................417

Victory In Vulcon............................431

Hilarious Nefarious..........................437

The Unawakening.............................447

The Lonely Cloud.............................449

Rising...459

First Reveal...................................463

Revelation....................................471

Epilogue One..................................475

Epilogue Two..................................485

Final word....................................489

Acknowledgements & Final Thought......490

By The Author

The Cloud Catcher
Adventures of Charlie Thatcher

Ella's Songg
& Other Tall Tales From The Distance

In Memory of

Sharran Russell
1958- 2024

&

Ronnie Lycett
1948- 2024

Prologue

Somewhere, in The Distance, an alarm was sounding. That somewhere was a small, almost forgotten about cupboard sized room, situated in the windowless basements of the 'Interrealm Free Will Monitoring, Intervention and Parallel Correction Headquarters,' or 'IFWMI&PCHQ' for short.

The IFWMI&PCHQ was housed in a monolithic, doughnut shaped construction, with a city sized footprint with more stories than one could ever count. The sole purpose of the IFWMI&PCHQ was to monitor free will decisions being made throughout the different realms, to ensure that any choices that were being made fell within the acceptable predetermined parameters of 'The Whole'.

The Whole contains everything.
The Whole is everything.
Everything that ever was.
Everything that ever will be.
Anyone that ever was.
Anyone that ever will be.

The primary responsibility of those working for the IFWMI&PCHQ is to monitor 'beings' playing out their little stories within any of the infinite array of different realms. Beings are tricky as they have within them a certain amount of perceived free will. Each time free will is exercised a new branch spurs off within The Whole and, whilst The Whole itself is infinite, there is simply not enough space to accommodate absolutely everything.

Therefore, when an act of free will creates a branch that significantly deviates from the preordained programme, the IFWMI&PCHQ step in to initiate a 'correction protocol.' This is essentially a pruning of the unauthorised branch, thus ensuring it can continue no further.

Currently on shift, in the room where the alarm is sounding, are the experienced, though relatively lacklustre technicians, Everett (57) and DeWitt (70). They had been assigned to this room for the unenviable task of monitoring activity within a rather unremarkable little realm that contains a rather unremarkable little planet called 'Earth'. Within that realm, within that moment, an unauthorised act of free will had just occurred, triggering the alarm to sound.

"Damn it!" Everett exclaimed, whilst at the same time spilling his cup of tea.

"What's happened?" DeWitt asked from across the room.

"According to my readout, the subject has just conceived."

"Just conceived! How the hell did that happen?" DeWitt questioned despairingly.

"Do you really need me to explain that to you?" Questioned Everett.

"No, idiot. I do not need to know how 'that' happened. What I want to know is... How did it happen?"

"I was monitoring the situation. A contraceptive device was there, on the side. I just decided to give them a bit of privacy. I only looked away for a minute then the alarm sounded. I can see now that the contraceptive device has not been used."

"Beezus!" DeWitt exclaimed. "You know how high profile this subject is. The boss is going to haul us over the coals for this one. Plus, this is like the hundredth deviation already, just on this shift."

"Well, that's not really our fault, is it? We're understaffed and underfunded. Nobody seems to care about this realm anymore. It's hardly surprising we have so many deviants these days."

DeWitt stopped talking and drew a deep breath. After letting it out he continued.

"One of us needs to tell the boss."

"Well, I'm not doing it." Everett protested. "I called him last time. It's your turn."

"Last time was for a nobody. This one is a high-profile case. I called in the last high-profile case so this time it's your turn."

The pair argued back and forth in this manner for a while. Eventually DeWitt produced a coin from his pocket. The coin was silver, an equilateral-curve heptagon in shape, patterned with clouds on one side.

"We'll flip for it." DeWitt announced.

"I call clouds." Everett insisted.

Dewitt flipped. The coin landed cloudy side up. Reluctantly, DeWitt made his way to the communication device which in this case, due to the budget restraints, was an old antique telephone. Picking up the mouthpiece DeWitt dialled the number and waited as it rang on the other side.

The call was answered.

"Yes?" Questioned the receiver.

"Your highness. This is technician ER10 to the power of 123, calling from the IFWMI&PCHQ."

"Yes..." A pause. "DeWitt. What do you want?"

"Well Sir, we have had, um... Well, we've kind've had another deviation event."

A sigh came from the other side.

"You seem to have nothing but deviation events these days. Why are you calling me?"

"Well Sir, I'm afraid that this one is regarding subject, LG101."

Silence.

"Sir? Sir? Are you still there?"

The call continued, and DeWitt filled in his boss on all the intimate details. After a time, the call ended, and DeWitt went back to work.

At the other end Sid turned to his assembled guests to make an announcement.

"Apologies all. It appears that our work for today is not quite complete. We have one more correction event that we need to arrange."

A collective groan went up from the small assembly. Reluctantly they proceeded to put down their various drinks and snacks, before returning to their seats at the table.

Living The Dream

We begin our story this time not in the sky, but on the ground. We are surrounded by shades of green, not blue. It is late spring. We are in a park. There are many species of tree here and they are all fully dressed in new coats.

Currently we are amongst the pines. If you care to be still for a moment you may well spot a squirrel or two, dashing from tree to tree, going about their business. Lend an ear to the sky and you will be rewarded with a myriad of songs from the birds above.

We are sitting on a bank. The park's landscape rolls away downhill, at the bottom of which is a large lake. The lake is filled with fishes, patrolled by ducks and governed by a family of white swans. The park extends beyond the lake, to a wooded area that contains a miniature railway track. The air today is gentle, warm and, thanks to the many trees, laced richly with oxygen.

Let us take a breath.
A deep breath.
Breathe in then.
That's it.
Breathe deep now.
Breathe deep into the bottom of your lungs.
Hold it.
Hold it.
Hooold it...
Okay, now let it go.
Let it all go and relax.

I think we are ready to meet the hero of our tale. There is no need to be nervous, she won't bite.

Behind you, further up the bank from where you are sitting, is a bandstand, forged to resemble an elaborate birdcage. Bands still sometimes come to play here. Today however, sitting on the edge of the bandstand, there is a young girl. Aged six, of Asian/British descent, straight silk black hair tied in pigtails. She is reading her favourite book. It is a book about clouds. This girl is lost to a world that only she can see.

This young soul has already proven herself independent. She is trusted to be alone in the park without adult supervision. You may have assumed that this park is a public space. One day it will be, but today this is the young girl's garden. Her father is the son of a wealthy couple that own a successful international business.

Her name is Ella. Ella Songg.

Ella has been reading for a couple of hours. Closing her eyes, she puts her book to one side and listens to the birds.

Ella has a gift, though she has yet to realise this. Ella can hear music in ways that the average human being never could. Her mind follows, distinguishes, understands each individual note as if it were a word.

Today the birds are generally content. Ella can't help noticing though that there is something agitated beginning to stir within their chatter. It seems that a storm may be approaching.

Ella is hungry. She puts her concern to one side, opens her eyes, stands then skips from the bandstand to make her way back to the house. Come on, let's follow.

On route to the house Ella runs into a man known to her only as Fozz.

"Hi Fozz."

"Hello Miss Song. How are you on this fine spring day?"

Fozz maintains the park grounds. He is Ella's favourite staff member. He will often take Ella for a spin in his buggy when out inspecting the grounds.

"I'm good thank you Fozz. I've just been reading my book on the bandstand. Now I'm going to get some lunch."

"Still reading the same book I see." Fozz nodded toward the book in Ella's hand. "Well, don't let me keep you. I have work to do. Would you like a ride back to the house?"

"No, that's okay. It's a nice day. I think I might quite like the walk."

"Very well young miss."

Fozz hopped into his buggy and Ella resumed her journey.

Ella's family home, or rather mansion, is a grand affair. Pitched at the top of the bank, built from old grey stone, it is perfectly placed to overlook the surrounding grounds, all the way down to the lake.

There are no less than seven high pitched windows adorning the southern facade of the ground floor. An additional seven windows can be found in parallel on the floor above. The central windows are framed in a grand stone arch. The overall effect is contradictory. Both imposing and inviting.

As Ella approaches the house, she spots her father's car parked outside. Her father is chauffeur driven. The car is a luxury model, top of the range, though this means nothing to Ella. To a six-year-old a car is just a car. The reason she does get excited when she sees it is that she knows that this is the car that drives her dad. If the car is here, then so is her dad. Ella breaks into a run for the final hundred yards to the front door.

Through the front door is the entrance hallway. The walls are painted soft red. The high roof, door frames, door arches and all other details painted a crisp white. A grand portrait of someone, supposedly important, hung to the left. To the right is the bottom of the staircase, that rises about halfway up the wall before taking a sharp left then disappearing into the floor above.

The floor of the hallway is wooden, laid in a dark rich oak. A relatively battered looking oriental rug has been centrally placed here. There are two doorways to the left, but Ella ignores these and makes straight ahead for an archway, and second hallway, that leads into a kitchen at the back of the house. Bursting into the kitchen Ella finds her parents.

"ELLA!"

Her dad shouted.

"What have I told you about running in the house?"

Ella stopped dead in her tracks, the wind knocked from her sails.

"Bruce, don't be so harsh." This was Mary, Ella's mother. "She hasn't seen you in over two weeks. She's excited is all."

Conceding, Bruce relaxed a little. Going down on his haunches he now opened his arms, offering a welcoming smile.

"I'm sorry Ella. Daddy has had a tough couple of weeks. How are you sweetheart? Come give your dad a hug."

Ella perked up and let herself fall into her father's embrace, who gave an affectionate growl as he hugged her tight.

"I've missed you button. How have you been? Have you been behaving for your mum?"

"Yes."

"And what have you been doing this morning?"

"I've been at the bandstand reading my book."

"Let me see which book."

Ella showed her father the book. Bruce put Ella down and let out a disappointed sigh.

"Ella, are you seriously still reading that? It's a kid's book. You're over six years old now."

"But I like this book. It has clouds in it, and dragons and monkeys and a boy named Charlie an..."

"Yes, yes, yes Ella. You have told me about it before. But don't you think it's about time you were reading something a bit more... I don't know, a bit more grown up maybe. Something about maths, or science perhaps."

At this point Mary chipped in.

"Leave her alone Bruce. She will only be six once. She has the rest of her life to read grown up books."

So, these were Ella's parents. Bruce and Mary Songg. Bruce was the only child of Vietnamese entrepreneurs, Thich and Tung Songg, who together had established a successful brewery business in Vietnam. Bruce had in fact just returned from a business trip to Vietnam. Over the years Thich and Tung built the business into the country's biggest brewery, home to the infamous 'Sing' beer. Success made them wealthy. So much so that they decided to send their son for an education abroad.

When Bruce turned six, he was put on a plane and sent to the UK for an English education. Growing up in the UK, Bruce inevitably went on to run a UK arm for the brewery business. At nearly six foot two Bruce was unusually tall for a man of Asian descent. Currently dressed in a slim fitting blue woollen suit, modern rounded glasses, and sporting a pristine swept over haircut, he was very smart looking too.

Mary was of mixed race. Unlike Bruce she had never known her parents, having been adopted as a baby. Shortly after being placed in a home her adopted parents split. Her adopted mother, Western in descent, found bringing up a child of mixed race difficult on her own. Mary was thus given up to the foster system and spent her childhood moving from one foster home to the next.

Mary was, by any standard, a very beautiful woman. Her hair was dark, shiny, and long, straight down to just below her shoulders. A slim, but round face, with almond shaped eyes. Dressed smart but informal, Mary wore a long sleeve, collarless cotton top, faintly patterned with cherry blossom shadows, buttoned down the front. This was complemented with an orange and blue checked scarf, draped around her neck, reaching down to her waist on both sides.

Mary had grown accustomed to wearing a scarf as it covered what she felt was a rather unsightly birthmark. Situated centrally on the back of her neck, the birthmark was in the shape of a musical note. Mary hated it and always sought to cover it up. Ella thought it was wonderful.

Black slim fitting jeans and a pair of casual white trainers finished off the outfit. Stylish but understated. No one would guess at the obscene amount each article of clothing had cost.

Mary was working behind a bar when she first met Bruce. He was meant to be attending a conference that evening, supposedly for aspiring billionaires, at a nearby hotel. Tragically, before the event had kicked off, someone was attacked and fatally wounded in the hotel lobby. The attacker had seemingly vanished as soon as they'd exited the hotel. The event was cancelled, and the hotel was cordoned off by the time Bruce arrived. Not wanting to go home he headed to the nearest pub for a drink. That pub happened to be the one in which Mary worked. Bruce was instantly smitten and soon enough he had charmed Mary into thinking that the feeling was mutual.

They did share an understanding of one another, Mary having grown up in care homes, Bruce in boarding schools. In everything else though they remained as opposites, Bruce oblivious to his many privileges.

A night of drunken passion came to pass, nine months after which baby Ella was born and the couple married. Mary felt wholly blessed by Ella's arrival. Bruce however, always with one eye on the business, would have preferred a boy.

Having been focused on work his whole life he certainly would have preferred his child to be away in some form of formal education by now. As it was, Mary, who felt that she and Bruce had both been denied a childhood, had put her foot down. Mary insisted that Ella would not suffer in any of the ways they had. Mary would stay at home with Ella for her earliest years allowing her to be the child that she was, safe in the knowledge that she was loved.

Bruce had relented, but as time wore on, he started to tire of this arrangement more and more. He was becoming especially concerned about her obsession with the silly book about clouds. He knew Ella tended to be a dreamer and he did not want to see her with her head stuck in those clouds forever.

"So how was your trip? It was incredible news to hear that your parents recovered so quickly. I know that they are still not sure about me, but I am very pleased for you." Mary gave the top of Bruce's right arm a gentle touch. "Have the doctors found out what was wrong with them yet?"
"No, not yet." Bruce replied.
"And how about how they recovered so suddenly. I mean, two weeks ago when you left, they were unconscious. At death's door."
Bruce rubbed the back of his neck with his right hand, looking away.
"No. No, they have no idea. Seems it's all a bit of a mystery."
"I'd say. To think two weeks ago that they would be back on their feet and on a plane coming to England. It's unbelievable. What time are they due to land?"

A month prior, both of Bruce's parents fell sick. Really sick. They had returned from a meeting, with a potential new client, and were both feeling a little out of salts. The next morning, they were located by house staff, having both fallen into a coma. In the days that followed their conditions deteriorated.

First the family doctor called, suggesting Bruce needed to come home. Then the family solicitor called. He felt it right at this stage to inform Bruce that he had been removed from his parent's will following Ella's birth. It was then that Bruce booked his flight tickets.

After Bruce had been in Vietnam for a couple of days both his parents miraculously awoke. A few days later and they showed no effects of having been sick and were seemingly both as fit as fiddles. The doctors had no explanations for either their sickness or their recovery. To all intents and purposes, they were both fitter than they had ever been, like awakening from a restorative sleep. So full of life were they that they declared they wanted to come to the UK and see their granddaughter and daughter in law. They would be bringing the family solicitor with them too, as they intended to write Bruce back into their will. They had only been to the UK once before, to inspect the UK arm of the business. That time they had been too busy to visit Bruce's family home.

For himself Bruce had booked an earlier flight back to the UK. He wanted to ensure everything would be to their standards when they arrived. He had landed in the early hours of that day. His parents would currently be somewhere over Dubai.

A radio had been playing music in the background whilst Bruce and Mary had been talking. The music stopped. The hourly news report began.

The newsreader was reporting on the cost-of-living crises and the worrying rise in petty crime. Bruce picked up on the story.

"Petty criminals. Pah. Nothing more than wasters and chancers if you ask me."

"Bruce. You can't say that. Some of the people out there are having a really hard time of things at the moment."

"Well, they could always get a job."

"Bruce, are you not listening to the news? A lot of these people already have jobs. More than one for some of them. The cost of living forces some people to make tough choices."

"Tough choices. Hah. They should try running a national business. All these people have got to decide is, 'do I steal or don't I?' Doesn't seem that tough to me."

Mary looked saddened.

"Talking about tough choices." Bruce went on. "That reminds me. I must let the motor dealer know this week whether I want red or blue leather trim in the new car." Bruce raised his hands to his head. "Argh. It's all too difficult."

Mary looked away from her husband, wondering when he had become so detached from the world. The newsreader then made an announcement that instantly changed the atmosphere.

"We interrupt this programme to bring you some breaking news. We have just heard that a UK airways flight, from Vietnam to the UK, has crashed. The crash has occurred five minutes out of Dubai airport. Concerned relatives can call the following number for more information. 0110 999 666."

Mary looked at her husband who was standing frozen, pale. This was the moment that the whole world, their whole world, was turned upside down.

Living The Nightmare

Ella is sitting in the bandstand, listening to conversations between the birds, reading her new book. Mary is sitting on a bench, opposite the bandstand, pretending to read a magazine. Anyone watching closely will notice that Mary has not turned a page now for at least half an hour. A small dog snaps her out of her reverie when it shuffles over and starts sniffing about, before cocking its leg against the bench to relieve itself.

"Oh my god, I'm so sorry. Jack!" The stranger shouted at the dog. "Jack, stop that. Naughty boy!"

Mary looked down at Jack with indifference. Jack looked back at Mary with the same indifference. Both Mary and Jack then looked at Jack's owner. Mary's eyes met but her lips made no effort to move. The owner then bent down, hooked a lead onto Jack's collar and swiftly led Jack away.

It had been almost a year since that fateful day when the plane had gone down. The world looked very different for the Songg family now. After the initial shock had passed the family flew to Vietnam for the funerals of Bruce's parents. With the family solicitor gone, Bruce liaised with a new solicitor, to enquire about his claim on the business and his potential inheritance. Unfortunately, no official update had been filed since Thich and Tung had written Bruce out of their will.

They had apparently written Bruce out to protect the business from Mary whom, at the time, they believed to be a mere opportunist. Mary to them was, after all, a nobody that had grown up in care and worked in a bar. She had no money, no real prospects and had, they believed, trapped their son into wedlock by becoming pregnant.

Following recovery from their illnesses the couple seen the world in a different light, and they had informed their family solicitor that whilst in the UK they would write Bruce back into the will. They would make it their first proper family celebration, including Mary. They had though taken no action before boarding their plane. There was nothing in writing, thus there was nothing in law, and the only credible witness to their intentions had been lost in the plane accident with them.

As a result, the business was entrusted to its senior board members, each receiving an equal number of shares. Collectively the board decided that they were no longer interested in the UK market, especially not since it had broken away from Europe. They voted nine to one in favour of immediately setting in motion the liquidation of the UK arm of the business. All UK employees, including Bruce, lost their jobs.

Adding insult to injury the house, that Bruce, Mary and Ella lived in, the car that was used to ferry the Songgs around, the flat in the city that Bruce used when working there. All these things were listed as assets of the business and all these things were liquidated at the same time. The Songgs had left the UK wealthy but returned homeless and a great deal poorer. Bruce did, thankfully, receive a very substantial payout to compensate him for his redundancy, but that was all he had received.

xx lol xx

After several weeks, following their return from Vietnam, a time where they had been living in a hotel near the airport, Bruce returned one evening, clearly excited and grinning ear to ear for the first time since the funeral.

"Mary, Ella. Pack your bags. We are getting out of this dump."

"Really?" Mary asked. "What's happened? Where are we going?"

"I've managed to rent us a place. Not far from here. Not as grand as our old house but it will only be temporary. Until I land one of the positions I have applied for."

Bruce had been busy reaching out to old contacts since they returned. He was uber confident that one of them would want to snap him up for a senior position somewhere. So far no one had.

"Bruce, how much is this place? Can we afford it?"

"Ah, relax Mary. You know how much money I got from those bastards that stole my company. It only has to last until I land back on my feet."

So far, whilst the family might have had to suffer the indignity of living in a hotel room they were, to all intents and purposes, carrying on as they had before. Bruce had insisted that they go out for dinner each night and the restaurants he had been choosing were not the cheapest. Mary knew he had been compensated a substantial amount of money. She also knew that he had never had to worry about money before. Budgeting was something that only poor people had to worry about and as far as he was concerned the Songgs were still flying high. It was a dark feeling of trepidation then that Mary now felt as she went about the business of packing up a bag for her and Ella.

Mary was surprised when they left the hotel and started heading in a taxi toward the city centre. Everyone knew the centre was the most expensive.

"Bruce. Why are we heading toward the centre? Won't the rents there be more expensive?"

"Relax." He said again. That word was starting to grate. "I got us a place in the centre so it will save me time and money commuting."

"Commuting to what? You haven't got a job yet."

"No, not yet. But I will have. It is only a matter of time." Bruce flashed a confident grin in support of his statement.

Mary started to fear the worst and soon enough the worst was confirmed. They pulled up in the middle of one of the quieter city streets, to the curb of a beautiful white Georgian style townhouse.

"Ta da!" Exclaimed Bruce. "Fully furnished too. Done pretty well, if I may say so myself."

"Bruce. What is this? We can't afford this. What have you done."

"Relax." He said it again. This though was one time to many. Through gritted teeth Mary responded.

"Tell me to relax again Bruce. Go on. I dare you."

Less confident now Bruce changed tact.

"Okay, Mary, I can see you have some concerns. But seriously, I have done the maths. This place is within our means. I want only the best for you and Ella. I'm going to have a new job in no time, then you'll be glad I slipped the estate agent a little extra to secure this place."

"You what! You know what, forget it. I don't want to hear any more."

The Songgs exited the taxi and entered the house. Bruce gave them the grand tour. The house was beautiful and, just for a minute, Mary managed to forget herself and their troubles and enjoy the moment. After the tour they ordered take out. Sitting down to eat Mary declared that she would get a job to help contribute.

"Ah, ah, ahh."

Bruce said whilst waving chopsticks in the air.

"No way. Nothing changes. The plan stays the same. You get to stay at home with Ella until she is ten. Besides, we have no staff now. Keeping this place clean will take up most of your time."

Turning his attention back to his food Bruce failed to notice Mary's expression freeze. He also failed to notice Ella noticing him failing to notice.

xx lol xx

So it went, from that day on, Bruce would leave the house early each morning to attend interviews, whilst Mary and Ella were left to tend to the house and each other. Every afternoon, to escape the house, they walked to the local park and sat for a while as the world passed them by. Whilst nowhere near as big as their previous grounds, the park did offer them both a sense of familiarity and comfort in what had suddenly become an uncomfortable reality.

They had been in their new house for over ten months. Bruce's promised CEO position had failed to materialise. Initially his expectations were so high that no one was willing to offer what he expected. As he started to face the truth, gradually reducing his expectations, he came to find that he had already reduced his options, burning down several bridges behind him. In the end he presented as a man that reeked of desperation, not confidence. No respectable business was going to touch him.

His mood had been getting progressively worse at home. Mary was no fool and knew that the money must be running out. Previously she had felt scared to broach the subject, but tonight she was going to confront him. Bring him back to earth. Remind him that together they could work out a way. Mary extracted herself from her thoughts, stood up from the bench and called to Ella.

"Come on Ella. Let's get tea on before your father gets home. Hopefully he will have some good news for us today."

"Huh." Ella looked up from her book, then muttered under her breath. "I doubt it."

"What was that?"

"Nothing mum. Nothing. Just tired."

"Hmm." Mary offered. "I see you have been reading your new book. How are you enjoying it?"

"I think I enjoy clouds more than numbers." Is all that Ella offered in reply.

When they arrived home Bruce was already there, sitting in silence in the kitchen. He looked dishevelled. He looked despondent. He looked broken. As soon as Mary saw him, she turned to Ella.

"Ella, go upstairs to your room for a minute please. I need to talk to your father."

"But I need a drink of..."

"Upstairs please Ella. Now."

Ella knew better than to argue when Mary used that tone so she swiftly obliged. Mary entered the kitchen, pulled out the stool next to Bruce and sat down with him. Mimicking him Mary started into the same middle distance as she spoke.

"It's gone isn't it. The money has all gone." It wasn't a question.

"Mary, I'm so sorry. I, I... I don't know how this has happened."

"I do." Came Mary's curt reply.

As if animated by lightning, Bruce suddenly jumped up from his stool.

"I know what to do." He said. "I know how to make this better."

"How Bruce? What are you going to do to make this better?"

"You have to trust me, Mary. I am going to go out there and make this better, you just have to trust me."

"How Bruce?"

"Trust me Mary. I will fix this. I will get our money back."

"But it's not about the money..."

Bruce wasn't listening. He lent over Mary's shoulder, kissed her cheek, then he was gone, down the hall and out through the front door. He didn't notice Ella sitting on the stairs. That would be the last time either Mary or Ella would remember seeing him.

Surviving The Living

Ella is sitting on a well-worn, tatty looking rubber swing, supported by a rust covered frame, located at the edge of the local recreational ground (aka 'the rec'). Ella is alone. It is spring again, early evening and still warm. The sun is still glowing but inside her soul is overcast. Today is an anniversary, though not the kind that one celebrates. Today, seven years ago, her father Bruce had walked out of Ella's life, never to return.

Neither Mary nor Ella had heard a single word from Bruce since that day. After a week had passed, they had reported Bruce missing. The police had apparently found evidence of Bruce's passport being used and concluded he had gone to start a new life back in Vietnam. They were busy of course with real cases so were satisfied enough at this to close the case down.

Bruce had left Mary and Ella on their own. They had no money to speak of and Mary did not have a job. The estate agent of their house eventually called, demanding payment of rent that was already, unbeknown to Mary, some way in arrears. Mary and Ella were evicted the following month. They left the house with only the possessions they could carry. Having no family to turn to, they spent the next three months together in emergency accommodations.

Between them they fell into a shared narrative that Bruce had abandoned them soon after Ella was born. This was easier, and much less painful to convey. In some ways it was also the truth.

Eventually they were offered a house in a nearby rural town. The house was situated at the heart of a council estate at the top of that town. Due to their mixed-race heritage Mary and Ella stood out amongst their new neighbours. Initial reactions to their arrival were generally hostile. Ella however was determined to make a go of it.

Ella's mind flashed back to those very first days on the estate. Their house was close to the rec so Ella had decided to venture there, thinking it would be a good place to meet some of the other local kids. She put on her favourite white trainers, which were also her only trainers, grabbed her latest library book and ventured out.

As it happened, on that day, Ella ended up sitting on the very same swing on which she was sitting now. Her new book at the time was a science book. It presented different theories as to the actual science behind bird song. By now Ella could understand all bird communications by ear. However, she still found the science that went behind some of it fascinating. Ella remembered being lost in that book and not noticing the gang of girls approaching. How could she have known then that reading in public was frowned upon by some members of her new community.

The leader of the gang was a girl named Angelica Wright. 'Angel' to her friends. Angel had thought of herself as a leader since birth. She took the role very seriously and always sought to lead by example. It was a shame however that the examples she led by were mostly bad. Standing at 5.8ft, Angel was tall. She was also very stocky. Angel was dressed in an oversized hoodie, with large print graphics. Currently she was wearing black leggings, arguably a little small for her size, and retro style treads, predominately white in colour. Her lank bottle blonde hair was pulled back into a tight ponytail and cheap bling was draped here and there about her person. The hoops in her ears looked big enough to hold a couple of hand towels. Angle's crew, bar one, all seemed happy to emulate similar stylings.

"What you doin sittin on my swing?"

"Oh, sorry. I was just... Well, I am new to the area an..."

"I didn't ask you if you was new to the area did I? What I asked is, what you doin sittin on my swing?"

This time the question was delivered more aggressively, rousing a few supporting noises and nods of the head from Angel's assembled crew.

"Sorry. I, I didn't realise that this swing belonged to someone. Here. I can move..." Ella spoke whilst moving to get up from the swing.

"Oi!" Exclaimed Angel, rather loudly. "Where d'ya think you're going? I didn't say you could go anywhere, did I?"

By this point Angel's little gang had circled around the swing. Ella started to realise she might be in danger. She could feel her heart rate increasing, panic rising in her chest.

"What's your name then?" Questioned Angel.

"Ella." Came the reply, a little un-certainly. "Ella Songg."

A few sniggers were omitted by the gang at the sound of her name.

"Ha. Song." Angel repeated the name but pronounced it incorrectly. "What kind of name is that? That ain't a name I ever heard before. So, what are ya. Chinese?"

Another member of the gang chipped in, offering, "Japanese?"

Then came, "Kidneys?" from a third.

Angel was about to say something else then stopped. She turned her head to glare at the member of her gang who had just spoken.

"What?" Questioned the culprit, under Angel's gaze. "It rhymes with Japanese, don't it?"

"Idiot." Is all Angel offered in return. Turning her attention back onto Ella now. "So, what is it then? What are you?"

"Well actually I..." Ella started.

"Well actually I, I, I... I don't care." Interrupted Angel, stealing the moment and earning a fresh round of cackles from the gang. "You all look the same to me anyway." More cackles.

Ella was going to tell Angel that she was of course British but now thought better of it and stayed silent.

"What's that you got there?" Angel demanded, looking at the book in Ella's hands.

Ella looked down. "It's a book." Came her simple reply.

"I can see that it's a book sweet cheeks. Do you think I'm thick or sumin? Give it here then. Let me have a look."

Angel snatched the book from Ella's hands.

"Bird song!" She announced out loud for the benefit of the group. "What are you? Some kind of swot, a teacher's pet?" Flicking through the pages, though not looking at them, Angel then stated. "You think you're cleverer than us don't ya. Think you're special or sumin?"

Ella had learned enough already to not say anything in reply. Instead, she took that moment as an opportunity to examine her shoes. She really would need a new pair soon.

Already tired of goading her prey, Angel tossed the book back toward Ella. The book landed at Ella's feet. Ella bent down to pick the book up. As she did so Angel grabbed her by the hair and yanked it. Hard.

Ella's hands instinctively went to her head. Satisfied with the resulting momentum of Ella's reaction, Angel let go and Ella went stumbling forwards toward the floor. She grazed both her knees and her wrists as she fell onto the concrete surrounding the swing. Angel then bent down herself to retrieve the book. After taking it from the floor she proceeded to tear out and screw up clumps of pages. When she was satisfied, she threw what remained of the book at Ella. Then she spat at her. Then she laughed. Then her whole gang laughed.

Collectively the group decided that they'd had enough fun. Whilst shuffling past, leaving the scene, each took a turn in calling Ella a loser. That encounter had set the tone for Ella's existence on the estate. She did not fit here, but she had nowhere else to go. From that moment on Ella did her best to become invisible to the world.

xx lol xx

Ironically, Ella had since learnt that the swing gave her the best view of who was entering and leaving the rec, thus making it the safest place for her to hang out.

Finishing her current contemplation, she looked up to see Angel and her gang entering at the far end of the rec. It was time for Ella to leave.

She exited the rec through an alleyway that ran between two houses, out onto a road at the centre of a street. Roughly in the middle of the street another road, again with houses either side, led away down a hill. Halfway down that hill was an offshoot into a cul-de-sac, then further on down was another offshoot. This is where Ella's house was located.

Ella's house was, some might say, conveniently placed opposite a local shop. This shop however was a magnet for the local kids, who liked to hang around outside each night until the early hours, smoking weed, drinking cider, swearing, and occasionally having fisticuffs with each other.

A past time that they often indulged in involved calling up the police for a chase. From a phone box they would call, pretending to be a resident, complaining that the local kids, aka them, were causing trouble, vandalising, stealing or fighting. Within minutes a police car would show up and they would scatter, like bed bugs in the light. Ella supposed that at least it gave them something to do, which kept them out of trouble. It suited the police too. Chasing bored kids was good training, low risk and justified the ever-increasing council taxes being imposed onto the rest of the district.

Arriving at her house Ella paused at the gate for a moment. A rusted, pointless addition to the house as it always sat open, wedged in by the surrounding weeds in the concrete pathway.

Behind the gate are the steps up to the house. Next to the steps was a small concrete drive. Also pointless as the Songgs did not own a car. Nevertheless, there was a large oil stain embedded into the concrete, but the area was home only to some random old red bricks and a few crumbled breeze blocks.

Ella walked through the open gateway, up to the yellow front door, put her key in the lock, opened it and went inside. The door opened into a short hallway. To Ella's right are the stairs up. Immediately opposite the top of the stairs is a toilet. This is partitioned and the room next door contains a green bath and sink. There is a shower attachment in the bath, the type that has rubber ends that plug onto each tap before use. The type where one must hold the showerhead when washing, waiting for the inevitable moment that the water gets too hot and scolds.

Coming out of the bathroom there is a short landing, with two bedrooms of equal size to the right. Squeezed between the two rooms is an airing cupboard that also houses a tank for hot water. Back downstairs the hallway leads directly to a small kitchen at the back of the house. The kitchen in turn leads to a relatively large living room that runs back down the house, parallel to the hallway.

A small table, below waist height, sits in the hallway. A mirror hangs above it. On the table is an old looking dish, a hairline crack running through its middle. The dish is meant as a place to put keys but is also home to a dead watch battery and a few crooked hair pins. A telephone might have sat upon the table, but Ella's mum could not afford a landline. Nor could she afford the internet.

Ella had to make do with 3G and the relatively small allowance her sim only PAYG deal offered. Her mobile was an old model. Her mum had been given it by a friend at work. It wasn't much but Ella was grateful. Besides, it didn't matter much as Ella was a loner without the same need for a social media presence as all the other kids her age seemed to have.

Mary had already left to attend her second job. She worked evenings as a health care assistant for a care home down the road. In the daytime she worked on the tills at the local supermarket.

When the pair had arrived on the estate they were in serious financial hardship. It did not take long before Mary had sought out and accepted the help of a legitimate local payday loan shark.

This business was run by a guy named Mick. He seemed nice enough, as long as Mary kept up with her payments. In fact, Ella was pretty sure that Mick had a thing for her mum. Especially as he made a point of coming to the house each week to collect Mary's payments. He said he wanted to save her the hassle of getting to the office. As accommodating as Mick was, it didn't seem to matter how hard Mary worked. She could never quite get clear from the interest on that original loan. This is why Mary worked two jobs, because it was necessary to make ends meet. Ella spent most of her evenings on her own as a result.

Tonight, like most nights then, Ella would have to make her own tea. The kitchen she was standing in was tired looking by modern standards. It was, however, fully functional. Opening one of the browning cupboard doors, that didn't sit quite right on its hinges, Ella peered inside. There she found a can of tuna fish, still in date. A half bag of pasta twirls. Some dried noodles. An almost empty bottle of ketchup, red crust hardened about the lid, and a box of instant mash, one sachet remaining. She opted for the pasta.

Ella filled an old looking pan with water from the drippy tap then placed it onto the electric plate hob to heat up. She then opened the door to the small under counter fridge that sat next to the cooker. Bending down she found inside a half box of passata and a plastic pot containing some already grated, though rather plastic looking cheese. Ella clocked the almost empty pint of milk, already two days past its use by date. She sighed. They would need to visit the foodbank again soon. The milk though put her in mind of a cup of tea, so Ella closed the fridge door and flicked on the old plastic kettle.

Ella paused to take a breath. Leaning against the kitchen worktop she looked around at her surroundings. They did not fit in here. They had no family. They did not know where they came from. They did not know where they were heading. Actually, that was not totally true. Ella did know where she was heading tomorrow, and that was worse. Tomorrow was Monday and Ella was heading back to school.

The kettle started to rumble, coming to the boil. Then came a loud click and all the electrics went off. Ella let out another sigh. Hopefully they were not on the emergency already, otherwise it would be dry crackers and water for tea again tonight.

Fallen Angel

Monday morning. Angel and her crew are sat round the shops, not far outside the school gates. They are sharing some banter whilst passing around a vape stick, getting a quick nicotine hit before starting the tedious school day. Ella, rucksack hanging from her left shoulder, walks past, head down, on her way to registration.

"Look at her, stuck up cow." Angel makes this casual observation to the others as Ella passes the group, just within earshot.

Michelle, or 'Shell' to her mates, exhales a large cloud of iced grape vapour, coughing a little.

"Yeah, stupid bitch. She thinks she's so special that one."

"Leave it out Shell. She's just keeping her head down." This is Beatrice, 'Bea' for short. The only voice of reason within the group.

"What you saying Bea?" Angel questioned. "Do you fancy her or sumin?"

The truth, if it were ever to be told, is that Angel herself secretly thought Ella was pretty. She could never admit that though. Not even to herself. So, she went on.

"You an Asian lover or sumin? Fancy a Chinese for your tea do ya?"

"Yeah Bea."

This was Jackie, who piped up now. Not the brightest by any stretch of the imagination. She did however hold the record for downing a whole bag of mixed jelly sweets in less than ten minutes. An achievement of which she was immensely proud.

"You love Kidneys." She jibed.

"Beezus Jacks! How many times do I have to tell you that 'kidneys' is not a race." Angel said this with a furrowed brow.

"Yeah Jackie. You're so thick sometimes. My mum reckons she's Chinese. Reckons her an her mum came here on one of them little boats so that they could claim our benefits."

"How is your mum Shell?" Bea questioned. "Still on the sick?"

"Yeah." Confirmed Shell. "It's her anxiety ain't it. She wants to work but the doc keeps signing her off. So unfair."

"Yeah." Agreed Bea sarcastically. "So unfair that."

Angel snatched the vape stick from Shell and took a long draw. Whilst blowing out the vapour she mused.

"Well girls, she definitely ain't one of us. We got hockey this morning ain't we?"

"Yeah." Confirmed Shell.

"Right then." Said Angel. "I think it's about that time again that we took her down a peg or two, what do you say? Remind her how we do things in our country."

"Leave her be Angel. She's not hurting anyone." Bea protested.

"How about we leave you alone." Was Angel's cold response. "You can be a 'billy no mates' like that little loser too if you want."

Bea held eye contact for a moment, then looked down at her feet.

"Thought so." Angel confirmed. "You just don't worry your pretty little head about it. In fact, when we're on the hockey pitch, all any of yous need to do is make sure she gets the puck. I'll take care of the rest."

Angel took a final long draw on the vape stick, then casually flung it at Bea's feet.

"Pick that up will you doll." Not even looking in Bea's direction whilst she said this, Angel turned to leave. "Come on girls. We don't wanna be late for school now do we?"

With that the girls all moved on, Bea a good step or two behind. She couldn't help but correct Angel under her breath.

"It's called a ball, not a puck. We play field hockey in 'our' country. Idiot."

xx lol xx

Later that morning Ella had arrived at what was possibly her least favourite place in the whole world. A sports field. Although to be more precise this one was a hockey pitch. As part of the retarded and archaic National Curriculum it was still deemed necessary by those in power that children should partake in at least two hours of physical education each week regardless of aptitude, ability or interest. Ella had no objection to the encouragement of physical exercise. It's just that for someone like Ella, being forced to partake in sporting competition felt degrading, demoralising and humiliating. Made worse by the fact that Ella's mum could not stretch to afford the school's sports uniform of choice, thus had to wear a second-hand outfit, snapped up in a charity shop, in the colours of a different school from somewhere out of town. Ella was also just not very good at sport, which inevitably meant being the last girl standing any time the picking of teams was carried out.

As it was then, Ella found herself standing in a left half position on a hockey pitch, on what had turned into a damp and dreary day. Ella was always placed in the same position but did not mind, nor care for that matter. Ella had players both in front of her and behind her. It was much easier to not get involved in the action here, to disappear in this position, to not draw the angst of her fellow players who believed that winning a game of hockey meant something. So far in today's game though things were panning out a little different.

Angel and her crew, Shell, Bea, and wacky Jackie were all on the opposing team. Normally the four would ignore her completely, which suited her just fine, but today they were all actively trying to play Ella into the match.

Angel would nod to one of the others, who would then knock the ball in Ella's direction. Angel would then start running full tilt, before another of Ella's teammates intercepted to catch the pass and reverse the flow of play. This had been going on for the whole first half, of which they were now approaching the end. It was clear that Angel was not happy with her fellow teammates and had been growing increasingly frustrated throughout the half. Now, in the last 5 minutes, Angel called out to Jackie. "Hit it to Ella. Now. Whack it!"

Shell, always one to do as she was told, hit the ball toward Ella with some force. Ella looked up and realised that there was no one around this time to intercept it. The ball, and Angel, were suddenly both thundering toward her from different angles. Ella had only one option, to intercept then hit the ball away from her as soon as possible. Angel on the other hand had seen that her prey was finally out in the open. With a look of sheer glee on her face she thundered as fast as her legs would carry toward her target.

Lost in both the moment and her previous frustrations Angel had failed to notice a shoe lace undo. For Ella the ball was almost upon her. She readied herself to hit it away. Ella drew back her stick into the air behind her then swung forward toward the ball. At the same time the ball hit a divot and bounced off to the right. Also, at that very same moment, Angel caught and tripped on her untangled lace. Due to the accumulated mass of momentum Angel carried on moving forward whilst falling toward the ground.

What followed was a moment of pure serendipity as Ella's hockey stick came up to meet Angel's face. The resulting 'THWACK!' sounded out across the whole pitch. A moment of eternal silence was followed by the crumpling sound of Angel's mass finally hitting the ground. A second silence followed as all those in attendance, a number with hands now covering their open mouths, looked upon the fallen Angel, watching for any signs of life.

The collective revere was broken only when Angel let out a low groaning noise which in turn triggered the teacher in charge to finally blow her whistle. Ella, albeit completely by accident, had just publicly taken down the school bully. There would be consequences.

xx lol xx

Following the incident on the pitch Angel had been dispatched to see the school nurse whereas Ella had been ordered back to the changing rooms to take an early shower. As Ella stood there, under the shower head, listening to the sing-song notes of the water dancing about her person, her mind started to replay the events that had just happened.

Ella was surprised to find that, whilst obviously concerned for her own safety, she was more concerned for Angel herself. A sense of guilt had overcome her, and Ella was wondering at ways she might be able to make amends for the humiliation she had inadvertently dished out.

Lost deep in her thoughts Ella turned off the water faucet and was about to step out the shower section when she heard the distinct 'clang!' of a locker being shut. Nobody else was supposed to be here. Ella froze, fearing it may be Angel coming for her revenge already.

"Hello." Ella called out. "Hello. Is anybody there?"

Nothing.

Then came the unmistakable sound of rubber soles, squeaking as they quickly turned. This was shortly followed by the sound of the changing rooms outer door swishing open, then closing again. Tentatively Ella stepped out of the shower area into the main body of the changing room. Whoever had been there was gone now. Everything looked as it should, so Ella convinced herself to think no more of it, instead opting to get dry, dressed and out of there as soon as possible.

Lunch break arrived. Ella's lunch today consisted of dry tuna fish spread, squished between two slightly stale slices of thin white bread. Sat on her own in the canteen, Ella quickly consumed her meal then started out on her usual circuit of the school building to kill time.

Lunch was normally a safe part of the day as Angel usually chose to leave the school grounds with her crew, so that they could hang about at the shops over the road and pass around a vape stick. Today though was not a normal day and as Ella was approaching the rear end of the school building, she looked up to see Angel and her crew were rounding the corner ahead of her, intent on blocking her path.

"Angel." Ella spoke first, wanting to apologise. "I am so sorr..."

"Shut it freak! You don't get to speak to me."

"But I'm sor..."

"I don't care what you are." Angel cut her off. "Nobody cares what you are. In fact, nobody even knows what you are. Japanese? Chinese?" Angel paused, looked toward Jackie then back toward Ella. "Kidneys!" She said this with a drawn-out sneer twisted into her face. "You're very brave all of a sudden don't you think?"

"What do you mean? I... Earlier on it... It was an accid..."

"I told you not to speak freak."

Ella stopped speaking. She also tried to stop staring at Angel's bruised face and the butterfly stitches crisscrossing her nose. Angel stood forward and grabbed Ella by the scruff with her left fist. She then reached into her right-hand pocket with her other hand, pulling out a plastic red nose and accompanying piece of paper. Holding these up to Ella's face Angel asked her.

"So, you think this is funny, do you? Think you're the perfect little comedian now do you? Eh."

"I don't know what you're talking about. I don't know what that is."

"Don't play dumb with her girly." This was Shell speaking now. "You was the only one in the changing rooms. We know it was you that put this into her locker."

"I didn't do..." Ella paused, remembering the sounds that she had heard and dismissed earlier on. 'That must have been someone...'

"Look at her." This was Jackie now, standing at the back, addressing the posse, and pointing. "Hers as guilty as sin that one. Stupid cow."

"Yeah." Angel agreed. "You must be more stupid than our Jacks to think you could get away with this."

Jackie looked a little put out as Angel held the scrap of paper up and started to read out loud.

'Dear Angel. Sorry I hit you in the face.
Please accept this new nose with my apologies.
Love L x
Ps It might even make you look more attractive.'

"What the..." Ella protested. "As if I would be stupid enough to write something like that."

"You were the only one in the changing rooms you stupid cow. There was no one else could have wrote it."

"But why would I do..."

"Shut it freak." Angel tightened the grip on her scruff. "You're a dead girl now. You know that right."

"But I. I would nev..."

At this point fear had risen high enough to choke off the words. As Ella attempted to talk, tears began to form in her eyes.

"Ha, that's right. Cry little freak." Angel let go of her scruff. "You don't belong here. You don't belong anywhere. After school I am going to find you and kill you out of my misery. The world will thank me for getting rid of a weakling like you."

Ella trembled. Angel went on.

"I guess that's what someone did to your dad, before you came to this country. Killed him out of your misery maybe? Was he a pleb too?"

Angel and her crew, aside from Bea that is, laughed heartily at this suggestion. Ella did not. In fact, for Ella something changed. Angel felt this and decided it would be fun to poke harder.

"Yeah, I imagine someone knocked him off for producing such a weak little baby. Your mum was a weakling too, right? Dumped by her parents 'cus they were so embarrassed at 'avin such a weak little baby I bet."

More laughter.

"You can't say that. You just can't. I won't have it."

Ella was surprised to find that her fear had been replaced with something else. Something new.

"Shame they didn't top your mum as well." Taunted Shell.

More laughter.

"Come on guys." Bea now. "Don't you think you're going a little far Angel?"

"Shut your face, Bea. It is good for this freak to know she doesn't fit in."

Suddenly all of Ella was anger.

"The world is a better place without your weakling dad in it."

'Stop,' Ella thought to herself.

She was trembling now.

"It means he can't reproduce any more weakling kids like you."

Laughter.

'Stop,' Ella thought again. 'Shut up!'

The anger was consolidating, into something pure, focused, brilliant.

"And the world will be a better place when I get rid of you."

Angel shoved Ella in the chest, pushing her backwards. The expectation being that Ella would fall over, onto her bum, and Angel could look down on her laughing, as her and her gang walked by.

What actually happened though was this.

Ella, anticipating the shove, let herself flail backward a few steps. At her most backward point she snatched the momentum, turned full circle on her heel, swinging her whole-body weight with her, then sprung the accumulated energy in the opposite direction, back toward her assailant.

With a clarity never experienced Ella's sight locked onto her target. Angel's nose. As Ella travelled forward, she cocked her arm back, clenched her fist, then released it in the direction of Angel's face. The resulting connection was so smooth, so focused, so beautiful, it could only be described as divine. The energy that Ella had released fired up from her legs and torso, before travelling down her arm, then into her balled fist, then finally into Angel's face.

Angel was lifted clean off the ground and flew six feet backwards. The movement was finished when Angel landed with a loud 'whomp' on the floor and lay there, out cold. Blood from Angel's exploded nose had spattered onto the faces of her friends who had just bore witness. All three now stood dumbstruck, in shock, staring at their twice fallen leader, whilst trying to retract their fallen jaws from the ground below them.

"ELLA SONGG!"

The teacher's shout snapped them all back to reality.

"REPORT TO THE HEAD'S OFFICE. NOW!"

So it was, for the second time that day, Ella had taken out the school bully. For the second time that day Ella knew that Angel would be obliged by reputation to come after her. For the first time that day though Ella was not scared. She would never fear someone like Angel again.

Little Pond, Big Fish

Meet Michael Summer, son of the once notorious Ronald Summer. Michael is commonly known in these parts as Mick, or rather, 'Mick the Fish'. Not the best 'gangster' name but Mick didn't mind as he did not see himself as a gangster. Mick did though see himself as a fish. A big fish. In fact, Mick liked to think of himself as a shark. Which is exactly what he was. Mick was a loan shark.

Loan sharks are generally viewed through a negative lens. Mick however did not see what he did as negative. On no. Mick was providing a valuable (very valuable in fact) public service. Besides, it wasn't like the bad old days anymore, when his dear old dad started the family business. Back then you had to break arms or legs when people didn't meet their repayments. These days you could just pay a solicitor and use the system to take all of someone's stuff. No violence necessary.

Mick is quite a good-looking fella. He is built well, spends a fair amount of his free time at the gym. He sports chiselled features, wears a constant short stubble, he keeps his hair short, and is wealthy enough to afford Hollywood style white teeth. He stands about 6.2ft, so is relatively imposing. He has very dark brown eyes, which lend to his fantasy shark persona. Personality wise, Mick is a natural charmer, to both man and woman. In summary, Mick looks like the sort of person that could well be dangerous and has about him a predatory aura. In reality though Mick would never resort to violence and finds the idea quite abhorrent. Mick is actually a nice guy.

In his own mind Mick is in fact a great guy. Whilst he could never agree with the way his father used to resolve things, he has never strayed from the belief that both his, and his father's role was to help people in their local community. It was not uncommon, especially these days, with the ever-increasing cost of living, to find yourself short one week. Unable to pay rent, electric, buy food etc. This is where Mick comes in. He can offer people small loans on the spot, that they can use to get themselves out of a jam. Yes, the associated interest rates were high. Very high in fact. But not everyone managed to pay back their loans, and the high interest rates were necessary to cover the risks involved in lending others money.

He also needed to pay for the shop. Since going legit Mick had opened his own little shop on the high street named, *'Interesting Financial Solutions.'* Mick had always thought this was quite a clever play on words.

The shop had made it easier for people to drop in and Mick had seen his customer numbers multiply tenfold in the time it had been open. To keep regular hours at the shop Mick also had to hire staff, and now had their wages to consider. Not only was he offering a valuable service to local residents, but he was also an employer, providing work for those in the community, helping to support the local economy. Sure, he only paid his staff minimum wage, but then that's what the government had worked out to be the necessary amount to live on and the government was full of people far cleverer and more qualified than Mick to know about these things.

Mick also had a life of his own to pay for. Take for example the car he was driving. It was a top of the range sports coupe, modified of course. It was important for Mick to ensure he gave the right first impression to his clients. He believed that the car a person drives speaks volumes about the kind of person driving it. A car like that though did not come cheap. Nor did Mick's other cars, all currently parked in his garages at home.

Mick's home was of a grand design. Perched on the side of a hill, on the outskirts of town, Mick liked to have sweeping views over his domain. The house had five spare bedrooms, an ensuite in each. A Master bathroom, with ensuite. A kitchen, bigger than most people's entire living space, with open plan into a lounge area where modern looking sofas framed an open gas fire pit. The whole south side of this space was glazed and could be opened onto a huge patio area, complete with its own bar and barbeque station, falling onto a landscaped garden below. There was no swimming pool out here though. Mick didn't want to rub people's noses in it. No, Mick was nothing if not sensitive. To that end he had decided to have the pool built inside, at the bottom of the house.

Mick was already wealthy then, but nowhere near wealthy enough. Mick admires the super-rich. His main ambition in life is to make a billion. He still has some way to go.

Anyway, the point here is that all of this must be paid for somehow, and that is ultimately why it was necessary for Mick's business to apply such high interest rates to its loans. To his credit, Mick understood that this could make repayments difficult. So, going the extra mile, Mick liked to offer the personal touch, often visiting his clients at their homes to collect their repayments. This is where Mick was today, out on his rounds.

xx lol xx

First up today was Robert Crow. Better known as Bob. Bob lived on his own. He had a little flat in sheltered accommodation. Bob had taken a bump to the head, a good number of moons ago, which led to his eventual decline and exclusion from normal society. Housed by the state, Bob was dependent on a cocktail of benefits, carers, microwave meals and prescription pharmaceuticals to ensure his day-to-day survival. His decline from a tax paying, home owning, participating member of society, to where he was now, had been a long one.

After the initial head injury, it was decided that Bob would be fine to go back to his old life. Damaged, just not quite damaged enough.

Unsurprisingly Bob proved incapable of holding down a job. He could not successfully maintain normal relationships either. First, he lost his work, then he lost his home, then most of his friends and all his pride. Bob had eventually landed here where only one or two witnesses to his continued existence remained.

A few years earlier, when he was still mobile, Bob shuffled into Mick's shop requesting a loan for £100. He said he needed it to help a special friend that lived abroad. Since that time Bob had been making weekly repayments. So far Bob had only ever chosen to settle the interest on the loan and nothing of the loan itself. Now that Bob's mobility was shot Mick visited him at his home to collect the weekly payment. In truth, the interest payment barely covered Mick's time. It certainly didn't cover the cost of fuel, but business was business and Mick was now one of Bob's very few visitors. Mick knocked on Bob's front door, then pushed it open to let himself in.

"Bob!" He shouted into the hallway. "It's Mick."
"Alright Mick." Came the reply. "Come on in."
Mick entered the flat proper and was instantly hit by a wall of heat. It was always hot as hell in Bob's flat. Bob liked to sit in nothing but his pants,

keeping the heating up high to stop himself getting chilly. Mick always wondered at how he could afford that much gas but could not afford to clear his £100 loan. After the heat came the odour. Not pleasant but not too horrendous either. A little like drowning, it was better to breathe it in rather than fight it.

"The oligarchs are coming Mick. Look at 'em, they're all over the news."

The news in question was concerned with recent sanctions being levelled at supposedly corrupt Russian businessmen. There was a war on, and leading politicians were busy trying to distance themselves from previous benefactors.

"Eh, I tell ya, it's a good job we're not rich eh Mick? Reckon they would be all over us by now."

Bob's banter was usually random, on account of that bump to the head. Mick had learnt by now to simply roll with it.

"I think you're right Bob. How you been keeping anyway. Good week?"

"Not too bad thanks."

"You mind if I turn the heating down a bit Bob? It's like the Australian Outback in here."

"Australia. You went there, didn't you? You were lucky to get out of there I tell ya. I was watching them border police at the airport. Crickey. They're tough out there. I'm glad you managed to get home Mick."

Mick had been backpacking to Australia, twenty years ago. Bob always referred to it like it was last week.

"Yeah Bob. You're not wrong. Tough lot them Australians. Anyway, you got your payment for this week?"

"Yes Mick, of course. Over in my top draw. Pull it open. There's a tin in there."

Mick knew the routine well enough. These days he came prepared. Using a disposable glove to open the draw (the handle was a little mucky) Mick retrieved the tin of coins. Mostly coppers but usually containing some silver, and sometimes the odd gold coin. Mick was entrusted to count out the interest amount himself. He also came prepared with money bags in his pocket. After counting out the appropriate amount Mick returned the tin and closed the draw. He then discretely dropped the used glove into the open bin bag that hung on Bob's kitchen unit draw. In the meantime, Bob had shuffled over to the kitchen area and flicked on the kettle.

"Do you want a cup of tea?"

Bob always offered. Mick always declined. Hygiene was not a priority in this flat and whilst

Mick felt bad for never accepting, he figured that the feeling of guilt was better than the feeling of food poisoning.

"Nah thanks Bob. Had one before coming round."

"Ah. You went to see one of them oligarchs I bet."

They both shared a chuckle at that.

Bob opened the fridge to retrieve the milk. Mick clocked the contents. Mostly filled with cold air there was a microwave meal, sat on the top shelf. A quarter block of mild cheese, out the wrapper, now more plastic than cheese. Some blackened lettuce, clearly out of date. A tub or cheap marge, no lid. Finally, the dreg of sour milk that Bob now added to his tea.

A layer of white bobbles floated to the surface after Bob stirred. Mick felt that strange twist in the base of his stomach before turning away. Other people's lives were not his problem and business was simply business.

"Right Bob. I won't keep you. See you next week."

"I'll be here." Came the reply.

The truth for Mick, if he was being honest, was that a little part of him always dreaded going to Bob's, but then always felt sad leaving. The world had forgotten about Bob, Mick would have liked to stay and sit with him for longer, but he had a schedule to keep. Time is precious right, and to Mick time meant money.

xx lol xx

Next stop on Mick's round was Madi. Mick had gone to school with Madi. They'd even had a little fling back in the day, before their paths diverged. Several years ago, a few years after they had left school, Mick spotted Madi coming out from the local food bank. She was carrying some heavy looking bags and Mick, driven by nostalgia, decided to stop and offer her a lift home.

Home for Madi is an old council house situated at the top of town. Mick offered to carry Madi's shopping to the door. In return Madi offered Mick in for a cup of tea and a catch up. During their conversation Mick learnt that immediately after leaving school Madi had been courted and fell for an older man. He was charming, seemingly with lots of expendable wealth. Her family however warned against him. Eventually they disowned her. Eventually Madi fell pregnant, and her charming man turned out not to be so charming after all. He turned out to be an abusive pimp.

Following the birth of their child, and frequent episodes of violence, Madi's spirit was broken. She was put to work by her charming man. He had moved out long ago but still visited once a week to deliver bruises and collect any earnings. Mick was upset to learn of Madi's lot. He couldn't fix things, but he felt he could help her out by offering a small low interest loan. Mick did not offer low interest to anyone so Madi, in that respect at least, could consider herself lucky. The loan was to help Madi with her daughter. To bridge the gap following her charming man's last collection and her next booking. Since that day Mick had been coming every week in service of the loan.

"Alright Madi. How are you doing? You look lovely as always." Mick offered the same complement each time, bruises or not.

"Ever the charmer eh Mick."

"You know me Mads. Got an eye for beauty ain't it."

Madi gave a soft giggle at this. She loved the way Mick made her feel about herself.

"So, Mick. You'll be wanting your money I take it?"

"Well, you know how it is Mads. A man's gotta make a decent living right?"

"Ha.   A decent man would let me off the repayments, then take me away for the weekend. Somewhere romantic."

"Times are hard Mads. What with the rising cost of living n'all. Gotta get the motor serviced next week and that don't come cheap you know."

"Pah. Fancy car. Does the same job as any other car you know."

"True. That is true. But this one does it in style eh." Mick gave a little wink of the eye to accompany this comment. Madi smiled.

"Well then Mick. I've got you're twenty. And two more pounds for this week's interest. But I'm running a little short again so how about you let me borrow that twenty back?"

This was how it went every time. Madi borrowed that first twenty pounds from Mick many years ago. Each time she made to pay it back she asked if she could borrow it again. She only ever paid the two pounds interest to service the loan. For Mick this arrangement made no money at all. The truth though is that he was glad that Madi never paid back the full twenty as he always had an excuse to drop in and check up on her.

"You know, one day you're gonna need to pay back that original twenty."

"Yeah yeah. An one day you're gonna need to make an honest woman out of me eh?"

"If only I was worthy Mads."

Another smile was shared, then Mick gave Madi a short, friendly hug and another cheeky wink.

"See ya again next week. Take care of yourself doll. And say hi to Angel for me."

xx lol xx

Winston was Mick's next call. An ambitious young man, or at least he was, until he had his accident. A mechanic by trade, two years ago Winston had been given the opportunity to take over a small workshop on the edge of town, fully kitted and with cheap rent. He had grabbed it with both hands.

New to the world of business Winston had no real idea what he was doing. He decided he would start with cash in hand jobs to build up the capital necessary to hire an accountant. The workshop was kitted with fairly decent tools, but there were a few items that desperately needed replacing. One of these being the main car jack.

Not being fully established Winston turned to Mick's company for a quick cash loan. Mick loaned £1,984. Exactly the amount Winston needed for a new car jack. Winston was aware that the interest on this loan would be high. However, he had a few jobs booked that meant he would make that amount back in no time. He intended to have the loan cleared by the end of the month. Unfortunately for Winston fate had other plans.

Toward the end of that week Winston was working under the jacked up front end of a friend's pickup truck when the new jack failed. The truck's nearside front wheel came down on Winston, crushing his left leg. It was over an hour before his friend came by to pick up the truck. Doctors were unable to save the leg and afterwards, Winston was unable to save the business.

He did not possess any insurance of any kind. This in turn invalidated any claim to the Jack manufacturer. To make matters worse, whilst Winston was in hospital the workshop remained his liability and he built up a large debt of rent arrears. As a final insult to add to his injury the tax office had gotten wind of his illegal trading and issued him with a hefty fine. All in all, Winston was well and truly up a creek with not a paddle in sight.

'Doof, doof, doof'. Mick bashed on Winston's door. He was used to Winston being slow to answer, on account of his leg, but today he seemed to be taking double long.
'Doof, doof, doof'.

"Hey Winston!" He yelled into the letter box. "I know you're there. I'm not going anywhere until you open up."

Another minute passed, then the door cracked open.

"I ain't got no money for you Mick. I barely got enough to eat these days without giving what I have got to you."

"Come on Winston. You're a businessman. You know how it works. You knew exactly what you were signing up too. Now you gotta honour that."

"Pah. Honour. What do you know about honour Mick. I've been paying off this loan for over two years now and I still ain't cleared a third of it."

"Hey, no need to get personal. This is just business. You know that."

"Business. Pah. Its robbery is what it is."

"You know what they say Winston. 'A rose by any other name' an all that."

"Hmph. It doesn't change the fact that I ain't got no more money for you. I've already paid at least three times the original sum I borrowed. Surely you can have a heart and write the rest off."

"It's business Winston. A heart has got nothing to do with it. I gotta make a living too, you know. Gotta get my car serviced this week and that costs a bomb. An unfortunately you ain't in no fit state to offer me a discount there are ya?"

"Man, you are cold!"

"Seriously Winston, you gotta make your payment otherwise I will have to take action."

"What action you talkin about?"

"Well, in my grandfather's day, he would have sent the boys round to break your legs."

"What the...! Are you threatening me?"

"No Winston, never. I'm not threatening you like that. Besides, there would be little point breaking your legs, on account you done that to yourself already. No. What I will have to do is take you to court Winston. That is the modern way. The civilised way."

"Ha, the court would never agree with you."

"But they would Winston. You signed a contract, remember? Crystal clear, black and white. They will force you to continue paying the loan, plus on top of that you will have the court fees and my fees added."

"Wow. Do you even have a soul?"

"Now then Winston, there's no need for that. Look, I know you are struggling, and I am here to help. What I am gonna do for you Winston is this. I will reissue your loan. We will take the balance you have left and reissue it to you on an increased term but at lower monthly minimum payments. Something you can afford."

Mick pulled out a pre-prepared sheet of paper, populated to demonstrate how this new arrangement would look. It reduced the minimum payment by over £50 a month but increased the term by 5 years. Winston knew he was cornered. The deal was ungood, but it was checkmate. He signed the new contract, which gave him a free month. Mick would be back at the same time next month to collect the first repayment on the new loan.

xx lol xx

The final stop on today's round was Mick's favourite customer. It wasn't just that Mick found this person particularly attractive. No, it was more than that. Mick felt different somehow, when in her company. He couldn't really understand it, but he could feel it, and he knew that he liked what he felt.

His client's house was at the heart of a council estate. Mick had developed the habit of parking up in a much nicer estate, a few streets away, then nipping down a couple of alleys that led to the client's house. This was quicker than driving in but also meant his precious motor was less likely to end up raised on bricks.

Mick had just entered the second alley when a hooded figure seemed to appear from nowhere. Head down, in a rush, the hooded figure walked straight into Mick. Bouncing off him the figure mumbled an apology and skirted around Mick. After recovering from the shock Mick quickly patted himself down. 'Phone, wallet, keys,' he thought as he went. Satisfied that he had not just been the victim of a crime he decided to let the matter go and continued down the alley.

Mick soon arrived at his destination. He raised his hand to knock, then stopped. Instead, he cupped his hand over his nose and mouth, then breathed into it to check his breath. Satisfied, he re-clenched his fist, took a new breath, then knocked on the door.

Becoming Undone

The door swung open, hard, crashing into the mostly disused radiator in the hallway that hung behind it.

Ella stormed in, slammed the door behind her and threw her keys into the key dish. Catching sight in the mirror of her own angry face she stopped for a moment and just stared. The face in the mirror changed. The person now staring back at her had tears streaming down their cheeks. What had she done? How had she gotten here? She had never been in trouble before and now she had been suspended for three weeks for an act of violence. How was she going to tell her mum? Ella stood and sobbed for a full minute before regaining her composure. Ella used her sleeve to dry her eyes and a slightly crusted tissue, from her pocket, to blow her nose.

It was then that she noticed a scent in the hallway. The scent was vaguely familiar. It was so faint that she could not put her finger on it, but she had smelt that scent before. Ella closed her eyes and reached deep into the recesses of her mind but the elusive thing she sought remained just out of reach.

A sudden noise from behind the front door broke her concentration. Her mother was home. A flash of panic rose up and she found herself making a dash for the living room. Ella sat on the edge of the sofa and switched on the TV. The local news was running a story on the good work and generosity of the local MP, who could be seen in the background talking and shaking hands with volunteers at the local youth centre. Presently she heard the front door open in the hallway. Mary entered the house. Hearing the television she called out.

"Ella? Ella, is that you?"
Ella's reply came as a croak.
"Yea... Ahem. Yea, yes. Yes, it's me mum."
"What on earth are you doing home at this time of day?"
Mary asked but wasn't at that moment interested in a reply. Instead, she continued.

"Well, I've got some good news for a change." Mary was talking whilst taking off her coat.

"On my way into work this morning I found a purse that I recognised as belonging to Irene. You know, one of our regulars. I got the boss to call her, and she was so happy when she came to collect it, she insisted on buying me a scratch card as a reward."

Mary kicked off her shoes, enjoying the sensation of release as she did so.

"Well blow me. The scratch card she gave me was only a winner. Twenty pounds! Can you believe it?"

Mary turned to drop her keys into the dish on the side.

"A whole twenty quid. I think we should use it to treat ourselves to a nice dinn..."

Seeing the dish Mary froze.

"Ella?"

"Yes mum?"

"Where is the money that was left in the bowl on the side?"

Ella had no idea what her mum was talking about. She shouted back.

"I don't know what you're talking about mum. I've not seen any money."

"Well, you must have Ella. It won't have just disappeared, will it? Mick is coming round to collect the loan payment. I left the cash here before going to the food bank."

Right on queue there came a rapping of knuckles on the door. Mick had arrived to collect his money.

Something New

It had been over half an hour since Mick had arrived to collect his money. Ella, the accused, with no opportunity to yet protest her innocence had opted to cower in the living room, television on but not watched. Mick and Ella's mum had been having tea and conversation in the kitchen. Ella was of course eavesdropping. It all felt a little pathetic, listening to her mum constantly apologising, Mick constantly reassuring. Mick had a reputation for being a cold profit driven businessperson. He seemed to be going soft on Mary though.

Their conversation concluded with Mick applying only half of the usual late payment penalty to Mary's loan. In this case twenty pounds. Mick had been willing to waive the fee completely, but Mary would not have it. Besides, she had just earlier that day gained twenty pounds so would not really miss it. It would just mean another humiliating visit to the foodbank tomorrow.

After showing Mick to the door Mary stormed into the living room to confront her daughter.

"What the hell did you do with that money Ella?"

"I didn't touch your stupid money. I didn't even know there was any money there."

"Well, it was certainly there earlier when I left the house. You're the only person who has been here since so it must be you that has taken it. Oh Ella, I know things are difficult, but you've never stolen before."

"I didn't take the money mum. I don't know what you're talking about."

Ella was starting to feel a little shaky.

"And what the hell are you doing at home anyway. Why aren't you still at school?"

"I've been... Um. I got suspended."

Ella muttered this under her breath.

"You got what? Speak up. What did you just say?" Mary demanded.

"I've been suspended mum!" Ella almost shouted it this time. "I got into a fight with Angel and the school suspen..."

"What the hell Ella!" Mary was shouting now. "What the hell is going on with you?"

Mary turned away for a moment, her right hand rising to her head, thumb and finger massaging her temples. In a deflated voice she continued.

"Fighting and stealing. This is not like you. Not like you at all. I don't need this, Ella. What is going on?"

"No mum. I, I... It wasn't like that. I..." She started but Mary cut her off.

"You know what Ella, I don't want to know. I've bent over backwards to keep you safe since your father left. I work two jobs. I save every penny I can get. I take the shame of having to visit a food bank once a week to keep you fed. It's not fair Ella. It just isn't fair. What about me. What about my life?"

Mary's eyes had welled. She was clearly at her wits end.

"I'm sorry mum. I'm..."

Ella's eyes had also welled, then spilled over as she was trying to talk. Trying to make her mother hear her.

"Just go to your room will you please."

A demand made in a whisper.

"I need you to be out of my sight,"

"But mum..." Ella pleaded.

"JUST GO!" Mary screamed back.

Stunned into silence Ella refrained from any further protest. She stood from the sofa edge. It took all her strength to move through the living room and ascend the stairs toward the sanctity of her bedroom. Ella gently closed the door behind her, sat down on the edge of her bed, placed her head in her hands and sobbed.

After a time, Ella lifted her head and the crying stopped. Dead. A thought had formulated that took Ella by surprise. In the top drawer of her bedside cabinet, she kept a small second-hand arts and craft set. Within this was a small Stanley blade, used for cutting out shapes and the like. Possessed by something she could never understand, Ella now retrieved that small Stanley blade.

She found a strange, almost familiar comfort in its handling. After a while she pushed the blade up from its protective plastic casing, then gently she drew the pointed tip across the top of her left forearm. A rush of adrenaline, followed by a release of endorphins.

All of Ella's pain was magically distilled down to a single wound. A wound that was now on the outside. One that she could watch and see heal. Ella, it seemed, had discovered something new.

Manipulating Person

The Rt Hon Josh Robertson, local MP, is a man who believes that he is of exceptionally good taste. This is why he takes his lunches, when he can, at the restaurant in which he is currently sat. They serve only the finest fillet mignon, which Josh has just consumed, partnered with a glass of Screaming Eagle Cabernet 92. Following his luncheon, Josh retired to the bar for a digestif whiskey-based cocktail.

Summoning the waiter for the bill, Josh proffers, as he always does, the credit card he has been provided with to cover MP expenses. Josh reasons that this is fair based upon the fact that he is taking his lunch within working hours. Why shouldn't the public purse pick up the tab. Besides, for Josh to be on top of his game it is important that he be well fed. In this respect he could conclude that the public were indeed getting good value for money.

Josh Robertson was, in fairness, a well-dressed man. He wore only the finest quality wool suits, tailored to best fit his rather generous frame. Josh would describe himself as slightly rotund. An honest observer would describe him as fat. Hanging over his shirt collar at any one time were at least two of his chins. He managed to stay clean shaven though and he liked to wear his silver hair tousled. He found it a useful tool in disarming people. Instead of seeing a fat, selfish, grotesque greedy pig, people instead saw someone who was, 'a bit of a cad', 'a fun guy', 'one of us' maybe. Maybe not.

Josh had just squeezed his fat frame into one of the restaurant lounge chairs. Slightly out of breath, and with some effort, he retrieved a mobile phone from his suit jacket inside pocket. Opening his recent contacts he pressed the call button for the contact labelled, 'Servant'. Josh had never understood why some felt the need to add the word 'Civil' in front of this. Josh was a man that liked to say it how it was, and he had never thought to use an actual name for any of his 'servants'. The phone was answered almost instantly.

"Yes Sir?" Questioned his current assistant upon answering.

Josh had warmed to this one a little. Unlike the usual woke-flakes he'd been assigned, this one seemed more than willing to act upon his commands. So far, she had managed to keep up. Carri-Anne was her name. She was hardworking, ambitious and attractive. Josh had considered whether Carri-Anne might serve him in other ways that could ultimately be beneficial to them both.

"What is in my schedule for this afternoon?"

"Well Sir, you have a PR visit at the local food bank scheduled to start in half an hour. I have kept the whole afternoon free so you can have time to tour the facility and meet volunteers."

"Pah, poppycock. We'll see about that. Pencil in a meeting with the PM will you, for 3pm. I think an hour of my time is more than enough to spare for these cretins."

"But Sir, I can't just pencil in a meeting with the PM. There are protocols I need to follow before we can book a..."

"Damn it Carri-Anne. I didn't say book me a meeting with the PM, did I? Why would I want to talk to that incompetent fool?"

Josh had always felt that he was the best person in the country for the top job. He was just biding

his time for the right moment to seize it. He had
been biding his time for a long time.

"I said..." Josh continued, "...pencil one in. Pencil
one in so that should anyone ask then that is where
I need to be at 3pm."

"Of course. Yes Sir."

Josh 'harrumphed' his approval.

"And where will you actually be at 3pm Sir?"

"That my dear is none of your business."

Silence.

"Is it?"

"No Sir. Of course not. My apologies Sir."

"Send the car will you. The sooner I get this visit
done the better."

"Yes S..."

Josh hung up before Carri-Anne could finish
speaking. He pocketed his phone then used both
of his pudgy little hands to apply what little
strength he had to lever himself free from the
lounge chair. Josh then belched out loud, before
waddling his way toward the exit to await pick up
by his driver.

xx lol xx

Josh's appointment was at a food bank located in
a local industrial estate, a little out of town. The

88

reason for Josh's visit was to announce a much-needed cash injection. The food bank was on the brink of closure and the money would not only ensure its survival, but also allow the means to relocate closer to the town itself, creating much easier access for the local people that had come to rely on the bank to make ends meet.

For Josh's part, he'd found himself left with some excess budget for the year. The money had originally been earmarked to provide affordable housing, but Josh had missed several vital meetings needed to get that work off the ground. As a result, the money sat unspent and Josh knew that if he didn't spend it his boss, the PM, would ask for it back, and he would struggle to get as much the following year. He also saw helping the ailing food bank as a great way to buy some good press and win some re-election favour with the locals.

Arriving at the bank Josh, rather ungraciously, climbed out from the rear of his car. It had started to drizzle but Carrie-Anne was there with an umbrella.

"Sir, our liaison is just over here. Her name is Philippa Bazquet and she..."

"Philippa Bazquet?" Josh interrupted.

"Yes Sir. Why do you ask, have you met her before?"

"Don't be so bloody ridiculous. Do I look like the sort of person that socialises with the sort of person that volunteers at a foodbank?"

"No Sir. Um, that's not what I..."

"It's just a rather appropriate name, don't you think? Philippa Bazquet. 'Fill up a basket'. Do you see. Do you get it? Ha ha ha."

"Yes Sir, very amusi..."

"Fill up a basket at someone else's expense though eh?"

"Um, well Sir, I'm not sur..."

"These people should maybe try filling up their days with a job. That way they could buy their own bloody food just like the rest of us."

"Right Sir, though you..."

"Philippa Bazquet. Hah! I do hope she isn't a 'basket' case. Is she foreign? Bazquet sounds foreign to me. Coming over here stealing our locals' jobs. She must be slightly tapped though if she thinks wasting her life as a volunteer is a good thing. Don't you think? Eh?"

"Very good Sir." This was all that Carrie-Anne could manage.

"Right then." Said Josh. "Where is the crazy old bat?"

Josh reached a small gathering of journalists who were there to cover the story. Carrie-Anne was doing her best to guide Josh to the planned liaison with Phillippa. Josh though had other ideas and decided now was as good a time as any to court with the press.

"Thank you, thank you. Thank you all for coming out to report on this truly fabulous feel-good story. We know. That is to say I. I and my government know. We know that people are struggling. We know that there is a cost-of-living crisis happening and it is making things tough for many, many people. That is why we are proud that so many food banks have been opened since we have been in power. It is now much easier for you people to gain some support during these hard times. And now, thanks to me, the food bank at which we currently stand, will be able to remain open."

Josh paused to nod his head in a positive fashion.

"Not only that."

Now lifting his hand, pointing a finger into the air.

"These people will be able to locate their little charity close to the centre of this town. This is not only thanks to the monies I am allocating but also thanks to the fact that there are many empty shops. Empty shops that have been made available so that other businesses can grow. All since we came into power. This means that the poor will no longer have to walk five miles to get here. This also means that shoes will not wear out so quickly. This will result in real time savings for the poorest within our community."

Josh again waggled one of his pudgy sausage fingers in the air for emphasis.

"My government is thus putting money back directly into the pockets of the poorest members of our society."

It was Josh's experience that journalists started to get excited at statements like this, shouting over each other to ask their pointless little questions whose answers they might use to try and catch him out. From these they could create counter stories to run in parallel, helping to sell more of their glorified toilet roll to an insatiable public, all under the guise of news.

'Pah!' This was not Josh's first rodeo. He was a master at smoke and mirrors. Just at the right moment Josh looked up to see two members of the public exiting the food bank. Fortunately, they were both women. More fortunately neither of them appeared to be ugly.

With an unaccountable turn of speed Josh moved to intercept the ladies before they had a chance to realise what might be going on.

"Why hello ladies." He'd intercepted the pair, blocking their path. "How are you both today?"

"Um, I. Erm, we... We are fine thank y..." One of them started.

"Good, good. I can see you have just been into the foodbank. Did you manage to get any nice goodies?"

"Goodies?" Questioned the second.

"Yes. What treats did you secure for yourselves today? I can see that you are both carrying a shopping bag, so I assume you have gotten yourselves a good haul?"

"Uh, we, um. What? Who are..."

"Of course you have." Josh Continued. "You needn't worry. I'm not after any of your goodies." Here he gave an inappropriate laugh and turned to offer a theatrical wink to the gathered press. Turning back, Josh began to rub his stomach. "No, no. I've had my lunch already, thank you. But you can thank me, and my government, for your good fortune today."

"Mum, it's him." Ella said aloud. "You know, the one from the telly."

At the mention of telly, Mary's senses recovered enough to realise that both her and Ella were now at the centre of a small press pack, one of which carried a camera on their shoulder. Another waved a furry microphone about in the air.

"Miss, miss. Excuse me miss." Said another. "Are you able to say what difference the food bank has made to your life?"

"Um, well, I um. Is this going to be on telly?" Mary asked the reporter.

"We are just shooting a small section for the local news later today if that's okay?"

"Oh, okay."

"Great." Said the reporter. "If you could, then, just answ..."

"No. No I don't mean that it is okay. I would rather not be on the telly, if that is okay. Okay with you that is."

Josh intervened.

"Look, it is quite clear that this..." He leant into Mary and whispered behind his hand. "What is your name?"

"Mary." Said Mary.

"Good. And who is this? What is her name?"

"Ella. She is my daughter.

"Excellent. Right, leave this to me."

Josh resumed his talk to the press.

"As I was saying, it is quite clear that neither Mary nor Ella here wants to be bothered by the press. They are obviously too humble to try and take any credit away from the good work I and my government are doing here. Please could you let them pass so that they might be on their way."

Like the red sea the gathered press parted to let Mary and Ella though. Josh then turned his back on the scene, looking for Carrie-Anne to escort him onward toward his liaison with Philippa.

As he turned, he bumped into a tall man, wearing a dark hoodie, who had been standing amongst the press pack but was now directly behind Josh.

"What the...?"

"Sorry. So sorry." Mumbled the guy in the hoodie. He was looking down, already making a hasty exit. Josh shouted after him.

"Hey you! You can't just... Bloody hell. Somebody stop that man!"

His shout had re-attracted the gathered press, who all turned again in his direction, swallowing the stranger into their midst as he made his escape. Josh quickly regained his composure. He would just have to let this one go.

Then there was another commotion and the press pack swung back the other way. To pay Josh back for his, albeit, very small act of kindness, Ella had attempted to block the stranger's path. The stranger had barged into Ella, shoulder first, knocking her to the ground and sending her shopping bag flying. Ella could not be certain, but she was sure the stranger had used her name as he barged past, hissing, '...get out of my way Ella.'

Now led on the floor, in a daze, Ella looked up to see the gathered press all looking down, a camera recording the moment for prosperity. Littered about her were the remnants of the bag she had been holding. Glass from a jar of coffee intermingled with the fresh meat and vegetables that was meant to be feeding them for the next few days. Ella had let her mum down again and this time, thanks to the press, the whole town would get to witness her humiliation.

Ella got to her feet and ran. She ran hard against the tears that were trying to push their way through. Ella would not stop running now. Not until she made it all the way home.

Josh, who had been watching this scene play out, muttered to Carrie-Anne about what a waste of the taxpayer money that was, referring to the spoiled contents of the shopping bag dropped by Ella. He then turned his attention back to his new target and switched the charm back on.

xx lol xx

"Mr Robertson." Philippa seemed awkward and even performed a little curtsy upon greeting the MP.

"Oh my." Josh whispered behind his hand to Carrie-Anne. "She really is a basket case."

He then turned to face Philippa, extended a clammy hand and plastered on his best fake smile.

"Miss Basket, how lovely to meet you." He said.

"Actually, it's Mrs. And it's Bas..."

"What?" Josh cut her off. "You're married? Really?"

"Um. Yes. What do you mea..."

"Ha. Well, I never. I just expected you to be the sort of woman to have lots of cats is all. But never mind that. I understand that you are nervous. It has to be quite something to meet your saviour, eh?"

"Well, sir, we are all very grateful here at..."

"Yes. It's not every day you get to meet a real knight in shining armour, eh?"

"Well, sir, yes. Um. I, um... I was hoping to take you on a tour. We can show you what we do here, and the staff can show their appreciat..."

"Ah, we are a little pushed for time as it happens."

Josh stared at Carrie-Anne, who was staring into thin air. Josh tried again.

"Ahem." This time a little louder. "We are a little pushed for time. Aren't we Carrie-Anne?"

Jolted back into the moment Carrie-Anne pulled up her tablet.

"Yes. Yes of course. Sorry. Yes. You have that meeting with the PM scheduled that you can't afford to miss."

"There you go see Philippa. As disappointing to me as it is, not to be able to take your wonderful tour, you will appreciate that I can't stand up the PM."

"No, no of course not. I underst..."

"So, if we could just get a couple of quick pictures together."

Josh turned himself around, so that he was standing by Philippa's side. He put his arm across Philippa's shoulders, telling her in her ear to smile for the press. Feeling both intimidated and trapped Philippa did as she was told. Satisfied with the number of flashes, Josh then turned his back toward the press once more. He grabbed Philippa's hand in both of his, offering insincere apologies for having to dash, saying that he hoped she would make good use of the money he had very generously given her. After that he was quickly back, into the safety of his car, and away.

"Well..." Started Josh to his driver. "That was just about as unpleasant as one might have expected."

The driver did not respond.

"Bloody peasants the lot of them. Eating out on the taxpayer dime eh. Who do these people think they are?"

"The driver stayed quiet.

"Take me home please. It's been a very stressful day and I need to relax."

"Very good sir." Came the eventual reply.

The thought of being safely back at home made Josh feel good. He would go straight to the attic and spend some time with his coveted toy trains. He thought he might even treat himself to a shower. Wash the scent of 'poor' off. At that moment Josh instinctively patted the pocket of his jacket where his house keys should have been. That pocket was empty.

xx lol xx

Josh arrived home in double quick time. After realising he'd had his pocket picked, Josh called his friend, the Chief Constable. A police sergeant was already waiting for him at the front door.

"Sir." Said the sergeant, offering up a salute at the same time.

"Yes, yes. Stand down sergeant. No need for formalities."

"Yes Sir. Of course, Sir."

"Well, what have you found?"

"Well Sir. It's the oddest thing. When we arrived, the front door was slightly ajar. However, we have completed a rec of the house. There is no one here and nothing seems to have been disturbed."

"What are you saying, sergeant?"

"Well Sir, if this was supposed to be a robbery, I would have to say that it wasn't a very good one."

"Not a very good one you say. What, do you normally give these things a score. Marks out of 10. Is that what you are saying?"

"No Sir. I didn't mean it like tha..."

"And what criteria do you score it on eh? Value of goods stolen. Damage done. Personal injury. In fact, do you score all crimes you attend? Bonus points for a murder maybe?"

"No Sir, of course not. I was just saying..."

"What you were just saying is that this wasn't a very good robbery. Which means, at the same time, you are implying that there is such a thing as a good robbery. Am I right?"

"No Sir. I... Err, I... Um..."

"Have you ever been robbed, sergeant?"

"No Sir, no. I have not."

"Well keep going the way you are, and you will be. Robbed of your career that is. I will make damn sure of it. Now, what else have you found? There must be something."

"Well Sir..." The rather flustered sergeant continued. "The only thing we did find of any note was your keys. Sat on the dresser in the hallway."

"Oh." Josh was genuinely shocked.

Picking up on this the sergeant braved a question.

"Is it possible Sir that you just forgot to take your keys with you when you left the house this morning?"

"WHAAAT!"

Came the very loud and very angry response.

"Are you calling me a liar?"

"No Si.."

"Suggesting I am losing my mind then. Is that it?"

"I. No Sir. Or course not, but we have to consi..."

"I will have your badge for this sergeant. Just you mark my words."

With that Josh stormed through the front door, slamming it behind him.

Feeling quite out of sorts Josh decided to make a beeline to the attic. The attic was Josh's happy place. Josh was very important. He knew hundreds, if not thousands of people. He didn't though have a personal connection with any one of them. No. Far safer to spend his personal time surrounded by his beloved trains. Here he was in total control. Here he was the Prime Minister. He decided what train went where, and when. In this world he was the Master. Because of this he noticed instantly what was missing, the moment he walked in.

xx lol xx

Josh had finally come around after fainting. He had fainted when he realised that his prized toy train had been stolen. It was a small blue train. There were only two such models known to be in existence. Josh had one. Or rather used to have. The other was located at the local toy museum. This is where Josh was sitting now.

Josh was in the reception area awaiting a meeting with the museum's curator, Mr Paul Furst. Whilst waiting in reception Josh couldn't help but observe how tatty the place was. It had been many moons since he had visited this place. It appeared that Mr Furst had let it go to pot since then. Why was the receptionist out on the floor cleaning cabinet cases he wondered. That simply made no sense at all. Where were the actual cleaners? This was not the way to go about creating a good impression on visitors.

Eventually Josh heard an old door creak open, followed by irregular footsteps, making their way down the wooden floored corridor. The footsteps were irregular as Mr Furst walked with a cane. This was not because he was aged, though he was getting on a bit. No. Mr Furst required a cane after suffering a leg infection many years prior. He had come to favour the cane over the years and liked the edge that he felt it added to his character. Mr Furst was dressed in a smart but comfortable looking brown suit. He favoured a bow tie, which was presented atop a slightly creased white shirt. His glasses were round, and metal rimmed. If he were outside, he would also have been wearing his hat. A Fedora or course.

"Well, well, well. Mr Josh Robertson. You have finally come to see me."

"So, I have. You are looking very well Paul I have to say."

Josh was standing now, offering one of his pudgy hands in greeting, which Paul ignored.

"How many letters has it been, do you think? How many phone calls? How many times have I had to try and arrange an audience with your good self?"

"Ahem. I'm not quite sure what you..."

"Come now Mr Robertson. We both know that you have been ignoring me. An important man like you doesn't have time for the likes of little people like me. It doesn't matter that I am one of your constituents. I understand. You have real politics to be getting on with, right?"

"Ahem. Well, yes. Yes, of course. I do have a very bus..."

'BHAM!'

Mr Furst stamped his cane on the floor. Josh almost had an accident.

"Out of the blue you just show up at my reception. You demand to see me immediately. What are the chances?"

"Well, erm no. Look here old chap. I think you have gotten the wrong end of the stick."

Mr Furst looked down at his hand holding the cane.

"Well no. Not that stick of course. I mean a stick. You know, figuratively speaking."

"What do you want, Mr Robertson?" Came the stern response.

"Ah. Yes. Straight down to business. Very good. I do like a man tha..."

Josh caught the look in Paul's eye.

"Yes, well, never mind. Ahem. To business then. The business. Yes. I am here to acquire the blue train."

"The blue train?" Mr Furst asked in disbelief.

"Yes, the blue train."

"The blue train?"

"Yes, the blue train."

"The blue..."

"Are we going to keep saying the same thing to each other all night?" Josh broke in. "You know which blasted train I am talking about."

"I do indeed know which train you are talking about. You are talking about the blue one right."

"Yes, that's it. The blue train. Can I have it please?"

"Ha! Ha, ha, ha, ha, ha, ha, haaa."

Josh stood unmoving.

"So, let me get this straight. You ignore me for... Beezus, who knows how many years. Then, suddenly, out of the blue, no pun intended, you waltz in here, demand to see me, then ask me to give you the most valuable asset that this museum holds?"

"Well, yes."

"Just give it to you?"

"Well yes. Why not?"

"Ha! You really are a right honourable something aren't you Mr Robertson. I will certainly give you that for free."

"Ahem. Okay. So, what will it take for me to acquire the train?"

"What, the blue one?"

"Yes, the damned blu... Look, just name your price?"

Here Paul took a deep breath and stroked his chin with his left hand. After a moment he leaned in close on his cane and softly asked.

"Mr Robertson. Do you even want to know why I have been trying to arrange a meeting with you for so many years?"

"Um..." 'Not really', Josh thought to himself. Then said instead. "Well yes. I suppose it would only be right of me to as..."

"Look around Mr Robertson. Look around and tell me what you see."

"Well. I see a toy museum of course. Albeit a rather tatty one."

"Tatty." Paul seized on the word.

"Tatty, yes, good. You are on the right path. And why do you think the museum might be... 'tatty'?"

"Well, I imagine you must struggle to get good staff. Especially after my government sent all those foreigners packing, eh?"

Josh stated this as if he were sharing some witty banter with one of his racist colleagues.

"No Mr Robertson." Paul rebutted. "It is not staff that is the problem."

"Oh. Does it have something to do with you needing a cane then maybe?"

"A cay… a cane…" Paul stuttered.

"What the hell is wrong with you man? No Mr Robertson. It certainly has nothing to do with me needing a cane."

Paul banged it down on the floor again for emphasis.

"What it does have to do with, Mr Robertson, is being chronically underfunded for many, many years."

"Oh, I see. Well, what does that have to do with me?"

Exasperated, Mr Hurst countered.

"Look. Mr Robertson. If the museum is to survive then it… We… We will require a significant cash injection."

"Oh, I see." The penny finally dropped.

"I have been writing to you all these years to lobby for funds to be made available to help save this important museum. Here we not only preserve history, but we preserve the stories behind that history. In doing so we help to inspire young minds. Young minds that leave here full of ideas and dreams that will help drive the next generation. You see, Mr Robertson, it is of the utmost importance that the museum is saved and, rather sadly, it seems that you are the only person in a position who can do that."

"I see. Very well then. How much is it you need?"

"Three million pounds."

"Three million pou..." Josh spluttered before he could get all the words out.

"Yes. Three million pounds Mr Robertson."

"But there is nowhere near that amount left in the arts budget for this year." Protested Josh.

"You're a resourceful man Mr Robertson. Everyone knows that. If you wish to acquire the blue train, then three million pounds is what it will take."

"But, but... I need that train Mr Furst."

"Indeed, you do. And I need three million pounds."

Mr Furst handed Josh a business card.

"These are my details. Please contact me again when you are ready to make the transfer."

Mr Paul Furst then turned on his heel and made off back down the corridor.

xx lol xx

Two weeks later Josh was back in his attic, donning his fat controller hat and beaming with glee as he watched his newly acquired blue train make its way around the tracks. Sourcing the necessary funds had turned out to be much easier than Josh had feared. In the end all he'd had to do was redirect the monies allocated for the food bank.

The money was left over budget anyway and by spending it on the museum Josh had secured for the public an establishment of the utmost importance. A place of sustenance for the mind. A place where dreams were created. A place now safe for future generations to visit and enjoy. This was money much better spent than on something as temporary and as fleeting as a food bank. Yes, there may be a cost-of-living crisis now, but that would pass. The museum, if it were lost, would be lost forever.

No, Josh had done a good thing here. An excellent thing in fact. He was so pleased with himself that he had reserved a table at his favourite restaurant where he intended to take himself tonight for a slap-up meal to celebrate. He would of course be charging this back to his expenses. It was, after all, only right that he be rewarded for his service to his public.

ACT 2

Unfinished Sympathy

Two years have passed since we last caught up with our heroine. Ella has been on quite a journey since then. You will recall that Ella was suspended from school, following the takedown of her arch nemesis Angel. As it happened Angel never sought to settle the score in her usual violent fashion. Instead, she chose to give Ella a wide berth and encouraged all their classmates to do the same. After what had happened, and what had happened after that, it was not hard for Angel to convince others that there was something not quite right about Ella.

Mary's disappointment at her daughter's suspension, coupled with the unfounded belief that Ella had taken Mick the Fish's money, meant that Mary was not there to hear her daughter when her daughter needed to be heard the most. The unfortunate succession of events was just enough, at just the right time, to nudge Ella onto a darker path. The light truly faded out when Ella self-harmed for that first time. Angel could not have known, but the isolation she had orchestrated for Ella suited her just fine.

A fresh blow came when the local MP had withdrawn funding promised for the foodbank. Local volunteers tried desperately to keep the foodbank going but, in the end, the inevitable happened and the bank closed. For Mary and Ella, the consequences of this were great.

Mary had to take on more shifts at the care home. Whenever Ella saw her, Mary was always exhausted. Ella was consumed by guilt for their current situation, feeling she'd somehow contributed to it all. Eventually she resorted to helping in the only way that she could think how. Ella started to shoplift food. She found that she was surprisingly good at this and got away with it so many times that she'd began to believe she was uncatchable. Her appearance however was changing in line with her demeanour. It wasn't long until Ella was dressed all in black.

Growing taller, coupled with a general lack of both food and appetite, Ella started to look unhealthy. She stayed indoors most of the time and her skin became very pale. Ella wore only long sleeve tops, to cover her arms, even at the height of summer. The overall sense of darkness that had settled upon Ella was being projected and soon enough she started to attract the attention of store staff as soon as she entered any shop. It was only a matter of time until Ella was caught red handed.

Ella got herself arrested and was taken to the local police station to be questioned and body searched. Being a few days shy of sixteen at the time, Mary had to be called as guardian and witness. The disappointment in Mary's eyes when she arrived was too much for Ella to bear so she stared at her feet the whole time. Because of this Ella did not witness the horror, then the heartbreak, in her mother's eyes when, after being instructed to remove her top, Ella's scars were finally revealed.

Following a tearful couple of hours, Mary took the police officer up on her offer of support. Within a couple of weeks Ella had been enrolled at the 'Ho-Bloom Therapy Centre', where she would embark on a series of counselling sessions with a trusted local therapist called Dr Eleanor Simian.

Despite looking a little bit like a monkey, Ella was to trust Eleanor explicitly. To her own surprise Ella had broken down, then fully opened up within their very first session. She had told Eleanor all about her feelings toward her father and her mother. How she felt that she did not fit in, anywhere. How she felt lost in the world, not knowing where her mother had come from. How she was being isolated at school by a bully. How she worried about the debt that her mother was in with Mick. How she worried about where their next meal would come from following the closure of the food bank. How she was floating through time, aimless, without direction or hope. Finally, she spoke of how she had found solace and comfort in the cold steel of a rust-tinged razor blade.

The big breakthrough came after Ella had finished school and Eleanor had encouraged her to find a job. Ella managed to land a position at a local chip shop. The idea of putting herself in front of the public in such a fashion filled her with terror. In fact, Ella very nearly turned tail and bolted on her first shift.

Then an old man shuffled in through the door and for some inexplicable reason, that Ella could not explain, everything felt different. All the colours changed and the world around her rearranged. The lights flickered back on, and Ella began to believe again that there was something else out there for her. Something better. Something good.

In Bloom

"Ella. You have made so much progress since starting your time here. I feel you have mostly come to terms with your past, and I think it is time that we turn our thoughts and attention toward your future?"

Ella was staring out the window, looking at nothing, absentmindedly fiddling with her most valued possession, a fifty pence piece that had clouds depicted on one side.

"I want to be a doctor." Ella responded, all matter of fact.

"A doctor? Well. I had no idea that you were interested in medicine."

Eleanor was teasing. She already knew full well that Ella did not want to become a Doctor of Medicine.

"Not that type of doctor. I want to be a head doctor. Like you."

"Oh." Eleanor replied, nodding thoughtfully.

"Yes. I want to be able to help people. Like you have helped me. I want to be able to help people get better. To be better. To be better people that treat other people better."

"I see." Replied Eleanor. "Well, I am obviously going to be an advocate of your career choice. We have already established that you have an extraordinary sensitivity towards the feelings of others. You have great emotional intelligence. You both listen and, more importantly, hear things very well. Yes. Yes, a head doctor. Why not? 'Dr Ella Songg'. Has a certain ring to it don't you think?"

Hearing this a big grin appeared upon Ella's face, driven by a rush of pride from within.

"Well Ella, if this is the path that you would like to take then it would be my pleasure to help you on your way. I would like to start by offering you an intensive hypnosis procedure."

"Sounds... intense." Ella reflected somewhat uncertainly.

"Ha, yes. Yes, it is rather. But you needn't worry. It is all perfectly safe."

"What is the difference between intense and not intense hypnosis?"

"That is a fair question Ella and one that I am happy to address. You see, I come from a long line of practitioners, stretching back over many generations. The school of therapy I come from. Or rather, 'house' of therapy I come from. Well, let's just say that it is much more varied than that of your typical practitioner. One of the tools that I have at my disposal is intensive hypnosis. The difference between this and your standard hypnotherapy is... Well, the latter will take you back. Back into your own past and your own memories. The objective is to seek out the key that will unlock the door to your future. My intensive therapy on the other hand... Whilst the overall objective essentially remains the same, the actual hypnosis will send you somewhere else entirely."

Here Eleanor beamed one of her joy filled smiles. This sealed the deal. Ella was sold.

"Okay. Let's do it then."

"Excellent." Said Eleanor. "Lets."

xx lol xx

The room that Ella and Eleanor now occupied seemed to be at the very heart of the Ho-Bloom centre. The pair had descended at least three levels below ground to reach this room.

Fascinatingly, Eleanor confirmed there were further levels still below this one.

The room felt enormous, easily matching the street level footprint of the building above. The roof was beautifully ornate, adorned in the fashion of an Edwardian mansion. Chandeliers, uniformly placed, hung from various points in the room, offering both warm illumination and dancing shadow. The walls were clad in dark, ornate oak wooden panels. Huge fireplaces sat, one at either end of the room, burning oak, gently crackling. In the opposite corner of the room was a large wooden door, similar to the one that they had just entered through.

Underfoot, the floor was fully carpeted in a deep, rich and intricately patterned Persian weave that contained depictions of people and animals and buildings and clouds and... All seemed animated by the soft flickering lights from the ceiling and fireplaces. One could easily lose themselves in the weave. Possibly many had.

Ella thought that the room was nothing short of miraculous. However, she could not help noticing a distinct lack of furniture. Positioned in the centre of the room there was a green leather chaise longue. Next to this was positioned a burgundy wing back chesterfield armchair. Between these two items was a very small, very low, mahogany table, currently holding two glasses of water. That was it. For the whole room that was all the furniture that there was.

"Why is there so little furniture in here?" Ella asked. "I mean, why have such a big room if that is all that you want to put in it?"

"Lesson number one Ella. It is not 'things' that fill up space."

"Right." Ella agreed, though wasn't sure she understood.

"Besides." Eleanor continued. "We need all this room so that our heads have space."

"Oh. Well, that kind of makes sense I guess."

"Come now. Let's get ourselves settled. Then we can begin."

Eleanor extended an arm out toward the chaise longue. Ella took her cue and the pair got themselves settled. Ella reclined on the chaise whilst Eleanor sat upright in the chesterfield.

"It may be an idea Ella if you drink a little water. Hypnosis can be quite disorientating the first time. It's important to be hydrated."

Ella picked up the glass closest to her, gulped down a couple of mouthfuls, then placed it back onto the table.

"Good. Now then. Are you feeling comfortable?" Eleanor asked.

"Indeed I am." Ella confirmed.

"Okay. Then let us begin."

Eleanor took a deep breath, followed by a long exhale.

"Okay Ella. It is all very simple. All I need you to do is lie back, close your eyes and clear your mind of any thoughts. I will count slowly down from 10."

"Will I then be hypnotised?" Ella enquired.

"Again, this is hypnotherapy Ella. I want to help you discover your true self and purpose, not trick you into believing you are a chicken." Eleanor paused, looked up to the ceiling then back at Ella. "You know what though, that could be quite amusing."

"Don't you dare." Retorted Ella with a smile.

"Ha, okay. Come on now. Lie back and close your eyes. Take a deep breath in. Then out. In. Then out. In... Then out..."

Ella closed her eyes and relaxed. Eleanor initiated the countdown.

"10"
Ella wondered if her sense of anticipation was like what spacemen felt just before blasting off.
"9"
She imagined spacemen would probably be less comfortable though.
"8"
'Spacemen. What is that all about? Surely by now it should be space people.'
"7"
'Had many women been blasted into space?'
"6"
'Eek. I was meant to be clearing my mind.'
"5"
'Maybe I should ask Eleanor to start again.'
"4"
'It's weird but Eleanor really does look a little bit like a monkey.'
"3"
'Wait, did she just say three alre...'
"2"
'Okay. This is clearly not going to wor...'
"1"
'Damn it. We'll have to start again.'
"0"
'Amazing. I hope Eleanor doesn't get cross.'

The Distance

"Open your eyes."

The command came to Ella's ears. Clearly it was Eleanor's voice, but it sounded wispy, distant, ghostly even, like a gentle breeze catching in her ear. With eyes still shut Ella started talking.

"I'm sorry Eleanor but I didn't empty my head. I think we might need to start aga..."

Ella opened her eyes. Then she dropped her jaw.

"What the actual...?"

The question was asked out loud to nobody, mostly because there was nobody there to ask. Ella sat up, finding herself on a solid wooden bench. The bench was situated on the hillside of a... A mountain maybe? Well, wherever it was situated the air was clean and crisp and fresh like nothing else. The views surrounding her were unreal, utterly stunning. Ella could see down into at least two valleys from here. Birds flew both above and below her.

The wind rose upwards, gentle and warm. All the trees were fully dressed and there were exotic looking flowers around in full bloom. 'What did she put in that water?' Is all Ella could think to herself.

Deciding to get to her feet Ella swung her legs off the bench and stood up. Her legs proved a little shaky but other than that she felt good. She stretched her arms high into the air, whilst taking a deep steadying breath, then turned to survey the rest of the landscape. It was something of a shock to find herself standing directly in front of a castle. 'What on Earth...?' Was all Ella could manage. But the castle was nothing on Earth. Nothing on the Earth that she was thinking of anyway.

The castle door that Ella stood in front of was huge, rectangular in design. Recently renovated maybe, freshly varnished certainly. It was a very proud looking door indeed. Cut into the bottom left section of the main door was a smaller people sized door. A door that had begun to open.

"Hello there Miss Ella. Are you alright? You seem a little lost."

In front of Ella stood a small, oddly stern looking figure. Rather short, dressed in an orange robe and sandals, head shaved, eyes that were focused and serene at the same time. Oh, and a tail rising from behind him, hanging over his right shoulder. This person it seemed was a monkey. A talking monkey.

Ella tried to offer a response but could only manage a rather odd gagging type noise.

"I'm afraid you are making no sense at all. Please, take a breath."

Ella took a breath, then tried again.

"You, you, you…" She pointed with her whole hand at the stranger. "You're a talking monkey."

"Pot calling kettle, I think is the expression young miss."

"But you can talk. You are talking to me."

Ella remembered again the water she drank then asked.

"Are you real or am I hallucinating?"

"I can assure you Miss Ella that I am quite real."

"Ha. I don't think so. There's no such thing as a talking monkey. I must just be off my head."

A little offended, the stranger crossed his arms. A second later though he relaxed.

"In all fairness it has been quite some time since you were here last. I can imagine it all does seem very strange to you."

"Since I was here last? I've never been here before."

"As you please."

"I don't even know where 'here' is. In fact, seeing as though you can talk, would you mind telling me where 'here' is?"

"Why 'here' is the residence of the Monkey King of course."

"Oh... Of course. Yes. Yes, that makes sense. I am at a castle so of course it contains a king. And as I am now in the land of talking monkeys it's only logical that said king is a Monkey King."

"Very good."

Ella sighed, then continued.

"What am I doing here exactly?"

"Well to that I would ask you, what do you think you are doing here?"

"Well, if I am here, in the land of talking monkeys, then I think, according to my therapist at least, that I must be here to find myself."

"To find yourself, yes. That would make sense."

"Okay, good. This feels good. Like we're getting somewhere."

"Indeed."

"So how do I find myself?"

"You will need to ask that question to the King."

"Oh, okay. So where is the King?"

"Can I assume it is an audience with the King that you seek?"

"Um, I don't know. Is it?"

"It usually is, yes."

"Okay. Well in that case, I am here to see the Monkey King."

"Very good. And what have you brought with you by way of an offering?"

"An offering? What do you mean?"

"Anyone that wishes to speak with the King must first present a worthy offering."

"But I don't have anyth…"

Ella pats at her empty pockets in protestation, then happens upon her lucky 50 pence piece.

"Ah."

Reluctantly Ella pulls the coin from her pocket. She hands it to the stranger for inspection, sure, it will be of little interest.

"Oh, my. Is this the one with the clouds on the back?"

"Yes. Yes, it is. But this is my luc…"

"Then that will do nicely. The King has an odd penchant for collecting 50 pence coins, I happen to know that he has been looking out for one of these for years. Very rare apparently."

"Yes, but it's my luck…"

The stranger pockets the 50 pence piece, turns on his heel then beckons Ella across the threshold. Ella lets out a defeated sigh then slowly begins to follow.

xx lol xx

Walking through the castle Ella is blown away by all the different coloured cottons and silks draped against the castle walls. Greens, purples, reds and oranges. Paired with beautifully intricate rugs to soften underfoot.

"Wow!" Ella exclaimed out loud. "Who is your interior designer? They are very good."

"Why thank you Miss Ella. I must admit I am rather proud."

"Wait. Are you saying that you did all of this?"

The stranger stopped, so abruptly that Ella almost bumped into him. Turning to face Ella he asked.

"You imply perhaps that a monkey would not be capable of such refined design choices?"

"No, no sorry. That's not what I... I mean... I didn't mean that. I'm sorry."

"Are you now?"

"Yes. Yes, of course. I'm sorry. I think it must be the clean air up here. I apologise if I have offended you."

"That's quite alright. There's not really anything you could say to offend me."

"Well, just sorry then. I think we got off on the wrong foot. I'm Ella by the way. Ella Songg."

"Yes. I know who you are."

"Hmm, you do seem to. Well, what is your name then?"

"My name is Kynome. Kynome Simian."

"Kynome." Ella tried it out on her tongue. "That's a nice sounding name. I don't think I've ever heard that name before."

"There is a first time for everything." Kynome replied. Then quietly to himself. "Appears that there is also a second first time."

"Simian?" Ella mused out loud. "That is the same name as my therapist. Eleanor Simian. Are you two related?"

"We are all related Miss Ella."

Nothing more was offered. Kynome then turned on his heel and again began to lead the way. Again, Ella began to follow.

Union

"Right Miss Ella." Kynome stopped outside a curiously small wooden door. "The Monkey King will see you shortly, though he will require a little time to prepare for your audience. If you will just wait here."

Kynome bent down and pushed open the small door. As it opened a wave of exotic aromas spilled out.

"You should find yourself most comfortable. Please help yourself to refreshments."

Ella could think of no-good reason not to enter the room, so decided to oblige. Even if doing so meant getting on her hands and knees to fit through the door. Once over the threshold Ella recognised what she would describe as a typically traditional Japanese room. A wood lined ceiling provided shelter to a beige tatami mat covered floor. A chabana flower display sat in an alcove at the far side of the room, positioned next to a hand brushed hanging scroll. Somewhere in the room incense burned.

At the centre of the room was positioned a low, rectangular wooden table. Running down the centre of the table were several small, ornate looking teapots. Next to each pot sat a container of leaves, each a different strain and flavour.

Kneeling already, on the far side of the table, was a woman, beautiful and striking. Her hair was rich and dark but caught the light in the room. Her face was smooth, radiant with youth. Her almond shaped eyes were smiling, as was her mouth. A full and beautiful smile that Ella felt was just for her alone.

"Hi. I'm Ella."

"Ella. Yes, I know. Ella Songg. Sid has talked much about you. Would you like some tea, Ella?"

"How does everyone know my name already? And what do you mean, Sid has talked about me? Who is Sid? Come to think of it, who are you? And where am I? Please don't tell me, 'The castle of the Monkey King'. I've heard that one already."

"My. So many questions. You are a curious one. One question at a time though. Starting with mine. Would you like some tea?"

Again, Ella could think of no reason to refuse so answered yes, indeed, she would very much like some tea. Ella took up a kneeling position opposite this new strange woman, then from the many assembled varieties chose a very satisfactory Cherry Blossom tea.

"So then, who are you?"

"Well Ella, since you asked so nicely. My name is Ebony. Ebony Thatcher."

"Ebony. That's a nice name. What are you doing here Ebony? Are you here to see the Monkey King too?"

"Sid, you mean?"

"Sid!" Exclaimed Ella. Then with a smirk questioned. "What kind of name is that for a king?"

"I know right. But seriously, you don't need to go there. His actual name is Siddhartha Gautama, but it's a bit of a mouthful and I think Sid helps him to feel humble."

"Fair enough. King Sid it is then. So, are you waiting to see him too?"

"Actually, no. We have seen Sid already."

"We?"

"Yes. I came here with my husband. We came to catch a cloud."

Ella raised her hand, a questioning finger extended toward Ebony. As Ella drew breath Ebony raised her own hand, palm facing Ella.

"Don't even ask. It's a long story."

Ella deflated, letting out a short sigh in response.

"So, anyway, he caught his cloud and had to leave already. He is on the next part of his journey, and I am still here."

"But why did he leave, and you stayed here? Why did you not go with him?"

"Well, where we are now, Ella, is a very special place indeed. Sid will explain more, but just know that I could not travel back with him."

"Okay. So, are you just staying here then?"

"No Ella. I'm not staying here. I am just stopping for a moment. Just for a cup of tea. Then I must leave to go back home."

"Oh. Okay. I guess. And how did you know my name? You look familiar. Have we met before?"

"The cosmos works in mysterious ways, it is true. But sadly, we have not met before. Sid has spoken about you to me though. He told me you were coming. He is quite excited I think."

"Excited? About me? I don't understand. I am just here trying to find myself. There is nothing special about me."

"Hmm. I think Sid would disagree. In fact, so would I."

Ebony gave Ella the warmest smile she had ever experienced. Then, at the far end of the room, a sliding door was pulled back from the outside and a beautiful open courtyard was revealed, brimming with lush greenery, a coy carp filled pond, a network of mini lakes and a gentle waterfall. Bird song could be heard all about the yard. No wind was there either for this courtyard was completely sheltered on all sides by the great castle walls. In the middle of the courtyard stood a beautiful ornate pagoda within which sat, cross-legged, illuminated, hands palm up, one rested upon each knee, the now fabled Monkey King. Poking his head around the open door was Kynome.

"Miss Ella. The Monkey King will see you now."

"Looks like you're up." Stated Ebony.

Ella looked back from the courtyard to Ebony. For some reason she appeared to have tears in her eyes. A little uncomfortably, Ella reached an open hand out over the table to shake and say goodbye. Ebony chuckled at this but took Ella's hand in hers all the same. She gave Ella's hand a big, warm squeeze.

"It was nice to meet you." Ella offered in response.

"More than you could ever know." Ebony replied.

After what felt like an age Ebony finally let go of Ella's hand. Ebony then stood and made her way to the small door. Looking back, she gave Ella the second warmest smile she had ever experienced. Then she was gone.

Sid

Kynome led Ella into the courtyard, to the pagoda where Sid was waiting.

"May I present to you, Miss Ella Songg."

Kynome waved his right arm in an ark and sort of half bowed as he gave this introduction.

"Hello." Said Ella. "My name is Ella. I understand that you are the King of Monkeys?"

"Something like that my child yes. But please, you must call me Sid."

"Sid. Yes, I know. That strange Ebony lady told me your name and I have to say that it's not very…"

"Yes, yes. Not very 'Kingy', I know."

"Ah."

"My full title is Siddhartha Gautama, Monkey King, representative of the House of the Blue Monkey."

"Nice."

"But I prefer Sid."

"Okay." Said Ella. "If I were a King Monkey though I would be using my full title. It sounds much grander. More important. "

"Well Ella, you will come to see that we are all grand and important, regardless of what names we are given."

"I'm not sure that's totally true. I once knew a girl called 'Elizabreth'. The other kids called her 'lizard's breath'. She had a terrible time of it, and I am sure that she never felt grand or important. Certainly not at school anyway."

"Hmm. I think you are missing my point there Ella."

"Hmm." Ella responded in kind. "I'm not sure that I am. A name can make a difference is all I am saying, and Sid does not sound like much of a name for a king."

"Okay. I will take your point. How about we park that discussion for a moment. Please, come sit with me so we can talk."

Ella took a seat, sitting on a gold embroidered cushion opposite Sid. Once settled Ella looked up and asked. "What do you want to talk about?"

"Well Ella, that depends mostly on you. Why is it that you are here?"

"I think I am here to find myself. Well, Eleanor hypnotised me, or drugged me, or whatever, and now I am here. Though I still don't even know where 'here' is.?"

"Okay then. Why don't we start there? The realm that you are in is known as The Equidistante."

"The a-quid-ee what now?"

"The Equidistante. Or 'The Distance', as we like to call it. This realm exists in a sphere that connects to all other realms. We are exactly an equal distance from each."

"Okay... I think. The Distance then. Is this like a dream world or something?"

"You mean 'realm'. Dream realm."

"Realm. Whatever. Is this a dream realm then?"

"No. The Dream Realm is another realm, much like the one you come from. You can access all realms from The Distance, including the Dream Realm. Though you really should be asleep if you want to go exploring there, otherwise the Sandman tends to get cross."

"The Sandma..." The word faded into a mumble before Ella could finish saying it.

"We are, to you I suppose, a little like the Dream Realm. There are various ways in which to enter The Distance, though sleeping is the most common. It is the only way that most souls will ever get to enter and only then whilst they are passing through toward the Dream Realm. In fact, humans especially often mistake time passing through here for time spent in the Dream Realm. It is those fragments of memory from just before falling and just before waking that they are recalling. Those are the times that they are passing through The Distance., either on their way to, or back from the dream realm."

"Wow. Okay. So, what about me? Am I not dreaming then?"

"No Ella. At this moment you are not. In your realm we have several representatives, working for the House of the Blue Monkey. Each of these representatives can open a doorway, if you will, that allows certain souls access to The Distance, in person. Like yourself."

"Ah, was that the hypnosis part?"

"Correct. Our practitioners are very skilled. You would not have been aware, but you were put under in a flash, then physically ushered through a doorway into our realm."

"Oh."

Ella wasn't entirely sure how she felt about this but decided to move on.

"How else can people get here?"

"Well, if a soul is desperate, or dying, the mind will sometimes create a crack that will let them through."

"That doesn't sound all that pleasant."

"It is neither pleasant nor unpleasant. It just is."

"Okay."

"Then there is always a cup of mushroom tea of course. Most who enter by these means though usually leave a little bewildered and end up convincing themselves it never really happened."

'Miaow!'

Ella turned toward the sound. A beautiful male Siamese cat had entered the bandstand.

"Aww. You own a cat?"

"Nobody 'owns a cat' Ella."

"Hmm, fair. Does the cat have a name?" Ella was already tickling the cat behind its ear.

"Schrödinger." Sid confirmed.

Schrödinger, now purring, curled up next to Ella and fell into a nap. Inspired, Ella asked.

"Has Schrödinger just gone to the Dream Realm then?"

"Weeeeelll..." Replied Sid in a very non-committal fashion. "The rules are a little different for cats."

"What is that supposed to mean?" Ella questioned.

"It's complicated." Confirmed Sid, leaving it at that.

A moment later Schrodinger opened his eyes, got up to stretch, then wandered off.

Sid resumed talking.

"You should probably know about time whilst you are here as well."

"Time?" Ella questioned.

"Yes. You will notice whilst you are here that clocks work... differently."

"Differently how?"

"There are only two times that we recognise here. There is the wrong time and then there is the right time. It will only ever be one or the other. We refer to this as 'DMT',"

"Sounds way too simple. How do you ensure you are on time for something?"

"The past, present and future all combine here. One can only ever be on time as one is only ever where one is supposed to be."

"Okay."

"Make sense?"

"No."

"Well, you are here now, but 'now' is not a real tangible thing. The 'now' is just the passing of a moment. A moment that passes only because you perceive it passing. In truth, nothing ever passes anywhere. Thus, everything exists, all at once."

"Everything?"

"Yes Ella. Everything. Making up 'The Whole'."

"Wow. That must be a pretty big hole."

"Quite. Though here it becomes a little more complex. Just because everything exists in The Whole, it doesn't mean everything is 'existing' at the same time."

"Ah."

"Because, as I have already explained, there is no time."

"No time."

"That's right."

"Just a right time and a wrong time."

"Very good."

"DMT."

"You've got it."

"Wait!" Ella exclaimed. "'DM', as in Dark Matter, right?"

"What's that?"

"Dark Matt... Ah, forget it."

"As you wish. DMT though refers to 'Distance Mean Time'. I believe you have something similar in your realm." This wasn't a question.

"Okay Sid. I'm not sure that I understand, but I am happy to just roll with it."

Sid gave a smile.

xx lol xx

The conversation went on. Sid gave a broad overview of The Distance and some of the characters within it. Sid talked Ella through the history of The House of Red Dragon and The House of Blue Monkey. Following this Sid outlined to Ella the principle of the four truths. In the main Ella was able to get on board but did take issue when Sid insisted that everyone always had a choice.

"So, you're saying that we always have a choice. But that's not really true, is it?"

"Well, as I have outlined, there may be occasions where choice has been taken away. But those occasions will arise only as a consequence of prior choices."

"Nah. I'm not buying it."

"The truth is not for sale Ella. The truth is just the truth."

"Okay. So, when I watch the news, and see silly little men, who think they are leaders, swinging their inadequate weapons about the place, throwing insults, then bombs, then missiles at each other. Are you saying that the people of their respective countries had a choice in that situation?"

"Well, those silly little men did not get to be leaders by magic. But I think here you are over complicating the point."

"Over complicating? That's convenient for your argument."

"No. That is not what I mean. It is just that in your example there are many variables to consider. Each member of a country will have a different point of view. It is easy to assume that one would not choose war. But in reality, a good number do."

"Okay. Let's just focus then on those that do not choose war as their preferred option. War goes ahead anyway, so their choice does not matter."

"Well, you are right. Their choice will not stop the war. Instead, they have now different options to choose from. They are presented with new choices. For example, they could choose to flee the country, to escape the war."

"They could. Okay, they could choose I suppose."

"There. You see. There is always a choice."

"Fine. What about a child in this situation?"

"A child?"

"Yes, a child. Born to parents in a country where war is played out. A child that would choose to be safe. A child that would choose to play with their friends. A child that would never choose war. A child that has no choice. Whose choices have been decided by the parents. Where is it that the child always has a choice?"

"You make a good case, but you are still missing the point."

"What point is that? You said, black and white, we always have a choice. I am saying that we don't always have a choice."

"Well Ella, what can I say. Most humans I speak with simply swallow it all up."

Ella crossed her arms and leant back a little. Sid continued.

"That said, most humans I speak with still believe that they have evolved from monkeys."

Sid looked up at the sky to reflect, then looked back at Ella.

"I can see now why she likes you so much." He stated.

"What? Who likes me?"

"The entity you are going to meet next." Sid looked at his wrist. He was wearing a timepiece of some sort. "Come on." He said. "It is time for the next part of your journey."

"The next part? I thought this was it."

"Oh Ella, you are a character. This has simply been an introduction. A chat. An interview of sorts. To gauge if you are ready."

"Ready? Ready for what?"

"You will see." Sid got to his feet and beckoned Ella to do the same.

"Come now Ella. Walk with me and I will take you where you need to go."

Ella stood and followed Sid's lead.

"Sid? A moment ago, you said something about humans believing we evolved from monkeys."

"I know. Have you ever heard anything so ridiculous?"

"But if it wasn't monkeys, then..."

"Octopuses Ella. Octopus."

"For real?"

"True that."

"Wow."

Ella made a gun using two of her fingers, pointed it to her temple, then blew out her mind.

Near Death Experience

Sid led Ella through the castle, down several corridors, until eventually they came to a doorway. It felt to Ella like they must be somewhere toward the rear of the castle. The door itself looked heavy and imposing, solid wood, well-aged, mostly black in colour. Ella noticed immediately that there was neither a door knocker nor door handle nor keyhole.

"So how do you get in then? Do we just have to push?"

"Why not give that a try Ella."

Ella did. Tentatively she reached out a hand, placed her palm flat against the door and gave a gentle push.

Nothing.

She pushed a little harder.

Still nothing.

She then placed the palm of her other hand against the door and pushed again.

Nothing still.

Now Ella set her legs, bent her arms, and pushed with all her might.

The door did not budge an inch.

"Okay." Ella conceded, now panting a little. "So, you can't just push it open then?"

"No." Sid confirmed. "You cannot."

"So how do we open it?" Ella queried.

"We don't." Came Sid's reply. "She does."

"This person we have come to see?"

"Person. Yes, you could say that."

"And how does she know when to open the door?"

"She knows everything."

"Excellent. Okay then. So why is the door still closed."

"Because you haven't asked to go in yet."

"What. Wait. You are saying I have to ask?"

"Well yes. It is you she wants to see."

"Okay. Helpful Sid. Thank you very much. So, what do I need to do then? Is there like a magic word or something?"

"Why don't you try knocking?"

"Oh, yes, of course."

Ella reached up a fist and gently knocked on the door.

"I meant with your mind." Said Sid.

"Wha... With my mind? What really?"

"Yes, really. Try knocking with your mind."

"With my mind. Okay, why not? It's not like this day could get any stranger."

Ella cleared her throat.

"Ahem."

Ella cleared her mind.

'Ahem.'

With her mind focused clearly on the door, Ella thought.

'Knock', 'knock', 'knock'.

A pause.

Then a creak.

The door began too slowly open.

"Well blow me." Ella offered.

"There." Said Sid. "Let that be a lesson. There are no closed doors that can't be opened if you truly put your mind to it."

Whilst no doubt delivered with good intent Ella couldn't help but feel just a little bit patronised.

Sid again took the lead and Ella followed him through the doorway, into the darkness beyond. The pair were then descending in circles, down a stone staircase, going deeper and deeper and deeper into the ground. Sid had lit a lantern at the top of their descent which was now their only source of light.

"I hope you're not scared of spiders."

Sid offered this comment with a little chuckle to himself. Ella, as it so happened, was not.

After descending for what seemed like an age the pair found themselves standing at the start of a long stone corridor. Decorated down either side by stone arches, lit from within by flaming wooden torches. The roof of the corridor was very high, especially considering the fact they had to be so far underground. There did not appear to be any actual rooms to speak of, but Ella could make out, at the opposite end of the corridor, a very ornate gothic looking archway.

Sid put down the lantern he had been carrying, on a ledge at the bottom of the stairs.

"Here we are then." He said. "We won't be needing that anymore." Referring to the lantern.

He then moved off down the corridor. Ella followed suit.

"What is this place then? Some sort of dungeon? Is this where you keep all the dead bodies?"

Ella couldn't see but this comment caused Sid to smile.

"Something like that." He said in reply. "Come now. We are nearly there."

A moment later Sid held out his arm to stop.

"Okay. That is close enough."

"Close enough for what." Ella questioned.

"Close enough for an audience with whom we have come to see of course."

"And are you ever going to tell me who it is, whom we have come to s..."

At that moment a rush of noise erupted into the hallway, sounding like a thousand tortured souls, all screaming out at once. The noise then cut off just as abruptly. A gust of hot wind blew into Ella's and Sid's eyes. Squinting now, Ella could just about make out a huge shape forming in the recess of the archway, shrouded in smoke, slowly moving toward them, at least 10 feet tall, dressed in a tattered black gown. The figure came closer, and Ella could make out a heavy black hood, but no face. Within the hood, two bright red eyes lit up, followed by a huge cloud of smoke.

Taking an involuntary step back, Ella's first thought was that they had come to see a hooded fire breathing dragon demon. The figure though was now so close that it was filling the archway in front of them, and Ella could see the giant scythe, held in the figure's bony left hand. She knew who it was that they had come to see.

The red eyes lit up again. Another cloud of smoke followed. This time though Ella could smell that smoke. Only it wasn't smoke that she smelt. No. What Ella could smell was banana flavoured vape juice?

"They're not your eyes, are they?" Ella spoke out loud. "You're vaping. Those are vape sticks."

In response to the charge, Death pushed back her hood a little and two vape sticks were revealed, hanging out of a bony mouth. Death grabbed them in her right hand. Then, coughing, said in a mighty booming voice.

"I HAD TO QUIT THE CIGARETTES."

'Cough,' 'cough,' 'cough.'

"THOSE THINGS WERE KILLING ME."

Sid and Death both burst out laughing, like this was the funniest thing either of them had ever heard. Death then casually tossed the vapes away down the corridor. As they clattered over the stone floor death continued.

"THE VAPES ARE RUBBISH THOUGH. THEIR BATTERIES EXPIRE SO QUICKLY. MORE QUICKLY EVEN THAN YOU MORTALS."

This triggered more laughter from the pair, though this time it seemed it was at Ella's expense.

"Wow." Said Ella in response. "You're a funny guy then eh?"

Ella paused. Her eyes looked up to the right whilst she thought. Then she looked at Sid and questioned.

"I thought you said we were coming to meet a woman, Sid?"

"OH MY LORD!" Exclaimed Death. "WHY DOES EVERYONE ALWAYS ASSUME THAT I AM A MAN?"

"Oh." Said Ella, looking up and placing a finger to the corner of her mouth.

"I don't know. Maybe it's something to do with that..." Here she changed body posture for added emphasis... "BIG BOOMING VOICE!"

"OH? OH YES, I SEE. OF COURSE. AHEm. AHem. Forgive me."

Now a significant number of decibels lower Death suddenly sounded very feminine.

"I always forget I've got the voice on. I like to use it as it often scares people to death. Saves me the job of having to use this heavy old thing."

Death swung her scythe in demonstration. Ella felt a very distinct chill run down her spine as it passed overhead.

"Anyway, my real name is Ivy. Or 'I', 'V' for short." Ivy used her bony fingers to make little rabbit ear shapes in the air for each letter, which elicited another burst of laughter.

"Ivy Profen, to give you my full name. Your realm named a class of drugs after me. We're both very good at pain relief apparently."

More laughter.

Honestly, this pair were like children. Ella was though genuinely surprised to learn that Death had a real name.

"But your name is Death." Is all she could think to say.

"Death is an occupation dear, not a name. I've certainly not met any humans called death. Have you?"

"Well, no. Maybe a few that looked like..." Ella trailed off. "But I, I..."

"But, but, but..." Interrupted Ivy. "But nothing. I think it's a little insulting, after all these years, that humans still think me not worthy of a name."

"I apologise for being shocked." Ella offered. "I just. Well, wow. Who would have thought that Death was called Ivy?"

"'I','V',"

Chipped in Sid. Now amusing himself.

"And who would have thought that death is a woman?" Ella continued, ignoring Sid completely.

"Seriously?" Questioned Ivy. "I mean. Really. Imagine this thing..." Ivy held up her scythe. "...In the hands of a male. One little knock to his ego and the whole human race would be gone overnight."

Ella glanced at Sid. Now it was her turn to smile.

"Seriously though." Death went on. "Releasing souls from their mortal coils is a serious responsibility. Most men would get bored after the first few centuries and start hacking away at goodness knows what."

"On that note." Ella interjected. "How do you manage to deal with so many souls on your own? I mean. I read somewhere that three people die every second. How on Earth do you attend to so many, all at different locations, at the same time?"

"Ella, for starters, it is not just your realm that I do business with. Can I take it that Sid has already outlined the fact that time works differently here in The Distance? There are only ever two..."

"Yeah, yeah. The right time and the wrong time."

"Yes. Very good. Then you understand."

"Uh, no. No, I wouldn't say that I understand. How can you be everywhere all at once to attend to all those people. I mean, shouldn't you be off decapitating some poor soul right now?"

"Ha, ha, ha. Oh Ella. I don't decapitate…"

"That's not totally true is it, Ivy?" Sid Interjected.

"Ahem. Fair. Okay, well I do decapitate. I just don't decapitate very often. Only the most vile and despicable will lose their heads. For everybody else I simply cut the thread that ties them to their realm. It would never do to arrive in the After without a head now would it."

Sid and Death shared another laugh here. Obviously, an in-joke Ella decided, as she could see nothing funny there.

"Decapitate, cut, slice, snip, chop, whatever. Whatever it is you do, shouldn't you be somewhere doing it right now, instead of standing here, talking to me?"

"You do make a fair point so I will try to offer you a fair answer. By way of its simplest explanation, I am Death and I have all the time in the Cosmos because behind me stands a special door. Whenever I choose to open that door, it will open to exactly the place I need to be at that moment. Whoever might be on the other side of that door gets the snip. Simple, no?"

"Well…"

"This door is what's known in The Distance as an Everywhere Door. This door opens to The Whole, which means that it opens to every moment that has ever and will ever exist. In terms of the performance of my duties I am in no rush, because whenever I open that door, I will be at the right place at the right time."

Not convinced Ella went on.

"Surely though, sooner or later, if working at that pace, then the number of hatches will outpace dispatches."

"I see that you are not fully grasping the concept so I will boil it down further for you. Here, in The Distance, time works differently, and that is all you need to know for now."

Frustrated though she was, Ella decided to let the conversation lie and moved on to a more pressing matter.

"Okay then Ivy. Different question for you. What is it exactly that I am doing here?"

Ivy gave a bony grin.

"As I understand it you have come here to find yourself. Is that not correct?"

"Well, that is why my therapist sent me to this place, yes. But that doesn't explain why you wanted to meet with me."

It was then that a rather obvious thought occurred to Ella, turning her a pale shade of grey as it did so.

"Ha, ha, ha. Oh Ella. If it was to give you the snip I would have come to you, in your realm. Not arranged to have met you here, in mine."

The colour returned to Ella's cheeks.

"Why then? Why am I here?"

"Well Ella, not many people know this, but there is more to life than Death. Have you ever heard of Lord Gangles?"

"Lord who?" Was Ella's reply.

"Lord Gangles. Wind chimes for fingers? Anything? No."

"Wind chimes f... What?"

"No. Of course you have not heard of Lord Gangles. The reason that you have not is because he is very good at his job."

"His job? What job? What are you even talking about?"

"Lord Gangles walks the line. Between The Distance and the realms. Lord Gangles is a creator of worlds and a healer of souls. When roads travelled get dark, the Lord may come and offer a light to illuminate a different way. The Lord offers choice."

"Oh, we're back to talking about choice again, are we?" Ella scoffed. "And how does he offer anything without real hands? Who has even heard of windchime fingers?"

"You misunderstand. Lord Gangles uses his chimes to create worlds in which souls can heal. Music is magic. One of the most ancient forms of magic in fact. Sadly, for most of your kind, music has lost meaning. Dark commercial forces at work in your realm have diluted and popularised the dullest of music spells. Masses hypnotised by repetition, primed to receive sinister messages that overlay the little ditties. Fortunately, though not all your kind are so switched off. Even those that are switched off remain susceptible to the real magic of music."

"So, what you are saying is that this Lord Gangles fella is a little bit like The Beatles?"

"Ha, ha, ha. Oh Ella. Majestic as The Beatles are, they would appear as the rock does to the mountain when compared to the mighty Lord Gangles. The Lord can hear notes between the notes. Align vibrations of the body with vibrations of the bass. Find melody within chaos. The Lord is truly mighty and by using his wind chime fingers, in just the right order, in just the right way, and at just the right time, the Lord can create worlds in which souls can traverse on tailor made quests for tailor made truths and spiritual enlightenment. The Lord is immense. The Lord is mighty. The Lord is great."

"Hallelujah!" Ella exclaimed, earning a rather stern look from Ivy.

"Sorry. Couldn't resist."

Ivy looked away, brushed some imaginary dirt from her left shoulder, then went on.

"Lord Gangles, you see, is an alternative to me. When beings get lost, generally heading in my direction, Lord Gangles may intervene and offer help to guide them to a brighter path."

"How is it then everyone knows about you, and no one knows about Lord Gangles?"

"In short, your kind tends to have a lot of near-death experiences. I've lost count of the number of times I have opened that door only to have it slam shut on me again. It may only be open a few seconds but that is usually enough for the poor soul on the other side to catch a glimpse of me and... Well, let us just say that my unique appearance, coupled with a brief moment of terror has tended to make me quite memorable to those that have seen me. You see, I never really know who is going to be on the other side of that door whereas Lord Gangles has the benefit of preparation. He is provided by the cosmos, via Sid, with a target. He will know who he is going to see as he needs to compose. Part of any composition will include a section to ensure the subject retains no lucid memory of the Lord himself."

"That makes sense."

"But some do remember subconsciously. Look closely and you will find your culture littered with references and reminders. Those who meet the Lord know that they have a memory of someone, something, someone important. But It will forever remain just out of reach, in The Distance."

"You know, Lord Gangles sounds cool. Do I get to meet him?"

"Well, that's the thing you see. The current Lord Gangles is due for retirement."

"Retirement? Can he do that?"

"Indeed, he can. Indeed, he must. Gangles is born of your realm and being born of your realm means that he remains tied to it. Whilst time works differently here, Lord Gangles is still subject to ageing, and thus expiration. The current Lord has served his time in The Distance and must now return to his home realm to see out his golden years."

"Well, in that case then I am very happy for him. Question though. Why are you telling me this?"

"Ella, this realm requires a replacement."

"And..?"

"Ella Songg, it just so happens that replacement is you."

"Pmph..."

Ella made this noise involuntarily, whilst at the same time turning to look at Sid with a very bemused expression on her face. By way of return Sid offered a, 'don't look at me' type look, accompanied by a hunch of the shoulders.

"I am serious young Ella. It is your destiny to be the next Lord Gangles."

"Ha. You must have confused me with somebody else. I mean, I don't know the first thing about gangling."

"Ah, but you do. You just don't know it yet."

"Seriously. Death. I mean Lord Death. Sorry, Ivy, whatever. You've obviously got the wrong person. I live in a council house and work in a chip shop. What good would I be as a gangleator? I mean, look."

Ella offered up both her hands like a little puppy dog.

"Fingers. See? Real fingers."

She gave them a wiggle.

"Not windchimes. I mean, how would I wrap chips up with windchimes? You've clearly got the wrong person."

"Oh Ella. Where you live and what you do has no bearing on what you are and where you are supposed to be. Let me tell you this. You have grown up in your world knowing that you don't fit. Am I right?"

"Well, yes, I suppose so. But that is the same for lots of people."

"Maybe so. But unlike lots of people, when you sit underneath a tree and listen to the birds singing, you can make out every single note. You understand what they are singing to each other. Am I right?"

"Well, I like to think I can, but I am sure other people can do th..."

"When you listen to the wind blow you can hear it converse with the trees. Am I right."

"I can... Well, I like to think that I can hear... But that's always just been in my head I'm sur..."

"When you listen to a piece of music you feel individual notes. You sense them like touch. You feel warmth and cold in their respective tones. You sense the notes between the notes. Am I right?"

"Well, I, I just... I don't know. I've spent a lot of time on my own. I just listen better I guess."

"Now is not the time for denial. The reason you have always felt so alone is because you are alone. The reason you feel unique is because you are unique. Many humans like to believe that they are special Ella, but you... You actually are!"

Ella's head was spinning now.

"So very special in fact. Only once every thousand years, your time, is someone born with the abilities that you have. You come from a long line of Gangles that stretch all the way back to the beginning. You came here to find yourself. Well Ella Songg, it is your destiny to be the next Lord Gangles, and it is my absolute honour to be the one who introduces you to yourself."

"No, wait. I want to be a doctor. I am going to save up and go to university and become a doctor. That is what I want to be."

"Alas, what is a doctor if not a healer, and what greater healer is there than the healer of souls?"

"But I... I mean... I..."

"You have many questions, I am sure. All will be answered in the fullness of time. For now, just know that it is your destiny to be the next Lord. Know that you will receive the best training for that position in this realm. Know that you will be a better doctor than any doctor in your realm. You will be Dr Ella Songg. You will be Lord Gangles.

You will be more magnificent than you could ever have imagined. It is, for you young Ella, written in the stars."

Ella moved her jaw and mouth but found that words failed her. All she could do was gawp, making facial expressions like a fish out of water. Sid was next to speak.

"Be calm Ella."

Sid took her hand within his own as he said this.

"You have nothing to fear, and you need not accept the position right now. Might I suggest you return home for a few days to ponder what you have learnt."

Staring into space, but anchored by the warmth of Sid's grasp, Ella took a breath then conceded.

"Yes. Yes. I think I would like to go home now. I think I could do with a little lie down."

"Very good." Ivy agreed. "Return home. Spend some of your time to think this over. Once you have arrived at your decision, please seek out Eleanor. She will let you back into The Distance so that your new life and your training can begin."

Staring at the floor, Ella nodded and made to turn back toward the corridor.

"Wait." Ivy commanded. "No need to take the stairs. You can use my door."

Ivy stood to one side and beckoned Ella, alone, toward the ancient looking door behind him. Ella shuffled forwards until stood in front of the door. The door seemed both solid and translucent at the same time. Featureless yet alive with all the activity of the cosmos. Ella could see no handle so turned to ask.

"How do I op…" Her question was broken by a soft creaking noise followed by a gentle rush of warm air.

"Simply step through Ella. We will see you soon."

Ella gave a little wave, took a deep breath, then made to step through the door.

"Wait!"

Sid shouted. Ella stopped and turned back to face him.

"You forgot this."

He rummaged in a pocket then pulled out Ella's prized 50 pence piece.

"My lucky coin. But Kynome said I had to pay for an audience with you?"

"The requirement was to make an offering. There is no charge."

"But Kynome said you collect 50p's. That you have been looking for that one for ages."

"Indeed, I do. Indeed, I have. The true pleasure in collecting though comes not in owning, but in seeking and acquiring. Seeing this coin reassures me that another will be out there. One that has my name on it. This one however belongs to you."

Sid expertly flipped the coin toward Ella, who caught it in her right hand. Feeling the coin there, a huge grin spread over her face. Ella then turned back and stepped through the door.

xx lol xx

On the other side Ella was stunned to find herself standing in the corner of a familiar looking room, with chandeliers hanging from the ceiling, crackling fireplaces either side and a beautiful chaise longue situated at its centre. And there, sat on a chair, next to the chaise longue was a familiar face.

"Ella!"

Eleanor exclaimed brightly.

"How was your trip?"

'Doof.'

The door swung shut behind her.

Back To Life

Ella's original intent had been to carry on like nothing had changed. When she'd first gotten back Ella was so relieved to be home that she ran into the house and gripped her mum in a huge embrace. This surprised them both, neither one being particularly affectionate. A slightly awkward disentanglement followed. The next day, a Wednesday, Ella was up early, keen to get to her shift at the chip shop. This was a role she understood. As the day wore on though the comfort of familiarity faded. For a start it was never the same after Charlie.

In the middle of her first shift back Angel and two of her gang waltzed in. They came at least once a week for chips. Angel never paid full price and Ella had gotten used to quietly making up the difference. Better that than to risk a public confrontation. This time though was different. This time Ella was different.

This time Ella called Angel out, stating that she would happily make up the difference but would be adding it to Angel's tab. Angel's first reaction was to laugh in Ella's face. Ella then calmly stated that she was arranging to sell the debt to Mick the Fish, who would be in touch.

It was public knowledge by this time that Mick had a thing for Ella's mum. In fact, just the other day Mick had asked Mary out to dinner. Mary almost accepted until Mick said he would loan her the money for her half of the bill. The date was put on ice but the idea that Mick may buy up Ella's debt, to win favour, was not outside the realms of possibility.

Back at the chip shop Angel had stopped laughing, turned tail and was now leading her followers away. She shouted over her shoulder as she left that she would not be back. In that same moment Ella realised that she did not want to serve chips anymore.

Returning home that evening Ella felt unusually weary. She perched on the couch, turned on the TV and unwrapped her dinner of slightly cold chips. The TV was tuned to the news. Ella just wanted something pointless and mindless to stare at whilst eating. The news was perfect.

Currently a piece was running with the Rt Hon Josh Robertson. He was waxing lyrical about how great he was for recently ridding the community of the local youth club. It was, he stated, a breeding ground for crime. A place where young hoodlums were freely encouraged to gather and make plans for mugging pensioners and the like. The youth club encouraged them to spray graffiti, to run amok on skateboards, to play loud music etcetera. They even provided condoms so that they could have sex with each other. The place was a disgrace and an absolute menace to society.

Josh was pleased to report that monies saved would instead be used to provide more police who would be empowered with greater stop and search powers, so that they could stop these wayward youths from ever having the chance to commit crime in the first place. Oh, he was also upgrading his office. This, he insisted, was so that his constituents could be more comfortable when they came to see him during open surgeries, not that Josh had held any of these recently.

Ella picked up the remote and switched the TV off. She sat there for a moment or two in silence, staring at the blank screen. She then got up, walked to the kitchen, dropped her cold chips into the bin and went to bed.

xx lol xx

Following those initial hours back at home Ella had started to seriously consider the opportunity that had been made available to her. Reflecting, as she was now able to reflect, on a potential lifetime of a thousand years, everything suddenly seemed far less important, less urgent. Being aware of The Distance took the edge off Ella's fears in this realm. So what if a giant meteor crashed into the Earth tomorrow? It might well mean peanuts to life in this realm, but life was everywhere. Attached to The Distance were an infinite number of other realms. Some perhaps just like this one. Ella, in her dreams, had revisited The Distance several times since coming back. She had talked more with Sid, the Monkey King, about life in The Distance. Ella had a better understanding now of how it served as a go between for all other realms. Ella also had a better understanding of the job offer that was on the table.

Ella would be required to reside in The Distance as a permanent resident. She would have to leave her life in the realm, and her mother, behind. The idea of leaving her mum saddened Ella greatly. At first, she would be permitted to visit whenever she liked. She had to understand though that because time passed differently in The Distance her mother would age whilst Ella seemingly would not. At some point this would become obvious, causing unnecessary distress to Mary and potential risks to Ella.

In the past, for example, one could have been accused of being a witch or a vampire. These days a time traveller would be more likely. Regardless, it was a fact that at some point Ella would have to stop visiting her mother.

In addition, was the fact that everybody Ella knew would die and she would be left to live over 900 years on her own. Aside from losing her mother this part didn't really bother Ella. She'd spent most of her life alone already. What was another 983 years? Anyway, Ella would not be alone. She would make real friendships in The Distance. A fresh start in a place where she was understood. Where she now knew that she belonged.

That's right. Ella had decided that she was going to take the job. Ella would train to be the next Lord Gangles. She would become Dr Ella Songg. She would be Lord Gangles. She would be magnificent. It was written in the stars. Hallelujah and amen.

First though she had to finish her last shift at the chip shop.

ACT 3

Living In The Distance

Ella had been living in The Distance now for some time. Following that final shift in the chip shop Ella had caught the bus home and packed a bag. The next morning, she gave her mum a hug goodbye. A cover story was provided and would continue to be managed by the Ho-Bloom centre. They had provided official looking communications that showed Ella had been randomly selected to receive part of a national levelling up bursary, being offered a once in a lifetime opportunity to train to become a doctor.

The training facility was located abroad and was residential. The bursary would cover initial travel costs, but any home visits would need to be paid for by either Ella or Mary. This made it easier for Ella to justify not visiting regularly. In time, as years passed, and Ella visited less, the Ho-Bloom Centre would assume different identities as required, offering Ella the necessary cover for her infrequent visits. Eventually they would deliver a final story, reporting to Mary that Ella had sadly been lost in a tragic accident and would not be coming home again. A final act of kindness.

Ella had arrived in The Distance with nothing more than a few possessions and the clothes on her back. After reporting back to Eleanor at the Ho-Bloom centre Ella re-entered The Distance via the door in the far corner of the underground room. This time no hypnosis was necessary.

Sid was waiting for Ella when she arrived. He had arranged a room, prepared in the higher reaches of the castle. The room was furnished with several comforts including a radio, that could pick up channels from her own realm, a four-poster bed and a huge desk situated by the window, ready for the pantheon of books that Ella would be required to read as part of her studies, set to begin the very next day.

Before that though Ella was first introduced to a young woman named Amari Animate. Both of a similar age, Amari was set to become Ella's partner in crime. Ella learnt that Amari was training to earn her Angel wings, and that part of that training meant undertaking the same rigorous course of study that was necessary to be the next Lord Gangles. It was fitting, Ella thought, that Amari should be training to be an Angel. She was, by far, the most beautiful person Ella had ever seen. Both of equal height it was here that the similarities ended. Amari had rich dark skin that seemed to shimmer in the light. She wore her hair in braided dreadlocks down to her shoulders. Her high cheekbones supported bright green eyes that shone like jewels. A regal nose sat atop full soft lips. An athletic physique, dressed in bohemian fabrics.

Amari and Ella would eventually graduate together, live together and work together always. But first they had to study.

xx lol xx

Several subjects were considered critical for the line of work that the pair were to take up. Sid took on the role of Philosophy & Psychology teacher. It was Sid's mission to create a safe space to provoke thought from Ella and Amari. Over and over Sid threw things at them that were initially shocking or offensive. Over time though they learned not to take offence but instead take the opportunity to think about things differently. It was essential that Lord Gangles could see the world from the view of the subject and not be led by any unconscious bias.

Kynome took on the role of Science and Biology teacher. Unlike classes delivered back in her realm, Ella found Kynome's lessons fascinating. His passion for science was infectious and through it he was able to show Amari and Ella how everything in nature is, literally, connected to everything else.

Maths and Physics were taught by Schrödinger the Cat. It turns out that cats can converse with humans whilst residing in The Distance. It also so happens that cats are very good at maths and have a remarkable understanding of Quantum Mechanics, particularly superposition.

Music lessons took up the main share of Ella's time. Ella had thought she already had a good grasp on music. She soon came to realise that she had known nothing of the art. Her music teacher, Ms Howlett, was a wise looking woman of roughly middle age. Quite the eccentric, Ms Howlett snubbed comfortable accommodation in the castle to live instead in an old weather worn silver campervan, pitched out on the common ground behind the castle. Ms Howlett confirmed early on that Ella had a strong natural ability, she just needed to be taught the skills to go with it. Ms Howlett's mastery of the art was a revelation to Ella, and she taught her how to start seeing music as the whole that it was.

A note, for example, was never just a note. Contrary to popular belief a note did not exist in isolation. Before a note could be registered its own resonance meant that other notes had already been created. Ella came to see notes as picture forming building blocks that could be combined in an infinite variety of designs.

An 'E' note was green in colour and curved in shape. E radiated love and warmth and felt like home. When combined with other notes whole shapes and additional feelings came into existence. E Minor, for example, created a deep cylindrical shape, like a hollow well. The length of the cord, or rather the sustain, could determine a shape's depth. A bend, on any of the notes, individually or collectively, could affect the colour, the width, the curvature, even the smell. Each note a different colour, each chord a different shape, each shape a different feeling. Music was no longer just sound. Music, Ella realised, was everything and everything was music.

The day came when Ella was introduced to the equipment that brought all her musical learnings together. She was presented with the outfit of Lord Gangles. Or rather, a very old prototype of the outfit of Lord Gangles. Never mind, the prototype performed in all the same ways. It was Amari who had been given the pleasure of presenting her friend with the costume. The pair were currently together in the castle changing rooms.

"Behold, Ella Songg, your new gear."
Amari bowed whilst stepping to the left and opening her arms to gesture behind her. There, in a neatly folded pile, a uniform of sorts was waiting on a bench. Ella pulled the kind of face that one pulls when they are not very impressed.
"Oh, come on Ella. This is amazing. It's like you're a proper superhero or something."
Ella had learnt early on that Amari had a rather endearing love of superheroes. Especially their costumes.
"Yes. A superhero that likes worn brown leather and smells like a charity shop."

"Okay, it's a little fusty, I agree. Nothing that a bit of fresh air won't fix. Come on, get it on and we can go outside. Test it out."

Ella let out a sigh, then began to survey the kit in more detail.

First was the mask. Not very flattering in truth but very striking in design. Looking a bit like a bird gone wrong, the mask covered the whole head, sporting a nosepiece that protruded away from the face to a point like a bird's beak. This face had clearly provided inspiration in Ella's realm for both plague doctors and masquerade ballers.

Goggles were used to cover the eye socket holes. There were though outlet valves, designed to emit dry ice, which could be fired outwards to shroud an area in a misty atmosphere, heavy with suspense.

Inside the mask there was a mouthpiece to blow air into. The air was directed up and into the nose. At the end of the nose were several tiny outlets where the air could be released in small bursts. These outlets were controlled by small balloons that sat under the outfit wearer's armpits.

Then there was a top hat that appeared to be primarily of decorative value. The hat however contained a telepathic headband, or rather, 'headband of telepathy', better known as a HoT-wire. Rare, even in The Distance, a HoT-wire allowed the wearer access to a subject's mind, where thoughts could be read and narratives planted. It was Lord Gangle's job to construct and upload appropriate narratives. It was the subjects themselves though that held all the finer details needed to bring their own personal journeys to life. The HoT-wire allowed Lord Gangles access to those details that could be used, in real time, to steer any narrative in a direction of the subject's choosing.

The boots of Lord Gangles were like those of a cowboy. Tough looking leather, rising to just below the knee. The sturdy heels in these boots were used to omit bass frequencies that brought solidity to any of Lord Gangle's creations.

Finally, there were the fabled wind chime fingers, an unparalleled marvel of engineering. The windchimes hung from a pair of very special gloves. Within each glove were a multitude of different sensors, both at the tips of each finger as well as along each finger's length. The tips were used to select notes whilst the rest of the finger was used to manipulate tension, allowing for notes to be sustained, flattened or bent in an infinite array of combinations. The wind chimes worked in unison with the mask and thus needed to be held aloft, one either side of the nose piece. Blowing into the mouthpiece, then using the armpits to control bursts of air, is how the wind chime notes were triggered. Gangles could then combine the controlled bursts with finger movements inside the gloves, to create the necessary soundscapes.

This is how Lord Gangles was able to build up just the right notes, in just the right order, played at just the right frequency and at just the right time, to entice a subject's mind into a world of revelations, on a journey of discovery and of their own making.

xx lol xx

Ella and Amari were outside, on a large expanse of empty common ground.

"You look amazing!" Amari exclaimed.

"I feel like an idiot."

Ella said this whilst looking down, awkwardly, side to side at her new outfit.

"And these things are soooo..." Ella lifted her new fingers into the air. "...heavy."

"Meh. You'll get used to them soon enough. Besides, that is the original prototype model right. Bound to be a bit on the clunky side."

Ella shot Amari a look, not that Amari could see, what with Ella's eyes being hidden behind a big gothic bird face mask.

"Right, come on you. Enough moping. Let's see what you can do with this bad boy. Why don't we start off with a beautiful white unicorn. What do you say?"

It was the job of Lord Gangles to create and plant appropriate narratives into subjects' subconscious. To deliver arenas that could facilitate journeys of wonder and self-discovery. To ensure that these journeys remained 'on-piste' it was also necessary for Lord Gangles to have an assistant on the ground, so to speak. That assistant would be Amari for whom, as part of the current 'Angel Development Programme', it was necessary to acquire at least a million hours of experience in the field assisting a Lord Gangles. So, before Ella could start creating new worlds as Lord Gangles, she first had to master shape shifting her trusted companion.

The pair had learnt in their studies that humans were often more receptive when they imagined themselves as animals. Amari then, in turn, would need to represent any species that might be associated with a subject. Not wanting to make life easy for Ella, Amari decided to kick off proceedings with a unicorn. To fully appreciate (aka judge) Ella's efforts, Amari had brought along with her a stand-up mirror, in front of which she now stood poised and waiting.

"Okay boss. Give me your best Unicorn."

Let There Be Light

Ella closed her eyes and drew in a deep breath.

'Okay Ella Songg,' she said to herself. 'You can do this.'

Ella cleared her mind.

Using the HoT-wire she opened a channel to Amari's mind. Initially all thoughts were lost to a dense fog until suddenly, a fuzzy picture of a unicorn started to emerge.

Ella drew in another deep breath, then blew into her mouthpiece. After a few primer breaths Ella lifted her arms, raising her windchime fingers up to the level of her nose. Next, clamping her armpits, Ella started to squeeze out the air from the nose vents. Finally, she began shaping the notes of the windchimes, flexing her fingers or pressing with their tips. Eventually a melody began to take shape and the air around Amari started to flicker and shake.

"It's working!" Amari excitedly exclaimed. "I'm changing Ella, I'm changing."

Encouraged by her partner's enthusiasm Ella blew, squeezed and pressed harder. Ella had of course practised each individual element in Ms Howlett's classes and had, she felt, mastered them all well enough. At least individually. Doing everything all at once though was quite the challenge. Ella was struggling to maintain a clear picture in her head whilst at the same time manipulating the elements in the right order in which to create that picture.

'POP!'

Amari transformed.

"Hee-haw!".

In front of the mirror posed a beautiful white donkey.

"Well, you got the right colour, I guess. But this is not the most elegant Unicorn I have ever seen." Amari quipped.

Ella concentrated harder.

'POP!'

Amari had morphed from a donkey into a pony.

"Alright. Loving the new hair." She commented whilst admiring her mane. "I'm still a little bit on the short side though don't you thin...."

'POP!'

There now stood in front of Ella, a stunning white mare.

"Yes! That's more like it." Encouraged Amari. "You certainly got the body right. But there is 'neigh' horn. Get it. 'Neigh'..." This time pronounced as a long drawn-out whinny. "...horn. Ha ha h..."

'POP!"

"What the fff...!"

Amari was disturbed to find a giant grey rhinoceros staring back at her from the mirror. "Um, okay. So, I got the horn now but it's not quite in the right pla..."

'POP!'

Amari changed form, mid-air, before she dropped to the ground. She was now looking at a rather cute little rhino horned lizard.

"Okay Ella. Enough with the rhinos. I'm supposed to be a bloody Unicorn. Come on now. Concentrate. You can do this."

Ella could feel sweat accumulating behind her mask. Her fingers were already sore, and she was starting to feel a little dizzy from a lack of oxygen.

Squeezing her eyes tight shut she urged herself to concentrate harder.

'POP!'

A Reindeer.

"Ahhh. I'm so pretty."

'POP!'

A Narwhal.

"That's a weird looking fish."

'POP!'

A Unicorn Fish.

"Okay. That's just plain creepy."

'POP!'

A little pony plastic toy.

"Should that even be possible?"

'POP, POP, POP, POP!'

Ella was becoming more and more frustrated. The harder she tried the further away she seemed to be. Eventually a rage overtook her, and she slammed down the heel of her right boot in frustration. The resulting resonance rippled up and out in all directions. In that same split second the anger evicted all other thoughts, emotions and self-doubt from Ella's mind. Adrenaline shot through her veins. Complaints of cramp from her fingers ceased. And just like that, Ella found herself tapped in and connected to the great cosmic flow of everything.

Amari let out a gasp.

"Oh Ella. What have you done?"

Ella still had her eyes scrunched closed. Although terrified at what she may have turned Amari into this time, she knew that she had to face the music. Slowly, she let her eyes open.

Standing there, in front of Ella, was the most beautiful Unicorn she had even seen. It was in truth the only Unicorn she had ever seen but this fact, Ella decided, was by the by. It wasn't this though that had taken Amari's breath away.

Ella soon realised that they no longer stood on an empty, open common ground. They were instead standing in rolling fields of fresh, bright green grass, framed all around by the most beautiful, colourful trees. Lining the horizon was a range of pink tinted mountains, snow capped at their summit, reflecting the light from warm afternoon sunshine. A magical looking castle stood nestled amongst the base of those mountains in which Ella could imagine a princess living. The sky had a hazy, surreal feel. Close by various insects mulled about in the haze and the pollen. Higher up in the sky various birds of prey circled, swooped and cawed.

"Oh Ella. How did you do this?" Amari's jaw was on the ground. "No previous Lord has ever created a world this early on in their training. Ella. How did you do this? It's so beautiful."

Amari looked at her reflection again, though this time in the crystal-clear waters of a lake.

"I'm so... beautiful." She whimpered. "How did you... I mean... Just... Just Wow. Ella, this is amazing!"

So it was that Ella had created her first new world as a Lord. It was only one of many that Ella would go on to create. However, it was this first world that the academy would talk about throughout the coming millennia, as they recounted to their students the day that the greatest Lord Gangles of all time came of age.

Gangle Manor

After that first world, training at the academy flew by. Ella and Amari spent all their free time creating and inhabiting different worlds. They had swum together in the deepest oceans. Sunbathed together on remote shores. Soared together in the highest skies. Drifted together amongst the brightest stars. Their bond was now something very special indeed. They could sense each other's feelings, read each other's thoughts. The pair performed seamlessly with one another, and Ella had truly mastered all the tools of the Gangle trade. Thus, when it came to the time of their final assessment the pair passed with outstanding distinction and the time had come for them to leave the academy. The time had come for them to inherit and move into Gangle Manor.

"Here we are." Sid announced, as the carriage they were in, drawn by two strong horses, breached a curve in the driveway that led to Gangle Manor and the house revealed itself in its full glory.

"My lord it's huge!" Amari exclaimed, whilst at the same time patting her palms against each other in giddy excitement.

"It's beautiful." Was all Ella could manage.

"Well, for the next thousand years or so it's all yours." Sid confirmed.

Amari and Ella instinctively reached out for each other's hands. When they connected, they stopped staring at the house and glanced at each other. A gentle, knowing smile was shared before they both quickly looked toward the house again, though their hands remained locked together.

The manor itself was just two stories high. Its footprint however was vast. At its core, the house was at least ten thousand years old. One could then see how the house had been added to over the years, with some outer sections seeming very modern. The front of the house presented itself as three peaks, the middle peak being shorter than those on either side. The windows were all leaded, set back within timber frames. If pushed Ella would have called the style gothic, or medieval maybe. On exiting the carriage Ella realised that the house was surrounded by a moat, though more ornamental than defensive. The house was set within acres of immaculately kept grounds and landscaped gardens. In truth it was all a little too much to take in.

"Come on." Encouraged Sid. "Let me show you the inside."

The main entrance door was solid, made from thick oak, set within a solid oak frame. It was hung on wrought iron hinges that spread out from the anchor points into beautiful ornate spiral decorations covering its face. It swung open to reveal a stone patio style floor, leading to a second door, directly in line, that then opened into a central courtyard.

Sid started the tour with the huge double aspect dining room to the right of the main entrance. He then proceeded to introduce them to the library, the study, the kitchen and the breakfast room. Next came the second dining room, the indoor pool, the gym, the cinema and the games room. Then there was a third dining room, multiple different bathrooms and an endless array of bedrooms. In addition, there were many outside spaces including the obligatory tennis court that a property of this size seemed to demand.

"How do we keep it all clean?" Ella questioned, with a hint of panic in her voice.

"The house comes with a contingent of staff. Hence the number of bedrooms. You will meet them all in due course. For the time being they have all been given leave, so that you two can have some time to yourselves, to settle in."

"I'm not sure how I feel about having staff."

"Well Ella, as Lord Gangles you will have your hands very full. The people that are here to support you are... Well. You are all part of the same team. The expectation is that you will work collaboratively together in the best interests of those that you work to assist."

Ella looked unsure but decided to concede.

"Come now." Said Sid. "I have one very important space left to show you."

Sid led the pair toward the centre of the house. Here it felt like all the different corridors of the house converged. A staircase descended into the space, built into which was a bookcase. At the foot of the stairs stood a small ornate wooden table.

On top of this, an antique telephone next to which lay a notepad and pen.

"Very quaint." Amari offered, stood with her arms crossed, sporting an unimpressed look. "A little underwhelming though when compared to the rest of the house?"

"That is the desired intention." Sid confirmed. "However, what you are looking at is the nerve centre. The key to the real heart of this house. Here, let me demonstrate. Amari, please could you select a book from the bookcase for me."

"Okaaay."

Unsure where this was going, Amari obliged, nonetheless. Spending literally zero-time pursuing book titles she simply pulled at the first spine that came to hand. The cover of the book was several different shades of red, with a Devil character depicted as the image. The title said something about algorithms. Amari offered the book to Sid, who simply shook his hand and pointed back to the case.

"It's okay. I don't want the book. I just wanted you to take one from the bookcase. Please could you put it back now."

Nonplussed, Amari returned the book back to the space left on the shelf.

"Now." Said Sid. "If I could draw your attention to the telephone. This is where you will receive your assignments from me. The notepad next to the phone is an infinity pad. Any notes you make will be transferred to a terminal downstairs, after which they will instantly vanish from view."

"Infinity pad?" Questioned Amari.

"Downstairs?" Questioned Ella.

"Yes Amari. An infinity pad. There will always be a blank page for you to work on and no danger of leaving notes that any visitors might see. And yes, Ella, you heard correctly. There is also a downstairs to this house. A cellar if you will. That is where we are going next. First though I need to make a call to that phone."

Sid produced a mobile from his pocket and punched in a number. The phone on the table gave a shrill little jingle.

"Wow." Offered Amari. "That's exciting. Not. I thought this was supposed to be a 'nerve centre'. The ring on that phone is more like a nerve relaxant."

"Your auditory stimulation is really none of my concern Amari. I am simply here to demonstrate to you the mechanics of the whole thing. Ella, please would you answer the telephone."

Ella did as she was asked and lifted the handset from the receiver. She made to raise it to her ear, but Sid shook his head.

"No need Ella. I am right here. Besides, I have already hung up. Please put the receiver back."

Ella obliged.

Immediately after the cradle clicked back into place Ella felt a sudden energy in the air. Something here had changed.

"Okay, Amari. Please could you retrieve for me another book from the bookcase. Anyone will do."

"Seriously?"

More of a sulk than an actual challenge. Amari, though obliged to Sid's request and made to pull another book from the case. This time however the book could only be pulled so far. A loud click came from behind the case and the book pulled itself out of Amaris hand and retreated to its original position. After that the whole case retreated, back into the space under the stairs. The bookcase then slid silently into the wall on the right, revealing in its place a warmly lit stone staircase that spiralled down, into the cellar and into the heart of the house.

"Wow...!"

Ella and Amari gave the expression in unison.

"So..." offered Sid, now rather smug. "Shall we go and see where the magic really happens?"

The pair did not need asking twice.

xx lol xx

Sid led them through the doorway, then down the stone staircase into the cellar. As he stood from the final step the bookcase could be heard sliding back into its closed position above them. Ella registered a twinge of panic, wanting to ask how they would get back out again, but quickly decided to park this question for later, assuming that the answer would be obvious. The other thing that happened, as Sid left the final stair, is that lights blinked on, all around the room, revealing a cavernous space that stretched out in all directions around them.

The Cellar was vast, essentially covering the whole footprint of the house that sat above them. The ceiling was unusually high for a room built underground. The lighting was rather antiquated. Soft light blazed from iron lanterns affixed at regular points around the walls. The impression was a little like that of candles burning. In addition, at various points around the room, there were positioned several Victorian style lamp posts all hosting a flickering light.

The whole space was roughly sectioned into four distinct areas. The trio were currently standing in the centre. Behind them, to the left of the room, was a living area. An old leather burgundy wing back chair sat next to a long green chesterfield sofa. Both were positioned on a very large and very worn looking Persian style rug, laid upon dark wooden floorboards that covered the whole of the cellar floor. A fireplace has been built into the wall and an old grandfather clock gently ticked away in the far corner, though Ella noticed that the arms did not seem to be moving.

Next was an open plan kitchen area, rather antiquated. Then next to that a sleeping area, partitioned off by a thick purple velvet curtain, currently pulled back to reveal a rather opulent looking four poster bed.

The next section, to the right side of the room, appeared more concerned with recreation. Filling out the corner was a very old looking bar, behind which hung a vast array of colourful vintage glassware. Pushed up against one of the walls was a well-worn looking piano, the sort that looked like it could play itself and would be at home in any wild west style saloon. Ella looked forward to making her acquaintance in due course. Next to the piano was an old vintage jukebox that appeared modern in its current situ. There were two tables with wooden chairs positioned around them. One set with a pack of cards and a stash of poker chips. Then there was a billiards table, not that Ella was sure what billiards even were. Finally, there was a stash of board game paraphernalia in a small cupboard area at the far end of the section.

Looking forwards, toward the front of the room, the left side had been sectioned into two halves. Sid explained that the closed off section contained toilets, showers and a dressing area. The other half included a row of oak wood Victorian style lockers, lined up against the back wall. Four sets of identical units stood next to each other. Each unit was six feet in height, four in width, split down the middle into two equal sections. The first half was split horizontally into four. The top section of each contained a hat. The section below contained a mask. Next was a taller section, holding a pair of tall leather boots. Underneath this was a draw section that pulled out to reveal a cravat and cufflinks. The second half was split vertically into two equal halves. In the first was hung a coat, a shirt, a waistcoat and some trousers. In the second half was hung a pair of wind chime gloves.

In front of them to the right was the last section of the room. About a third of the area was boxed in. This was the soundproof composition room where Lord Ganges could perfect the final scores for the worlds that were to be created. In the centre of the section was a huge wooden story desk. This is where Amari and Ella would work on putting narratives together. At the far wall, directly in front of them, stood a large storyboard, used for visually mapping out constructs. Then there was a computer console and a dot matrix printer, obviously the machine that was linked to the infinity pad upstairs.

The final thing of note, situated on the far wall to the right of the room, was a huge door. As they were standing in a cellar it appeared that this was to be a door to nowhere. It was in fact a door to everywhere.

"Behold!" Sid announced rather grandly. Ella could see that he was enjoying his moment, which was fair, considering he only got to do this once every thousand years or so.

"Behold." He said again. "I give you the Everywhere Door, of the great Lord Gangles."

The door itself was beautiful. Obviously very old, it was covered in carvings that included flowers, birds, monkeys and dragons. It had been painted to include all the colours of the rainbow, detailed with black edging, seemingly projecting its colours into the room. The door was set back a little into an arched wooden frame, itself adorned with various symbols and markings, appearing as if they had been scorched into the wood from the inside. Ella noticed that the door did not have a handle.

"An Everywhere Door knows when to be open and when to be closed. No handle here shall ever be required." Sid explained.

This triggered a discussion regarding the mechanics of the door and how it would open automatically when they presented themselves on a case or simply whenever it wanted them to walk through it. Amari would have preferred more detailed information, but Sid insisted that they would just have to trust and see.

With a visual tour of the room complete Sid suggested they adjourn to the bar for a drink, to mark the occasion. Absinthe was Sid's choice, and after all the glasses had been poured Sid raised his drink into the air and grandly confirmed that the new era of Lord Gangles had begun. The pair were now ready for their first real case.

After they had thrown back their drinks Ella, face screwed up, decided to ask her question.

"Sid. I do have one question. How do we get out of the cellar?"

"Ah." Said Sid, already pouring out another drink. "About that..."

The Hungry Dragon

It was several days before the Everywhere Door finally opened to let the trio back into the house. Just enough time to become familiar with the cellar room and all its various functions. Three months had passed since then. The house staff had returned in the third week and Ella and Amari had come to feel familiar in their company.

There was the groundskeeper, Jack Cawstost, a spirit of boundless energy, come from a realm where rabbits had evolved to succeeded as the dominant species. Successful evolution meant Jack's shape resembled that of a typical human, whilst retaining the main facial features of a rabbit. He could rotate his ears 180 degrees but did not like carrots.

Housekeeping and cooking were managed by twins, Poppy and Rosie Rena. Rosie was a master of flavour, Poppy of sustenance. Between them they kept the manor spotless whilst cooking up an endless array of incredible delights.

The final live-in member of staff was a butler, Alfred Pound-Worth. Alfred was reputed as being the best butler to reside in The Distance. Ella never saw Alfred in the house until she needed something, at which point she would find Alfred was already there, awaiting her instruction.

Getting to know the staff and their new home had been fun. The novelty though was starting to fade. Without a case to work, Ella and Amari were finding themselves to be a little bored.

"So..." Started Amari. "I have to be honest. I thought the great Lord Gangles would be a little busier than this."

Ella let out a sigh.

"Well, Sid did say it might take a little while for the first job to come through. The Distance has to adjust to the transition as much as we do."

The pair were sitting outside in the courtyard, tossing a ball at each other to catch whilst chewing the fat. Suddenly their conversation was interrupted by a shrill ringing noise.

"Shhhhh."

Amari demanded whilst holding up a hand.

"Do you hear that?"

 "Yes. Yes, I do. What is... Is that..."

"THE PHONE!"

They both shouted in unison.

Amari was first on her feet, dashing toward the door. Ella, a nano second behind her.

'Ring, ring', 'ring, ring'.

The shrill tone of the telephone increased in volume as they got closer. In her enthusiasm Amari practically dived at it and already had the receiver to her ear as Ella rounded the corner behind her. Amari picked up the pen and began to scribble notes onto the infinity pad. After a time, she returned the receiver to its cradle, looked up with a mischievous grin, and locked eyes with Ella.

"Well?" Ella asked impatiently.

Amari tipped her head back and yelled at the top of her voice.

"WE'VE GOT ONE!"

Dragons & Monkeys

After the initial excitement, Ella and Amari had managed to calm down a little. The pair had been in the cellar, storyboarding, for the best part of an hour. Their first subject was a young male, mid-thirties, of Asian descent. Blessed with a beautiful wife and a beautiful daughter, he had never realised. Instead of seeing what was truly important he had become obsessed with a financial inheritance.

"Definitely a dragon."

"Okay, okay. You can be a dragon."

"Good. He's Asian so he would totally want to be a dragon."

"Um, do you not think that's a little bit racist?"

"Well, if it is then it's good racist. I mean, who doesn't like dragons."

"Fair." Conceded Ella. "Dragons are pretty cool. Okay, so I was thinking of the old, 'one in the hand, two in the bush' routine. We can make him super hungry, then offer him a choice related to greed."

"Oh, I like that. Two what though? Birds aren't gonna cut it. Way too small for a dragon appetite. What about humans?"

"I don't think we should be encouraging him to eat other humans Amari. That's a bit cannibalistic, no?"

"Hmm. Okay, fair point. What about Monkeys?"

"Monkeys?"

"Yes, monkeys. Everyone knows that dragons and monkeys butt heads. We can give him an appetite for monkeys. Also, they like to live in trees, which are a bit like bushes, right."

"Okay then. I'm not sure what Sid would think about it though."

"Meh. Sid never needs to know."

Amari offered a conspiratorial smile. Ella reciprocated. The story was agreed. Amari would present as a dragon, taking their subject into a dark and barren land. Hunger would be the theme. The objective would be to recognise the blessing of a modest meal, compared to the lure of a potential feast. Ella then moved to the music room to compose, leaving Amari to work on the finer details of the narrative. Sometime later, with music and story complete, the two reconvened. It was time for Ella to don the suit, and for the new Lord Gangles to make her debut.

Standing there together, side by side, waiting for the Everywhere Door to open, Amari took hold of Ella's hand. Looking briefly at each other they both took a deep breath.

"You got this."

Is all Amari said.

Then there was a loud creak as the Everywhere Door began to open.

The One That Got Away

Their instructions stated that they were to liaise with their subject at a crossroads situated someway down the mountain. They exited the Everywhere Door through the front door of a small end terrace house. Immediately opposite them, across a road, was a bus shelter.

"I didn't know there were buses in The Distance?" Ella commented.

"Not everyone has an Everywhere Door you know. How do you think us normal folk get about?"

"Well, if the buses here are anything like they are in my realm they probably walk. And you're not normal by the way."

A shared giggle followed, then the pair agreed that the bus shelter would probably be a good spot to wait for their subject. Crossing the road, the pair approached the shelter from the right side. As they were approaching, they noticed a man exiting the shelter from the left side, walking away from them.

"That must be him." Amari suggested. "But where is he going? Isn't he supposed to be walking towards us?"

This is what Ella had expected. But this man was definitely walking away from them. Ella looked around and spotted a second man, standing under a signpost, marking the centre of a crossroads. Tall and lean, dressed sharp in an old fashioned 50's style pin stripe suit. Dark hair, short and slicked back with oil. A pencil thin moustache and skinny eyebrows. The man plucked a smoking cigarette end from a golden cigarette holder, threw it to the floor then crushed it with his heel. He slipped the golden holder into his left-hand jacket pocket. Then he turned in Ella's direction. Startled, Ella looked away, sure that she had caught a flash of fire from the man's eyes.

Ella reverted her attention back to the man walking away from them. He turned his head briefly, to check the road before he crossed. He did not see Lord Gangles, but Lord Gangles saw him.

A sickening wave of recognition rose up, then crashed back down into her gut. The wind went out of Ella's sails, and she stumbled backwards, slumping onto a plastic bus shelter bench behind her. Amari spun around, a look of concern on her face.

"Ella, what's wrong?"

"I, I... I think I know who that is. But it can't be. It can't be him."

"Can't be who? Ella, what is it? Who do you think that man is?"

"He, he... He looks like my father."

"Looks like your what now?"

"My dad. He looks like my dad."

Ella was remembering an image of her father from when she was a little girl. He had just returned from a business trip to Vietnam. Thinking logically, Ella reasoned that this was many Earth realm years ago. More, if you considered her time spent in The Distance. Her father would surely be much older by now.

"No. No, it's okay." Ella let out a breath. "It must just be a coincidence. I'm sorry. I think I'm just having a moment."

"Hey, it's okay. This is your first proper job. Probably just nerves getting the better of you."

The man in question was now in conversation with the sharp looking man at the crossroads. Whilst seemingly quite animated, with his back to the pair he showed no sign of turning around again. The sharp looking man then reached out a hand and placed it on the other man's shoulder. This seemed to calm him. After a few more moments, and much head nodding, the sharp looking man offered out his left hand. Following a brief pause the offer was accepted and the pair shook hands. As they did so the sharp looking man placed his right hand onto the other man's head, following which the other man began to fade, before eventually disappearing altogether.

xx lol xx

"What the hell!"
Ella started.
"That was our subject. Where did he go? What did he just do to him?"
With that she was off, quite cross, storming across the road in the direction of the crossroads man that had just made her first case disappear.
"You!"
She shouted.

"You there. Who are you? What did you just do to our man."

"Ella!"

Amari was on Ella's heels, trying to stop her.

"Ella, that's not a good idea. Ella. Ella!"

Ella stopped, just shy of the strange man, and turned on her heel to face Amari.

"What?" She demanded.

A little out of breath, Amari started.

"Ella, that... That man is... Well, he's..."

"Lucifer Morningstar." Announced the man now standing directly behind her.

Ella spun back around to face the man.

"Lucifer Morningstar?" She enquired. "What, you mean, like... Satan?"

"Actually, I prefer the name Lucifer. Satan has such negative connotations."

"Satan!" Ella exclaimed out loud to herself.

"It's Lucifer." Amari offered.

"As I live and breathe." Ella said, still talking to herself. "Satan..."

"I would really prefer that you call me Luc..."

"I am standing, talking to Satan."

"Lucif... You know what forget it."

"OMG!"

"Ahem. I would prefer it if you didn't mention 'that' name as well. Anyway, you must be the new

Lord Gangles. I've heard much about you. Very pleased to make your acquaintance."

Ella, head spinning, turned to Amari with a questioning look.

"It's true." Amari confirmed. "This is Lucifer Morningstar. The very first assistant to the very first Lord Gangles."

"Ahem, yes..." Confirmed Lucifer. "That was quite some time ago and we don't need to talk about that do we."

Ella spun back round to face Lucifer. Raising a finger into the air she declared.

"I don't care who you are. What did you just do with our first case?"

"Ooo, straight to the point. I like you."

"Don't patronise me Satan. What did you do to him? We were supposed to meet him here and we came through the Everywhere Door and that should have brought us out at the right time, but somehow, we were late, so you must have done something, so what did you do?"

"Well, young lady, as you have quite rightly stated, the Everywhere Door will always bring you to a place at exactly the right time that you are supposed to be there. However, to suggest that I have any power over that is ludicrous."

"Hmmm." Ella was not convinced.

"In fact, it was not I who did anything. Rather it was 'he' that did something. I saw the poor fellow standing, waiting cluelessly at the bus stop and he, in turn, happened to see me. He chose to come to me and tell me his woes. I, in turn, offered him a deal. Which he, in turn, and of sound mind I hasten to add, chose to accept. Deal done, I sent him back to his own realm."

"What does that mean?"

"It means, I suppose, that your services here are no longer required. Think of it as a good thing. You've both gotten the afternoon off."

"But I don't want the afternoon off."

"Well, we don't always get what we want dear. But there we are. First World problems and all that. Now if you'll both excuse me I have business of my own to be getting on with."

"But I... Wait... I..."

It was no use. Lucifer had already taken his leave, crossing directly over the road, toward a large warehouse looking building just below the dip of the hill.

"Well, I never!" Exclaimed Ella. "How rude is he?"

"Well, he is the Devil."

Amari offered rather unhelpfully.

"Come on. There's no use waiting around here. We'll just have to chalk this one up to experience."

Reluctantly Ella agreed and the couple took their own leave, making their way back toward the small terrace and the Everywhere Door that would take them home to Gangle Manor.

The Friendly Wasp

"Stupid cow!"

This was Angel speaking.

"That stupid, stuck up, useless little bint."

Pacing back and forth.

"Who does she think she is? Trying to show me up like that."

It was mid-afternoon, on a Wednesday. Angel and her gang were hanging out on some benches at the bottom of the high street. Neither Angel, Michelle nor Jackie had managed to land a job since leaving school. Beatrice was the only one that had but was currently on her lunch break. Weeks had passed, since Ella had called Angel out in the chip shop. The gang had no idea that Ella had already departed to a new life in The Distance. Angel was still hungry for revenge.

"I'm telling, you I don't know where she's been hiding, but a hiding is exactly what she's gonna get the next time I see the co..."

"It's been weeks now Angel!"

Beatrice interrupted Angel's tirade with this observation.

"Don't you think maybe you should just let it go?"

Turning on Beatrice, Angel responded.

"I know how long it's been Bea. Weeks, yes. And not one of you mugs has been able to find her. I mean, what is wrong with you all, eh? How hard can it be to find a snowflake like that?"

"More like what is wrong with you?"

The words were out of Beatrice's mouth before she even knew that she was saying them.

"What did you just say?" Angel, flushed a deep red, putting her face so close to Beatrice's that the tips of their noses gently touched. "What's wrong with me? Have you forgotten who you are talking to?"

The truth of the matter was that these last weeks had been zero fun for Beatrice. Seeing her friend, completely obsessed with some vendetta, against a girl that she, truth be told, secretly admired, had made her think about who she really wanted to spend her time with. She hadn't planned to speak up against Angel just now, but the moment had happened, so she decided to follow it through.

"What I mean is... Well. When she called you out in the chippy, she was right wasn't she. You have been underpaying and she just called you out on it."

"You think that's what this is about do you?"

"Well, it is, isn't it? Ella called you out and you don't like it."

Jackie and Michelle both remained very quiet as the scene in front of them played out.

"Maybe I should take this out on you instead, eh Bea. I mean, you've gotten all high and mighty since you got that job, treating the rest of us like charity cases with your big wage packets."

"Is that what you think?" Beatrice challenged back. "I buy stuff for you guys because I know your skint. Cus I'm a mate."

"Mate. Pah. You're lording it over me now Bea. You don't know what a real mate is. If you did, you'd be here with us all day. Not swanning off to your fancy new job and your fancy new mates."

"What are you even talking about?"

"You know very well. You ain't one of us no more Bea..." Angel drew the name out, then added. "...ich!"

A pause.

"Why don't you just get stuffed."

Shock was Beatrice's first reaction. Then she pondered the attack and quickly decided that enough was enough.

"Maybe you're right."

Beatrice took a step back, turned to leave, then stopped. Turning again to face Angel, now shaking a little and holding back tears.

"You know what Angel, we left school ages ago. Ella has moved on. It's about time you grew u..."

'Thwack!'

Angel slapped Beatrice across the face. Jackie and Michelle froze, hands covering their mouths in shock. After a moment of silence Beatrice defiantly turned her reddened face back towards Angel. There were no new tears. She held Angel's gaze, for what felt like an eternity, then turned on her heel and confidently walked away.

Angel quickly spun on her heel to face Michelle and Jackie.

"Either of you two got anything you want to say?"

Both shook their heads.

"Eh. What's that? Speak up will ya."

"No." "No Ang." "No, of course not."

Both were talking over each other.

"Good. That's what I thought. Just remember who the leader is here. We don't need that stuck up cow in our gang anymore. She can go an hang out with her new friend Ella for all I care. Then I can take them both out."

Angel spat on the floor, then hopped onto a bench, resting her feet where her bum should be. She pulled a disposable vape stick from her pocket. Sucking on the stick she found that it had expired. Unfortunately, Beatrice was no longer there to buy her a new one.

xx lol xx

Angel went home early that night, leaving Jackie and Michelle sitting on the swings in the rec. Angel told them she was feeling unwell but in truth she was feeling down and wanted to be on her own. Reaching her house Angel opened the front door. The door was a sort of off yellow in colour, with a frosted glass panel, reinforced with wire mesh, cracked down the middle. A kick to the bottom left corner was required for it to open. Angel's mum was in the living room. It was immediately clear from the pungent odour and psychedelic soundtrack that Madi was stoned, again. Angel headed straight up the stairs to her bedroom.

The door to Angel's bedroom was a cheap hollow faux wooden affair. This one complete with holes, on Angel's side, where she had, on more than one occasion, vented her anger upon it. Pictures, torn free from magazines, of historical leaders, better described as dictators, adorned the walls. These were Angel's heroes. They also helped to cover up the worst of the 1970's woodchip wallpaper.

In terms of furniture, the room included a wardrobe, of sorts, and a small chest of drawers. The wardrobe listed slightly to one side. The chest of drawers was four high, the fascia of the second drawer supported by the fascia of the third from underneath, the innards of each drawer bowed. The bed though was the worst. A single bed that had been Angel's resting place all her conscious life.

The base was constructed from MDF, supported by a coaster leg in each corner, each with a small wheel on the bottom. The mattress appeared thick enough but quickly gave in the middle when lying on it, and there was more than one slightly rigid spring that would poke into Angel whilst she slept. The mattress was covered with a cheap, slightly furry feeling bed sheet, topped with a thin quilt and single foam pillow, dressed in faded covers that had survived from Angel's childhood.

Finishing off the room's ambiance were the curtains. Two in total, one for each side of the window. They were in fact quite thick. Angel's mum had been given these free by a kindly neighbour. They were red velvet on the outside, with a now yellowed water-stained lining. The curtains were just about long enough to cover the window. Unfortunately, though several of the plastic curtain hooks, and their associated bindings, had failed so that the curtains now hung in a rather unruly fashion, sagging in places to let the light in. This usually made Angel cross but tonight she didn't care. She pulled them together, as best she could, then climbed into her bed. There was a chill in the air, so Angel kept her clothes on.

As she lay there she reflected on the day's events. Doing so she became aware of a stinging sensation in the palm of her hand. This was followed by a more violent stinging sensation deep in her heart. Eventually this was followed by sleep.

Meanwhile at Gangle Manor

Ella and Amari had been a little subdued since their false start and subsequent run in with the devil. Since then, Ella had mostly been practising compositions, whilst Amari had taken to DIY. Apparently, she was making some home improvements, though Ella had yet to see any evidence of these. The next call came about a month later, whilst the pair were spending some time together in the courtyard, sharing a bottle of wine.

"You really should have a theme tune."

"I've told you before, I'm not a superhero. I do not need a theme tune."

"Aww but seriously you are, and you do." Amari had become a little obsessed with the idea of a

Lord Gangle theme tune. "It will help with your branding." She said.

"What branding. What are you even talking about Amari?"

"Seriously. Listen. Just listen. I've been working on a little tune that is well catchy."

"I don't want to hea..."

Ella tried to object but Amari burst it out anyway.

"Dinna, dinna, dinna, dinna.
Dinna, dinna, dinna,
Here comes Gan-Galls..!"

"Obviously a work in progress, but what do you think?"

Ella's face was frozen, mouth agape.

"Good isn't it." Stated Amari, all self-congratulatory.

"Amari. You literally just sang me the Batman theme tune."

"The bat man what now?"

"Batman Amari. That tune is Batman's tune."

"I literally have no idea what you're talking about Ella. There's no bat man in The Distance. Sure, we got Death, and the Sandman and even Satan, but I never heard of anyone called the bat man. What does he even do with a name like that? I guess it would be sport related?"

Ella released a long sigh, following which she took a large glug of wine.

"So anyway, you like it. It's got potential right. I can work on..."

The conversation was interrupted by a very loud noise.

'AA-OOO-GAA! AA-OOO-GAA!'

Ella spat out her wine in shock and nearly dropped her glass to boot. Accompanying the very loud alarm were red flashing lights going off all over the place.

"What the hell is that?" Ella spluttered.

"Good ain't it." Came Amari's response. "I thought we could do with something a little more... exciting. You know, for when a call comes in. Get us into the right frame of mind."

"What!" Ella exclaimed. "You mean that is an actual call coming in?"

"Yes Ella. And you must admit, this is much better than that dreary old telephone tinkle. Come on, let's go. I've updated the telephone too."

Sure enough, the previous antique telephone had been replaced. The replacement was still retro in appearance, though now it was made of red Perspex and currently it was flashing.

"What do you reckon? Cool eh."

Slightly perplexed Ella offered a brief, "Whatever," then, "...Okay, just answer it will you. That noise is hurting my ears."

"Yes. Sorry. I forgot you're a little sensitive to loud noises. Okay, I will turn it down a bit for next time."

Amari said this whilst reaching out and lifting the handset. She then started to scribble down some notes onto the infinity pad. Ten minutes later the pair had descended and were sitting at the narrative table in the cellar.

xx lol xx

"This is so crazy." Stated Ella. "I know this girl. She used to bully me at school."

"Awesome. Well now you can get some revenge on her."

"I don't think I have been entrusted with this role just so I can dole out personal vengeance Amari. No, my job is to try and help her do right. See if she can't turn things around."

"Whoa. Ella, you are way too soft."

"What are you saying? You're supposed to be training as an Angel."

"Ha. You obviously don't know much about Angels yet."

This rebuttal came with a smile.

"Fair enough. I am though, going to try and help her, and I have the perfect transformation in mind."

"Okay maestro. Please feel free to share with the group."

"An angry wasp!"

Ella's revealed.

"Buzzin!"

Amari approved.

The pair high fived, then got down to work.

Prince Albert

"Wake up. Excuse me, miss, you need to wake up. You can't sleep here. Come on now. Open your eyes."

The voice was a male, drifting into her consciousness from across an abyss. Slowly Angel conceded and began to open her eyes. It quickly became apparent that she was no longer in her bedroom. Instead, she was led on a wooden bench. The bench had its back to a stone wall, a few stones missing, set at the back of a small triangle of grass, either side of which was a road. Obviously at high altitude, Angel could see out across a valley. Directly opposite her was an old looking public house. Standing directly over her was a young man. His was the voice that had summoned her from her slumber.

"Who are you? Where am I?" Angel asked, slowly sitting up.

"Well miss, my name is Wspeta. Wspeta Horn. You are currently halfway up a mountain in The Distance."

"Wes what? Did you say 'wes-pet-aa'? What kind of a name is that?"

"A very common one, I think."

"Common? I've never heard a name like that before. Are you one of those boat people?"

"Hmm. If you've not heard the name Wspeta before then maybe you ought to get out a little more."

Angel was sitting upright, rubbing the back of her stiff neck.

"Maybe you're right."

Angel was surprised to hear herself concede this fact. Then continued.

"Well, clearly I'm dreaming as this is definitely not my bedroom."

"You're not dreaming miss. If you were, you'd be in the dream realm. But seeing as though you're here, in The Distance, then you can't be dreaming, can you? You may have been dreaming before I woke you up though."

This guy was making Angel's head spin. She decided to change the conversation.

"Alright then Wes…mond. Whatever. I don't really care where I am, but I can see a pub over there. Are you gonna offer to buy a lady a drink?"

"Actually miss I tend the bar in that pub. It was one of the locals that told me you were out here sleeping. Normally I would have let you carry on, but today we have a bit of an event on. Prince Albert is coming to give a talk on leadership in the back courtyard."

"A talk on leadership." Angel repeated. "Well Wes… ley. I'm a leader myself. I think I would like to listen to that. What time is he on?"

"Well, that'll be the right time of course. You are more than welcome to come along. For entry though you need to buy a drink, then have one gold coin to give to the prince."

"One gold coin." Angel almost laughed. Then started patting down her pockets in a slightly exaggerated fashion.

"You got me wrong there Wes… mate. I haven't got a pot to pi…"

A bulge in her left tracksuit pocket stopped her mid-sentence.

"Wait there. What is this?"

Angel extracted a small leather purse from the pocket, that looked like something from the Middle Ages. The purse was tied at the top and positively bulging. 'Of course,' she thought. 'I'm dreaming. Why wouldn't I have loads of money.' Pulling open the purse Angel was very pleased to find it brimming with gold coins. 'All right,' she thought with a smile to herself.

"Well then Wes'er. Lead the way. What's your most expensive drink?"

xx lol xx

A short time later, Angel was already into her second glass of champagne. Whilst being the most expensive drink in the bar Angel, in truth, was finding the drink somewhat disagreeable.

"Hey Wez, you sure you're not having me on. This stuff tastes like fizzy cat's urine."

The truth of that matter was that Angel's taste buds were more accustomed to two litre, brown bottles of cider and supermarket brand vodkas. She was quite unable to appreciate the supposed quality of the grapes that she was swigging now. Angel was killing time, waiting with several other punters in the bar for the prince to begin his seminar. He and his little entourage had shuffled through to the back courtyard some time ago. Angel would have left already if she'd had anything better to do.

A bugle sounded at the other end of the bar. The offending bugle player was dressed in royal garb. Once satisfied he had caught the attention of the room he dropped his bugle arm to one side. Then, in a booming voice, he proceeded to announce.

"Gentleman. Ladies. Anything in between. Please be advised that his relatively high highness, the Royal Prince Albert, is ready to begin. All here are welcome..."

A pause.

"All here are welcome, for the admission fee of a single gold coin."

There was, no doubt, many in the bar that might benefit from the prince's wisdom, but unless they could cover the entry fee they would miss out. This issue did not apply to Angel today and soon she found herself seated in the courtyard with several other well-heeled punters.

The seating was a rather ad hoc array of wooden benches, metal stools and anything else one might find to sit on. Everyone in the courtyard was facing toward a pair of wooden gates that opened onto the main road outside. A couple of pallets had been used to form a small stage. A projector had been set up to the left of this and a very cheesy image, of what must be the prince, wearing a winning smile framed by a thumbs up, was currently being beamed onto a projector screen set up in front of the gates.

The bugle playing assistant popped up and started to gesture downwards with his arms and hands, palms face down. The gathered crowd slowly dispelled with their various conversations and soon a hush had settled over the courtyard. The assistant then spoke.

"Gentlemen. Ladies. Anything in between. Please put your hands together."

Here he started to clap to the person closest to him on his left. As that person joined in, he worked his way in an arc across the audience. His clapping became more enthusiastic as he went. By the time he had gotten to the person closest to him on his right, the gathered crowd were all on their feet whooping and cheering in anticipation. Angel was surprised to find herself stood up as well. Fully caught up in this moment.

"I give to you, the one, the only, the amazing... Rooyaaaal Prince ALBERT!"

The crown went wild.

Albert entered stage left, bouncing into the centre stage. There he stood, soaking up the adoration, until eventually the audience resettled, and Albert was able to begin.

Ultimate Corporate BS Success

"Hello, peasants. How are we all?"

A couple of attendees close to the stage made to answer. The prince continued.

"That was a rhetorical question. Please don't answer because I don't care."

Angel was impressed already.

"All of you are here today because you obviously have good sense. Many times, I have been asked. 'Albert, what is it that makes you such a great leader?'. Well, I say, you don't have to be born a leader to be a leader. I mean, social standing helps, and most of you here today will never rise past the general scum line, it's true. For a lucky few of you though here today, what I am about to share will transform your life."

Applause followed. Angel was sold, albeit a little distracted by an unpleasant odour that was starting to build.

"That's right folks. I am going to share with you my secrets to success."

'What is that smell?' Angel thought to herself.

"Yes. For the price of a single golden coin, I am going to give you 'Five Golden Leadership Rules' in return."

'Cow manure!' Angel realised. 'That's what it is. Must be a farm near here somewhere.'

Satisfied that she had identified the offending whiff Angel turned her attention back fully to the stage.

<u>Rule 1</u>

If You Want To Do Well, Don't Ask - Tell

"Many leaders make the mistake of asking subordinates for their opinions. The truth of the matter is that if you ask someone what they think, then they will waste your time offering you their pointless opinions. These can only distract from any necessary task at hand. Much more efficient is to just tell someone what you expect them to do. Remembering also the golden ratio."

Albert pointed to his ears.

"Two of these."

Then to his mouth.

"Only one of these."

Angel thought she knew what was coming next, but to her pleasant surprise the prince followed with.

"It is impossible to speak directly into both ears at once, so often you will have to SHOUT! to make sure your subordinate hears you. Also, when shouting, the more aggressively you can shout then the more likely it is that your instructions will get through."

Rule 2

Meetings Are For Bleatings

"I myself am a modern man. I fully understand that in these modern times we want to give our subordinates the impression that they might have an input into the way things are run. Instinctively meetings may feel like a good way to achieve this. All they really do is waste everybody's time.

People like the sound of their own voices and generally believe that they might have something valid to say. Being in a meeting though is like being in a field full of bleating sheep. Everyone feels a need to contribute noise. Meetings are a waste of precious time when your subordinates could be getting on with real work. You should avoid calling meetings at any cost.

That said, if you do ever feel your subjects are becoming especially disengaged then a meeting is a good way to bring the bleating sheep back in line and make them feel like you might actually care. The trick works especially well if you provide free sandwiches."

Rule 3

Dispel With Fear
Tell Them What They Want To Hear

"That's right. As a leader you can be up to all sorts of no good. Despite reality staring your subordinates right in their faces, you will be amazed at how willing they are to believe you if you just tell them what it is that they want to hear. The truth of your actions literally does not matter one dot.

An especially excellent trick here is to devise some sort of vision, or value statement. You know, 'we believe in always doing the right thing,' that kind of nonsense. If you can get your subordinates to buy into the values, then they can continue to feel good about themselves even when they are blatantly doing the wrong thing. As an aside, the trick of telling people what they want to hear works equally well upwards. However, applying it this way is a lot riskier and could end less well for you."

<u>Rule 4</u>

Increase Deeds By Understanding Needs

"As a leader you will repeatedly find the need to squeeze your subordinates for greater output. This is incredibly easy. All you need to do is understand that your subordinates all have needs. Ultimately, they all need to feel good about themselves. They have primitive needs, like needing a family, needing to own a hovel, needing to wear fashionable clothing or needing to drink excessive amounts of alcohol. For all the above they will require money.

As you are in control of the money, their 'wages,' then you already have them by the short and curlies. If someone is not performing all you have to do is threaten them with dispatch. Once they realise that they will no longer be able to pay for their needs they will soon fall back in line with your demands."

<u>Rule 5</u>

Buy Them, Tie Them Or Die Them

"The most important rule of all. If you want to be the best, then be the best. Never, ever waste your time competing. Don't compete, defeat. Crush potential competition by any means necessary."

Albert raised his left arm into the air, clenched his hand into a fist, then dragged it back down. The action was more that of an 80's pop video star than that of a fearless leader. Still the audience lapped it up.

"Most of you peasants have a price. If a potential competitor appears to be doing well then simply buy them out. If a threat to your leadership emerges from within, simply overload that threat with pointless unnecessary administration type tasks. Tie them up in knots. If that fails, tie them up in chains and throw them in the dungeon. If all else fails, then..."

The prince slowly drew a finger across his neck. "You may need to 'die' them."

He used his fingers to make little speech marks in the sky to accompany the word die.

Having delivered his five golden rules, the prince moved to wrap up his presentation.

"So, peasants. To recap my rules for success, remember."

Albert clicked a button and the first rule projected onto the screen behind him.

"Everybody. Say them with me."

The gathered audience obliged, repeating in unison.

'IF YOU WANT TO DO WELL, DON'T ASK, TELL!'

Albert shouted the word 'tell' for extra emphasis.

'MEETINGS ARE FOR BLEATINGS.'

"Meh. Baaaa. Mehhh..." Added the Prince for effect.

'DISPEL WITH FEAR. TELL THEM WHAT THEY WANT TO HEAR.'

"That's right, peasants. Remember, attending this seminar will change your life for the better and is a gold coin very wisely spent."

'INCREASE DEEDS BY UNDERSTANDING NEEDS.'

"Woo wooo, choo, chug, chuff. If you wan' 'em to work harder then you gotta treat 'em tough."

'BUY THEM, TIE THEM OR DIE THEM.''

"Yes, peasants. When someone else shows signs of doing better than you, then apply this rule. You'll soon turn that frown into a crown."

Albert used both hands to create an arch (supposed to represent a frown), then used his opposing thumbs to make something like a circle, which he then, rather awkwardly, lifted to place on top of his head, as if it were a crown.

"That's right folks. If you want to be a successful leader like me then don't debate, dictate. Don't compete, defeat." Albert put his arms out toward the audience. "Rise, and..." Palms facing the sky, he lifted his arms into the air, encouraging the audience to rise with him.

"Never, ever, compromise!"

The audience were once again worked up into a frenzy, applauding enthusiastically.

Albert then used his arms in reverse, to pat down the crowd's energy.

"Now, before I go. Does anyone have any questions?"

Several hands went up in the audience. The prince surveyed the raised hands briefly then responded.

"You idiots with your hands in the air were obviously not paying attention. As for the rest, you will be pleased to hear that I have copies of my book for sale."

A faint buzzing sound became audible. Albert started to gently waft at the air around him with one hand, whilst holding up a copy of his book in the other.

"'Five Golden Rules - Ultimate Corporate BS Success.'"

He was wafting a little harder as the buzzing started to circle his head.

"Pft, fff. 'BS' by the way is... Pft, fff. 'BS is short for business by the wa...'"

The Prince was now quite animated in his attempts to waft away the offending buzzing.

"Pft, fff. Forgive me. There appears to be a rather friendly wasp here on the stage with me. Pft. fff. As I was saying. Unfortunately the title was a little long for the publishers so I had to abbreviat.."

The wafting had now turned into full attack mode as the prince tried to slap down his new friend.

"Pft. fff. Damn it. Look, if you would like to buy one of these for only two gold coins, please come to the stage no..."

The wasp landed on Albert's nose. In his distracted state Albert's reflex was to strike at the wasp with his book. The wasp was too quick, and Albert proceeded to slap himself in the face. He decided to retreat back to the safety of the bar.

"Stuff this. If you want a book I will be inside."

With that the Prince was gone.

The gathered audience took this as their cue also to begin their shuffle back into the bar.

All this time Angel had not moved from her seat. It had been her first time attending anything like this and she was feeling a little overwhelmed by it all. As she sat reflecting on the presentation, she became aware of a buzzing in her ear. Somehow Angel knew that this wasn't the same wasp that had just scared off the prince. This wasp settled on Angel's shoulder.

Angel did not flinch.

"What a wuss." Said the wasp in Angel's ear.

Angel flinched.

In fact, she jumped clean out of her seat.

The wasp remained anchored to her shoulder.

"What the actual..."

"Calm down Angel. What's the matter? You never spoke with a wasp before?"

"What the... Where the... Where is that coming from? Who said that?"

Angel was looking frantically this way and that. Looking for the source of the voice. Refusing to believe a wasp could be talking to her.

"Calm down will you. Please. Remember where you are, what you are doing. What is wrong with a talking wasp?"

"Wha, whe, what..." Angel remembered to breathe, then started to relax a little. "Oh yeah. I'm dreaming, I think. I kind've forgotten for a minute. Okay. A talking wasp. What the hell. How you doing? My name's Angel."

"I know. And my name is May."

"Oh, I get it. Like May Bee?"

"No. Like May Wasp, thank you very much." Introductions over, May continued. "As I was saying, what a wuss?"

"Oh yeah, the prince." Angel relaxed back into her seat. "He danced off stage like a scared little kid."

"I'm not talking about the prince. I'm talking about that wasp. I Mean, did you see him? He landed on the prince's nose and didn't even sting him. What was that all about?"

"Oh," said Angel. "I see. You mean the wasp was acting like a wuss. Right. Fair. Gotcha."

"That's right Angel. That wasp is part of a cult that is growing and starting to do some real damage to our reputations. That is why I am here, Angel. We need a strong leader to help get things back on track. I heard you were here, so I came looking for you."

"Looking for me?" Angel was surprised that anyone other than the police would want to look for her.

"Yes Angel, you. You are already a leader. You must know that you are one day destined to become a great leader."

Angel was shocked to hear such a thing said by someone else, especially as that someone else was a wasp. In her heart she liked to believe that she was destined for bigger things, but that belief had started to feel more like fantasy as she had gotten older. Now though there was someone else, something else, saying it out loud to her.

"Well yeah, yes. Ahem, of course I know that."

"Good." Replied May. "Then you will help us? Help me? Be the great leader we so desperately need right now."

It has been said that flattery will get you everywhere. May's flattery certainly had the desired effect on Angel, and she found herself quickly agreeing to May's request.

"All right then." May was happy. "We are on. There is though one thing I should mention."

"Oh. What is that?"

"You will need to become a wasp, like me."

"Say what!"

"Just for a little while. Just until you have helped resolve the crisis. Then you will be turned back. I promise."

"Will I be able to fly?"

"Yes."

"Will I be able to sting humans?"

"That is desired, yes."

"Okay. In that case count me in. What do I need to do?"

Angel became aware of a faint tinkling sound in the air, accompanied by a growing, settling mist.

"Oh, not much."

The tinkling grew louder. The wind started to pick up. The mist turned into a fog.

"Just sit back."

Quite loud now were the twinkling and chiming sounds. Quite strong now was the wind. Quite thick now was the fog.

"Take a deep breath."

Breaking out of the fog was a tall figure with a creepy bird-like face and really long dangly fingers.

"Relax."

"Wow. Are those fingers made of wind chimes? I think I'm starting to feel a little sleepy. Hey, what is in that fuug..."

"Close your eyes."

Angel dribbled a little. Powerless to resist she let her eyelids shut.

"Now let go."

Angel did as she was told.

Sting In The Tale

"Open your eyes Angel. Come on. Wakey, wakey. We've got work to be getting on with."

Angel opened her eyes.

"There you are."

"Aaaaaaahhhhh!" Angel screamed.

She had opened her eyes to find herself face to face with a giant human sized wasp. In fact, Angel was now a wasp sized human. Or rather a wasp sized wasp. She just hadn't realised this yet. Angel instinctively made to swipe at the giant wasp but found that she now had very little arms.

"What the..."

"Calm down Angel. It's May, remember? You agreed to become a wasp. You agreed that you would help me."

Angel remembered, then began to calm down.

"I remember. This is seriously freaky though. I mean, wow. Look how tiny my arms are."

"That is a matter of opinion." Said May. "I suggest that before we get to business it might be a good idea to undertake a few orientation exercises."

Angel then received a crash course in being a wasp. Once she was semi confident in the control of her new vessel May offered to show her around the place.

xx lol xx

"So, where are we?"

"We are at The Bee-Hive."

"The Bee-Hive. Really? It doesn't look very 'hivey.' Is hivey a word? I feel like it should be a word."

"The Bee-Hive is a pub, for humans. Our colony lives in the beer garden and has done so for many moons."

"Oh."

"And no. Hivey is not a word."

"Shame."

First stop on the tour was an area of brightly coloured flowers.

"Welcome to The Nectar Inn."

"A pub within a pub. Nice. Is this your place by any chance?"

"Very intuitive of you. Yes, indeed. This is my bar."

"Alright. Owning a bar is awesome. I have to say though, it looks pretty quiet. Is it open?"

"Yes, the bar is open. Sadly, my fellow wasps stopped coming. The place used to be absolutely buzzing. The colony would all pile in, day and night, to get loaded on nectar. They would then fall out of here, fight with each other a little, then pile into the beer garden and start annoying the humans."

May let out a sigh.

"Those were the days."

"Sounds amazing. What happened?"

"Bon Lemon is what happened."

"Bon who?"

"Bon Lemon. Come on, I'll show you."

xx lol xx

The pair lifted into the air leaving The Nectar Inn behind. They flew past a children's play area, then over the top of a short hedgerow. As soon as they had crested the hedgerow Angel could hear the buzzing of noise, of song, of energy. Groups of wasps were clustered all over, busying themselves with this or that. 'Quite the colony,' Angel thought to herself.

At the very centre of the chaos a large group of wasps were all sitting on the ground, surrounding a single, slightly larger looking wasp that was singing and playing a guitar. Clearly a trick of the light but Angel was sure that the wasp had a beard and long hair. The group surrounding him were singing and clapping along. Angel could just make out the words.

'...all we are saying, is give bees a chance...'

"What is that all about?" Angel asked. "Who is the wasp in the middle?"

"That..." May replied. "...is Bon Lemon."

"That is your problem?"

"That is 'our' problem." May confirmed.

"Fair." Conceded Angel. "I have to say though that he just looks like a harmless old hippy to me. Why is this guy a problem?"

"Well Angel, it all started to go wrong several moons ago. Bon used to be one of our best. One of the angriest wasps you had ever seen. So much passion and energy. The other wasps used to hero worship him. Then, one sunny day, he got fully loaded on nectar at the bar. He'd had a couple of fights with other wasps, stung a few humans in the beer garden, then decided to round the night off with some greasy pollen from the takeout. He was so drunk on nectar though that he took a wrong turn and landed instead on a recently grown patch of mushrooms. Greedily he ate his fill and then..."

May paused.

"Then what?"

"Well, then he left the colony. He spent the next seven and a half years thinking he was a beetle."

"A beetle!"

"I know right. Nothing really changed whilst he was away. He was still considered a hero and all the younger wasps kind of built up a cult, where they all idolised him, even though he wasn't here."

"Then what happened?"

"Then he came back."

"Oh."

"He'd realised by this point that he wasn't a beetle. He had however chosen to identify as a Bee instead."

"Identify as a Bee!" Angel was confused. "Can you guys do that?"

"Apparently so. When he returned the young wasps all flocked around him and started to hang onto his every word. Whilst he was away, he had come to renounce violence. He told his followers how their lives were empty. There was more to life than just irritating the humans he said. He had spent time watching bees. He saw how they lived in harmony with the humans. How they spent their time pollinating and helping to make the world a more beautiful place."

"Wow."

"He declared that he had identified as a Bee and wanted to work towards living in harmony with the humans. Soon after most of the youth of the colony had also identified as bees. Then, soon after that, the adults started to follow suit.

In pursuit of a more productive life the colony slowly stopped coming to my bar. Instead, they started spending more of their time in the beer garden with the humans. Slowly building up trust that they were no longer angry wasps. Once the humans realised the wasps had changed, they started to bring offerings of fruit. The colony was now living in peace and harmony. Eventually they learnt to produce honey, just like the bees. Now it's all '...ooo, let's make honey for the humans. That way they will know that we love them.' Soon they were being rewarded with piles of fruit. They had never had it so good."

"Wow." Angel said again.

"You know, there hasn't been a single pint glass fatality in over a year now. In fairness it's no wonder that they started to refer to Bon as the second coming."

"The second coming! You mean there was a first?"

"Yes, of course. Lord Beezus. He died Cross for us. He showed us the way. We are supposed to be wasps. We are supposed to be cross. We are supposed to be irritating to humans. That is the natural way of things. This guy though is all peace and love and flowers, and it is, quite frankly, not acceptable."

"What is it you want me to do about it?"

"Well, I need a leader to rival Bon Lemon. I need someone who reminds his followers of the Wasp that he once was. Of the Wasp that they idolised before he turned into a hibbee. In short Angel, I need you to take back control and get these little fellas all fired up again. What do you think? Do you think you can do that?"

Angel took a moment to reflect, remembering her one great desire, to be regarded and remembered as a great leader. Taking a deep breath, Angel replied.

"Yes. I think I can do that. First though let's go back to your place and get a drink. I really wanna try some of that nectar."

The one drink turned into an all-night session. The pair spent the night necking nectar and plotting, then fighting, then eventually hugging, then gorging on greasy pollen. The next morning Angel awoke with a little sick encrusted down her front and a very sore head.

"Woman, that nectar is serious! Not sure I'm ever gonna drink it again though. My head is banging."

"Ha. Give it a few hours, you'll be begging for more."

"I think not."

"Come on. We'll go get a pollen sarnie. That will sort you right out."

"Oh my... I think I'm gonna be..."

'WRETCH!' 'HUEEY!' 'DURK!'

After Angel had stopped being sick, again, she found that she felt a lot better.

"So, I know we made plans last night. But I'm not sure I remember what we said."

"Well Angel. I think we agreed that you would just talk to Bon in the first instance. See what he says."

"We agreed that?" Angel was surprised.

"Sounds a little passive for me."

Then she remembered the rules learnt from the prince. Rule five: buy them, tie them or die them. By having a conversation, she would know which of those three options was necessary.

"Okay, I will go and see Bon. Have a little chat."

Angel crested the hedge, as she had done the previous day. Sure enough, Bon was again sitting at the centre of a large group, leading them all in song. With her little right arm Angel rubbed at her chin and wondered. 'How am I going to get him alone for a chat?'

At that same moment there came a commotion from behind, as humans started to appear in the beer garden, taking up places on their favourite benches for the afternoon. This was quickly followed by a chorus of chatter within the colony, along the lines of; 'Ooo, ooo, ooo. The humans are coming, the humans are coming. Quick, quick, quick. Let's go and see them. Let's go and see our friends.'

The colony rose up, forming into a tightly packed swarm, which then descended onto the humans.

To Angel's utter disbelief not a single human made to run or expressed any concern at all. Quite the opposite in fact. The humans held out their hands, encouraging the wasps to land on them. They started to 'coo' their affections in return.

"OMG!" Angel said out loud to no one. "That is actually disgusting."

Charged up with a greater sense of purpose than before, Angel turned from the scene to find Bon still sitting there, amongst the flowers, alone. This was her chance.

As she descended in Bon's direction Angel was surprised to find that she felt a little nervous. The realisation distracted her so much that she didn't notice she was hovering in front of Bon until she noticed.

"Hi there." Bon spoke with a Liverpudlian accent. "Can I help you? Do you need somebody?"

"I uh, ah. I, um. I, I..."

Was she starstruck? Angel didn't care about celebrities, only great leaders. Though wait. Maybe Bon was a great leader? 'Come on Angel. Pull yourself together,' she thought to herself.

"Ahem. I have come to talk to you Bon."

"Ah, you already know my name I see. So, what's your name then?"

"Oh, yes. I'm Angel."

"Oh, you're an Angel. So, are you an angel of hope or an angel of death?"

"A wha... No, my name is just Angel."

"Okay 'Just Angel'. Very nice to meet you. What can I do for you?"

"Well first of all, why are you still here when all of your followers have buzzed off to play with the humans?"

"My followers? I'm nothing but a humble bee. They are free to follow whichever path they choose. They are free to bee whatever they want. All I have done is show them a way."

"Why aren't you over there though, showing them the way?"

"How many bees get to say that they changed the world from a flowerbed?"

"What? You think you're changing the world? You're just misguiding a small bunch of young impressionable bees... I mean wasps."

"As I said, we are all free to choose what we beelieve."

"I think you mean who we believe."

"Semantics. It's up to them if they choose to listen to me or not. I'm just here and nowhere man. Nowhere and everywhere."

"Well, that makes literally no sense at all. Bees nee... I mean wasps. Wasps need a proper leader to follow. Wasps are supposed to be cross. Everybody knows that."

"Ah. Beezus and the whole cross thing. Imagine, though, just for one second, if it didn't end that way. Imagine if Beezus had more time. Maybe mellowed in his old age, learnt to see things differently, as we all do with time. What might the message from the past have been then do you think?"

"I think the message would have been the same. Bees... Wasps. Wasps. Wasps are meant to be cross. They are supposed to annoy humans. That is their job."

"Heavy."

"Humans have stressful lives. They need something that they can collectively direct their frustrations towards. Otherwise, they just direct it at each other."

"That sounds like a human problem to me. Don't you think? They have a choice too. They can choose to bee happy. All they need is love."

By now Angel had concluded that Bon was too far gone for reason.

"I think you're wrong Bon. In fact, you're Bon gone wrong. That has a ring to it. Don't you think?" An excellent insult Angel thought.

"If an Angel thinks so, then who am I to disagree?" This was Bon's retort.

Frustrated, Angel turned to leave with a humph.

"Do you need anything else?" Bon asked after her.

"No. No sir." Was all that Angel replied.

She then rose to the air and went looking for May. It was clear that the more drastic solution was required.

The Assassination Of Bon Lemon

Back at The Nectar Inn, Angel explained to May how Bon Lemon was not for turning. There would be no 'buying' of Bon as there was nothing he wanted. As for 'tying', this was not an option as it would encourage the hibbees to start having peaceful protests. Sadly, the only option here was 'dying' him. Bon had to go, and Bon had to stay gone.

"So…" May started. "I have a friend in the BIA."

"The BIA? Shouldn't that be WIA? 'W' for wasp?"

"The 'B' is for buzzing, not Bee. The BIA covers Wasps, Bees and Hornets. I happen to know Bon has been on their radar for some time. I think that they will be more than happy to help."

By sundown the next day the whole colony was in shock. News had spread that whilst the colony were in the beer garden, playing with their human friends, a hornet, posing as a fan, had approached Bon, then stabbed him in the back with his giant sting. Attempts had been made to save Bon, but all efforts failed, and he had passed at the same moment the sun had set. The wasps were now dispersed throughout the night garden, holding a glow worm vigil and sharing memories and songs of their fallen chosen one. They all agreed that there would never bee another quite like him.

An Angel's Ascent

Angel had the decency to wait until the next morning before moving to install herself into the now vacant leadership position. She opted for a prominent sunflower as a stage from which to address her captive, rather vulnerable audience.

"Friends. Insects, country-wasps, lend me your antennae."

'Were bees not wasps!' Came a shout from the crowd.

'What's an insect?'' Came another.

"Listen, fellow wasps. Toda..."

'Were bees!' Came a new heckle.

Angel took a breath, then tried again.

"Fellow wasp..."

'Bees!' Came a new heckle. 'Bees not wasps!' Came another. Soon it seemed that the whole crowd was shouting the same thing. Angel stayed calm and remembered rule two, how the prince had suggested 'meetings were for bleatings.' Angel could feel herself losing the crowd and it was too late now to offer sandwiches.

'Okay,' she thought. 'Rule one. 'If you want to do well, don't ask, tell.' She also remembered the prince's advice that shouting could help.

"YOU'RE BLOODY WASPS!"

Angel did indeed shout this at the audience, and with a fair amount of aggression in her voice too. The crowd were not used to this style of leadership. This was something new. The gathering instantly fell silent. Most looked away awkwardly or stared down at their tiny feet. Fearing that she may have gone too far too soon, Angel decided to initiate rule three. 'Dispel with fear, tell them what they want to hear'.

"Okay. What I meant to say is that you are bees. Yes. Today you are bees, but tomorrow you will be wasps."

A few stopped looking away and, out of curiosity, turned their attention back toward Angel.

"That is right. I happened to be the last Was... Ahem, Bee. The last Bee to have an audience with

Bon, and he told me how he had come to realise that the only true path to happiness was for us to return to our true nature. To reclaim our status as the crossest creature in the realm. Once again, the time has come to make the humans dance to our tune. Bon told me that it was time to re-identify as wasps."

The crowd were engaged. Angel found her flow.

"For too long we have lived in confusion as to our true identities. We have in fact received complaints from the BIA for stealing honey making jobs from the Bees."

'What about our human friends? They love us as bees and we love them.'

"That is a good question. I spoke with a human the other day and concerns have been expressed. Have you not noticed how they have all become fat and lazy? For some, the only true exercise they had was running away from wasps. Now we roll over and let them tickle our bellies. What kind of friends are we to the humans if we are actively helping to bring on coronary issues?"

A gentle buzz started to rise throughout the crowd. Those gathered looked to each other for reflection.

'But they bring us fruit. Without them we might starve an..."

"Poppycock."

Angel was a little surprised to hear that word come out of her mouth but carried on regardless.

"What they bring is their cast offs. The stuff that they were going to throw away. No, my friends. You have clearly forgotten. When we were glorious wasps, we did not wait for them to bring us what they chose. No. Instead we chose what we wanted, and we took it. We chose, not them. We. Us."

Another louder buzz swept through the audience.

"To the young that are gathered here today, I bet that they have never experienced the exotic flavours of smokey bacon or cheese and onion. Have never felt the rush of abseiling into the neck of a bottle of strawberry and lime cider. Have never experienced the serene feeling of warm greasy fish batter underfoot. You see my friends, by accepting the human cast offs we have forgone our previous riches and freely accepted slavery. Where once we were queens, we are now mere peasants."

'But it's fun to play with the humans.' Came one retort from the crowd.

"You think it's fun now. You wait until you see them dance."

'So, what are we supposed to do?' A new question from the crowd.

"Fear not, for I will show you the way. I will help you to remember and reclaim your former glory. I will teach you to rise, to sting, and to fight again."

'But what if we don't want to fight dude? What if we think that peace is like way better?'

Rule four came to mind. 'Increase deeds by understanding needs.'

"Well, my peace loving hibbee friend. In answer to your question. If you value your liberty, then you will fight. If you value the liberty of your family, then you will fight. If you truly value peace, as you say you do, then the only way to achieve that peace is to fight."

Angel noticed several heads nodding in the audience.

This was the moment.

This was her moment.

She launched into her final rally.

"We shall fight them in the beer garden.
We shall fight with growing confidence and
growing strength in the air.
We shall defend our nectar bar, whatever the
cost may be.
We shall fight on the garden benches.

We shall fight on the pub playground.
We shall fight in the flower beds and in the pub
car park.
We shall fight all day until the night
We shall never surrender."

Angel lifted her little arms into the air for
emphasis.
It worked.
The crowd let out a cheer.
"We will be glorious wasps once more!"
The crowd went wild.
Angel had done enough.
The bee... Ahem, sorry.
The wasps.
The wasps needed a new leader and it appeared
that they had found one.
Angel rose into the air and led the crowd over the
hedge to May's bar. It was time to get this lot back
on the nectar.

xx lol xx

What followed was a week-long nectar binge and
cementation of Angel's leadership. Soon every
soul in the colony was fully back on the nectar, all
drinking and fighting and swearing and just

generally being cross. They were identifying as wasps once again and the youngest amongst them were now super keen to get some action in the beer garden.

Being a great leader though, Angel, not sure how the humans might react, insisted that the adults would take the first flight out. Sunshine was forecast for the next day, which meant the beer garden would be full. As soon as the lunch time rush arrived the wasps would make their comeback.

Battle Of Beehive

The next day arrived. Angel chose an early hour to move her troops into the hedgerow that edged onto the beer garden. Being a great leader Angel would of course be leading from the front. May was Angel's wing wasp. Behind them would be a great swarm made up from all the adults within the colony.

Lunch had begun, the pub garden was almost completely full. The colony was itching to get started on this mission.

"Wow Angel. I knew you were going to be a great leader. Just look at us. Look at them. We're wasps again. All of us. And it's all thanks to you."

Angel wanted to be modest and even felt a little embarrassed in taking this praise.

"Save the complements May. At least until we have completed this first mission. You and I both know that when we start attacking there is a high risk that one of us may not make it back."

"Death or glory!" May offered.

With that, Angel raised her little right arm and gave the order.

"CHARRRRRGGGGGGEEEEEE!"

The beer garden was packed. Many humans were sitting on benches drinking, eating, vaping, texting, chatting and laughing. All enjoying the sunshine and the moment. All happy and grateful to be alive. The sudden incoming cloud of wasps did not alarm the humans. In fact, several smiles lit up when the first sounds of buzzing were detected. The wasps swarmed in as usual, then spread out amongst the humans. Angel had devised a strategy that would take full advantage of the humans' trusting nature.

The colony would start by pretending that nothing had changed. The wasps landed onto offered human hands. Some crawled, on top of human ears. Some nested themselves into haircuts. Some on the tips of toes exposed by flip flops. A few were bold enough to land on noses. The humans, unaware of what was coming, all giggled and laughed and took pictures of one another covered in what they believed were their friendly wasps.

Then Angel gave the order.

"NOW!"

With the command given, all the wasps proceeded to plant their stings. They stung fingertips, ear lobes, heads, toes and noses. The humans, totally in shock, began to scream. Chaos ensued. Glasses were knocked over. Humans hit themselves and others, whilst trying to get the wasps off them. A good number broke into wild dance moves.

"AGAIN!"

Another sting.

The humans were in disarray. Nobody was left sitting down. The garden was in utter chaos. Plates, drink glasses, vapes, sunglasses, were dropping all over to be broken by the ground.

"AGAIN!"

Another sting and that was it. The humans were done. All running now for the cover of the pub itself.

Angel and May hovered side by side, watching the human retreat. Once the garden was empty, they turned to survey the scene. The humans had left sugary drinks, exotic flavoured crisps and various half-finished meals all over the place. The other wasps were busy taking all of this in when May grabbed Angel's little hand in hers, raised her little arm into the air and shouted.

"Long live Angel."

May chanted this, and it wasn't long until the rest of the colony joined in. Soon all the wasps were chanting Angel's name. She'd done it. She had taken back the beer garden for the wasps without a single reported casualty. Tonight, they would celebrate their success and feast upon all the riches that the humans had given up.

That night, back at May's bar, the wasps could talk of nothing else. Angel had been instantly elevated to legend status. Bowing to pressure Angel agreed that the young wasps could have their turn the following day. The adults would join as a second wave if needed, though with it being such easy pickings today nobodbee thought that would be necessary. Being in such high spirits the singing, dancing, swearing and fighting went on into the early hours. Nobodbee in the colony really slept that night and the wasps began the next day all a little hungover. Angel especially so.

Weeping Angel

Due to the thumping that was occurring within her head, Angel opted this time to hold a position at the back of the charge. The young pups, despite their hangovers, were fully charged with an energy and enthusiasm that Angel did not quite possess this day. When all the young wasps were in position, and with the beer garden almost full, Angel gave the order they were waiting for.

"Charge..."

Angel managed a shout but the delivery this time was a little half-hearted. The colony flew on. Angel and May took up the final two positions at the rear. It was whilst on their final approach toward the humans that Angel realised something was wrong.

All the humans had their backs turned against the oncoming onslaught. Angel felt her gut drop as she realised that nobody had any fluids in their drinking glasses.

"Beezus, it's a trap!"

"RETREAT!" She shouted

"RETREAT!"

The wasps were buzzing so loudly that they did not hear Angel's order. They flew on, deploying the same agreed tactic and dispersing themselves amongst the humans as their parents had done the day before. This time though no wasp was going to get close enough to make a landing. This time the humans were prepared.

Suddenly they turned to engage. Amongst them Angel saw that they had bats, they had cans of spray, some had cans of deodorant and lighters, some had pots of jam. Others were armed only with empty pint glasses. The first of these Angel witnessed as it crunched down on top of young Johnny Good. In a state of shock Angel did not see the bat being swung in her direction. May however had her back. She grabbed and pulled Angel into a dive below a bench. Above them the scene was carnage. This time however it was the colony that were in trouble.

Wasps were being swatted, stamped, sprayed and slammed in every direction and in every manner possible. Many were taken as prisoners, locked up in half filled jam jars.

"Angel. You are our leader. What do we do? What do we do?"

Angel did not react to May's questioning. She was shell shocked and frozen and could do nothing other than stare off into space.

A new wave of buzzing could be heard, rapidly approaching the scene. Angel realised this was the adults, the second wave, flying in to try and rescue their young. They themselves were immediately subject to the same onslaught. The pub garden had turned into a killing ground, the gutters running in shades of yellow and green as wasp after wasp succumbed to one of many grizzly endings.

xx lol xx

The sound of buzzing began to fade, then eventually ceased altogether. This was replaced with a cheer from the humans. Oblivious to the genocide that they had just wrought they seemed elated to have rid their beer garden of the annoying wasps. May used the moment to push

Angel out from under the cover of the bench so that they could both make a fly for it. A nearby human, holding a can of bug spray, reacted to the movement. The human turned and fired. Too slow to hit Angel but May, who had left the safety of the bench just a second later, was caught by the edge of the resulting gas cloud. Breathing in she began to cough and splutter but managed to fly on.

The pair made it back to The Nectar Inn and landed outside. Well, Angel landed. May sort of crashed into a heap. Having been poisoned by the bug spray May could barely breathe at all. She was dying and these were to be her last moments. Angel held onto her as she began to fade.

"Oh May. What have I done?" Angel was snivelling. "This isn't how it was supposed to be."

"Wars often are no... 'cough' ...not. Yet they alway... 'cough', 'cough' ...they always end the same way. Don't you think?"

"But I was supposed to be their leader May. I was supposed to be their great leader. Now they are all gone."

"You were their great leader, Angel. At least for a... 'cough', 'cough', 'cough' ...at least for a short minute."

"But who is there to remember me? Everyone has gone. What was the point? I just wanted to be a great leader."

"You still can be. You are still he… 'cough,' 'cough' …here. You can start again Angel. Be the leader yo… 'cough', 'cough', 'cough'.'"

It turned out that May did not have enough time left to finish the sentence. Gently, her eyelids closed, and May went to sleep.

"Please don't leave me May. What am I supposed to do without you? I need you."

Tears were streaming down Angel's little cheeks, falling onto the upturned face below. May's little arms went limp, her hand slipped from Angels and dropped toward the floor. Angel squeezed her eyes tight, looked to the sky and let out a scream.

"NOOOOOOOOOOOOOOOOOO!"

The Awakening

Angel's mum came running into the bedroom at the sound of the scream.

"Angel. Angel love. Wake up. Wake up. Come on love, open your eyes."

"Wha... where, wha..."

Angel opened her eyes.

Angel's eyes were now open.

Disoriented and clearly quite distressed.

A curtain had fallen away in one corner.

The light coming in was blinding.

Angel looked around the room, at the posters of her previous heroes.

Her mum hugged her and stroked her hair.

Angel knew that something had changed.

The Lone Shark

It had been a long, grey, chill to the bone type afternoon, a storm from the previous day still making its presence felt. Mick the Fish had been out on his usual rounds and was now sitting with Bob, in Bob's flat. He had saved his visit to Bob for last, anticipating that he might need cheering up and hoping also to benefit from some of his mostly untapped wisdom.

"I don't get it Bob. I mean, it's obvious she likes me, so why won't she come out for dinner with me?"

"Well Mick, you know what them women can be like. From another planet I tell thee. You wanna watch em too. They can be worse than them feevin oligarchs you know."

"Ha. I hardly think Mary is comparable to an oligarch Bob."

"Maybe. But she is a woman. At least that's what you told me. If you're not careful she'll have all of your money off ya and you will have to stay here with me."

Mick had a little smile to himself.

"Do you wanna cup of tea? I'm gonna have one."

"Thanks Bob, but I had a cup before I got here." Mick lied. "I'm all tea'd out.'

"Ah well. Maybe next time."

A small silence followed.

Bob then reflected.

"In all fairness Mick. If you really want her to go to dinner with you then you probably shouldn't ask her to pay for herself."

"I told you Bob. It's not that I wouldn't pay to take her out, it's just that I don't want to offend her pride."

"That's very admirable of you Mick. But I'm not sure that offering an interest free loan, just so's she could join you for an expensive dinner, is the right way to go about not offending someone. Just my thoughts there Mick. For what they're worth."

"Hmmm. Maybe you're right. But what if I did just take her out and then she decides she's not interested in me. Then I would have wasted my money, right? I'll never make it to a billion if I go around doing that?"

"Ain't you wealthy enough already Mick?"

"Ha, not really Bob. I'm doing alright but I've got some way to go before I make it to a billion."

"What do you want that much money for Mick? You wanna be like one of them oligarchs? They'll end up coming for you if you get that rich. Then you won't be able to visit me Mick."

"Don't you worry Bob. As long as you owe me money, I will be coming to visit you."

"Seriously though Bob. What do you wanna be a billionaire for anyway? Better to be rich in memories I say."

Bob tapped at his forehead for emphasis.

"Well then Bob, it's just a shame that you bashed that head of yours and can't remember anything eh?"

Certain words, put together and delivered in a certain way, at a certain moment, are capable of inflicting more hurt and pain than anything else in this universe.

Bob gazed at the floor and let out a sigh.

Then he raised his head back up and turned to make eye contact with Mick.

"You may be right there Mick. You may well be right. But the heart..."

Bob bashed a fist against his chest.

"The heart Mick. That never forgets."

xx lol xx

After seeing Bob, Mick returned home. For some reason he found himself feeling down. To cheer himself up he decided to retreat to his home office and conduct a review of his finances.

Mick's office was as you would imagine it to be. Very modern with expensive looking furniture. Three monitors for the PC (he only ever worked on one) and another, very large flat screen, hanging on the wall behind. Also hanging on the wall were pictures of Mick's heroes. 'Billionaires row,' as Mick liked to refer to them. These were all self-made people in business that had achieved making a billion. These were Mick's inspiration. Winners in the game of capitalism. It was Mick's long-term ambition to count himself amongst them. When he finally made his billion, he intended to commission a portrait of himself that he could hang alongside his idols, ensuring that he too would be remembered as a success.

After conducting a full review of his wealth Mick found he was feeling a little better. He also found that he was feeling a little hungry. On autopilot

Mick made his way to the oversized refrigerator in the kitchen. The kitchen itself was huge, including both a large kitchen island and a twelve-seater dining table. Mick opened the fridge door out of habit. He already knew that the contents were minimal. Some butter or course. An array of ageing condiments. A few pots of gut friendly bacteria drinks. A carton of juice. A half-consumed block of smoked cheese. A random selection of chilled craft beers.

"Looks like takeout again tonight then Mick."

He said this out loud to nobody but himself. Opening the bottom kitchen drawer Mick pulled out a wad of menus to peruse, eventually settling on Thai. He ordered satay chicken and spring rolls to start, and a main of green curry accompanied by coconut rice. When the food arrived Mick plated up, grabbed a beer from the fridge, then took himself and his meal into the lounge area.

At the centre of the room was a huge sofa arrangement, forming three sides of a square, in the middle of which sat an indoor firepit. In front of the sofas a huge widescreen television set was mounted onto the wall. Embedded into the walls was a state-of-the-art surround sound system, worthy of any current day cinema complex. This was a momentous space and an incredible setting in which to experience the best that any movie producer might have to offer.

Mick turned on the TV and found a programme about antique celebrities driving around in antique cars looking for antique antiques to sell at a local auction house.

After dinner, and two hours of mindless TV, Mick took his dirty plates to the kitchen and washed them up. He did this even though he paid for a cleaner to come in once a day. When everything was tidy Mick decided it was time for bed.

After sorting himself out in the bathroom Mick climbed, literally, into his huge custom made 'Super Duper King' sized bed. The sheets were all 3,000 thread counts. Mick insisted on clean sheets every day. As he lay there, savouring the rich feeling, he clapped his hands, activating the automatic curtains to close. As the motor whirled Mick reflected on his day. More specifically he reflected on his visit to Bob's. As he did so he felt a fresh bubble of melancholy rise and burst inside his chest.

'Poor Bob,' he thought. 'His life is so sad.'

Mick had no way of knowing that at that exact same moment Bob was himself led in bed, eyes closed and drifting. A huge smile was spread across his face, lit by a warm glow from his heart, as it remembered.

  Right before it stopped.

  "Good night, Bob."
Mick said out loud.
Then he closed his own eyes and went to sleep.

Meanwhile At Gangle Manor

Amari and Ella were enjoying some downtime, lounging about, streaming movies and chilling out together. Both were still buoyed up by their experience with Angel, considering the mission to have been a success. At this moment though Amari was struggling with the plot currently playing out on a movie they were watching.

"So, what you're saying is that X is from the future?"

"Yes."

"But the current X, in the present, doesn't know that yet?"

"Yes."

"But then there is the X from the past, who is also in the present, and who does know that the X from the future is that same X as in the present?"

"Yes."

"And he knows this even though he is from the past and not from the future?"

"Yes."

"Well, that doesn't make sense does it? If X from the past knows now, then why doesn't present X remember."

"Well, X from the past gets a bump on the head and then forgets about meeting X from the future. That's why X from the future was okay with telling his past self... About himself. Because he knew that his present self, in the past, would forget."

There followed a long pause, after which Amari simply exclaimed.

"I don't get it!"

"What's not to get?" Questioned Ella, a little exasperated.

"Nah. The film is rubbish anyway. Can't we watch something els..."

A cacophony of beautiful bird song rang out in the room, and all the other rooms within the Gangle Manor. Loud, but not too loud, the alarm was actually quite pleasant.

"Phew. Saved by the bell." Said Amari. "You can turn that rubbish off. Sounds like we've got work to do."

"Wait. Is that the Gangle alarm? You changed it?"

"I did. You like bird song right?"

More of a statement than a question, said with a knowing smile. Ella felt her heart warm as it forged a new memory.

"Enough of that please miss. We've got work to do. Come on. To the Gangle Cave!"

"The Gangle wha..?" Ella started to question, but Amari was already up and out the door.

xx lol xx

Ella took her time and eventually caught up as Amari was pulling at a book on the shelf. The shelf obliged and sank back, before disappearing into the wall. When it had fully retreated Ella was surprised to see a fireman's pole instead of the usual staircase.

"Well, that's new."

"Yeah, I know. Fun right. Come on. Come see what else I've done."

Amari flung herself at the pole then zipped out of view. Ella, a little more cautiously, followed.

'Doof.'

Ella's feet hit a padded floor at the bottom of the pole, closely followed by her jaw, after she'd looked up and saw the other changes that Amari had made.

The whole basement area had been completely transformed. The space was now full of bright white led lighting. Gone were all the original features. The lounge area looked like an advert for a Swedish furniture store. The bar looked like something from a bowling alley, all modern, marble, framed in neon pink and purple lighting. The story desk area looked like the office space of a modern minimalist architect, whilst the old wooden lockers in the changing area had been modernised. Central to the space was a full ensemble, displayed in a cylindrical glass cabinet, illuminated by up-lighters surrounding the cabinet base.

"What the actual...!"

"Good, isn't it?"

"What have you done?"

"I've brought the old place up to date. Made it more like our very own bat cave. It's awesome, do you not think?"

Amari had since gotten up to speed on Batman. Needless to say, she was now a huge fan.

"No. I do not think Amari. And clearly you don't think either. Why would you replace all those beautiful original things with modern tat like this?"

"Modern tat! Excuse me, but this was all very expensive."

"I don't care how much it cost. It has no character. And where have the bloody stairs gone? You think everyone is gonna want to slide down a pole?"

"Well, 'everyone' shouldn't even be down here should th…"

"THAT'S NOT THE POINT! GRRRRRRR!"

"Alright grumpy pants. Keep your hair on. I saved everything from the room. Maybe we can put some of the old things back if you like."

"Maybe. I do like. Yes."

Ella took a breath.

"Look, let's just talk about this later. We have a new job we need to focus on for now."

The conversation was parked there, then Ella led the way over to the shiny, ugly, new story desk.

xx lol xx

"Right then" Ella enquired. "What have we got?"

"Subject is single, male, yey old… Quite fit and looooves money."

"Loves money you say?"

"Yeah. Like, really, really, really loves money. The guy is totally obsessed about becoming the next big billionaire or something. Thinks money is how you measure success."

"Only if the measure of success is having more money than anyone else."

"Yes, quite. Thank you for stating the obvious there." Amari looked up from the brief sheet to offer Ella a smile.

"Okay." Said Ella. "So, the guy likes money. Wants to be a big fish. Does he have any experience with money?"

"As a matter of fact, he does. He runs a loan business. Gives people short term loans at high interest rates."

"Like a loan shark you mea..."

Ella stopped mid-sentence.

"Wait. What's the guy's name?"

"Michael Summer. Likes to go by the name: ""...Mick the Fish...""" They both said in unison.

"How did you know that?" Amari questioned.

"I know this guy. He gave my mum a loan once and hasn't stopped coming round the house since. Well, when I lived there, I guess I... I um... Sorry."

Thinking about her mother had caught Ella off guard. She looked down for a moment to regain her composure. Amari reached out and gave a little stroke to Ella's forearm.

"Ahem. As I was saying." Ella continued. "He gives out loans and he liked to come around and see my mum. It was so obvious that he liked her, and I think she liked him too. She was just put off a little by his obsession with money. Having been there with my dad already."

Ella paused, took a breath, then carried on.

"Okay. Well, we must help this one. If my mum likes him then let's make sure he is worthy eh."

"That's the spirit. What are you thinking?"

"Well, it seems obvious. He wants to be a big fish, so let's make him one."

"Oooo. What fun. We'll have an absolute whale of a time!"

"Whale! Yes, you can be a whale."

"Hey! I know I've been taking it easy this past couple of weeks, but I've only put on a couple of pounds."

Amari said this whilst patting her slim tummy.

Ella, ignoring her, carried on.

"Yes. You can be a whale, and Mick can be a shark."

"Right, that's settled then. I'll go find my swimsuit whilst you get to work composing."

"Perfect."

"Talking of composing." Amari continued. "I've been working on a new theme tune."

"Not this again. I've told you I do not need a the..."
Too late. Amari was off.

"Dun dun dun dun dun dun dun dun,
Dun dun dun dun dun dun dun dun,
Lord...
Gan-Gaaallllls
Wah waaaah
Saviour of the Dis-e-Tance..!"

"Oh lord!"
Ella slapped a palm against her forehead, turned
and simply walked away.
"What do you think?"
Amari pleaded after her.
"I know it could do with a little wor..."
Ella slammed the sound booth door shut behind
her, signalling an end to the conversation.

Father Thomas McKenzie

"Ahem. Excuse me young man. I say, ahem. Young man, come along now. Open your eyes. I'm afraid you can't sleep here. This is a place for resting, not sleeping."

Mick opened his eyes. The man leaning over him slowly came into focus.

"Where am I?" He asked. "Who are you? Why are you wearing a dog collar?"

"First of all, this..." The stranger pulled at his collar, "...is called a clerical collar. Made for humans, not dogs. My name is Father Thomas McKenzie, which I believe answers two of your questions at once. Pleased to make your acquaintance."

Father Thomas offered a hand but was left hanging. After a moment he withdrew his hand and carried on.

"You asked where you were. Well young man you are in a church graveyard, which is not an appropriate place for sleeping rough."

"A church graveyard?" Mick asked the question as he turned around to find that he was currently leaning against a headstone.

"Urgh!"

Mick scrambled to his feet and started frantically dusting himself off.

"What am I... I mean, what is... Wow. Why would I do that? Sleep there I mean."

"Well, it does seem to be a little disrespectful. One could at least expect dinner before you hop into their bed."

The father had a little chuckle to himself, Mick looked horrified.

"Oh, forgive me. Gallows humour I think they call it. I spend a lot of time with the residents here and we do like to share the odd joke. Helps pass the time."

"Maybe you should get out a little more."

"Hmm. Maybe you're right. Maybe you are right. But all these souls have been placed under my charge. I feel it my duty to stay and keep them company."

Mick quickly calmed down, regaining most of his composure. He took in his surroundings whilst

Father Thomas continued talking, finding that he was in the grounds of a beautiful little church that appeared to be quite high up on a hill. The graveyard he was standing in doubled as the staging for a rather elaborate model train set.

Tracks were laid out everywhere, running various courses between and around the headstones. In some areas the track circled and climbed a headstone, as if climbing a mountain, before bridging to the next and descending back down. Various train related paraphernalia, like stations, signals, tunnels and the like were spread out across the breadth of the scene. Standing here, looking down, Mick felt like a giant surveying a strange new civilised land below.

"Well father, I have to give it to you. That is some train set you have got going on. Very impressive."

"Do you care for trains, Mr... Um?"

"Sorry, yes. Michael. Mick. Mick Summer. Mick the Fish even. And um, sorry about sleeping in your graveyard. I'm not sure how I got here to tell you the truth. Oh, and no. I don't really care for trains. At least not toy ones. Real trains are okay though. Good thing to get into if you want to make a lot of money."

"Ah so, money is your thing. That's a shame. It won't bring you happiness. I should know. The church has got loads of it."

"You say it won't bring happiness father. But I'd rather be unhappy and rich, than unhappy and poor, eh?"

Father Thomas gave a shrug.

"Seriously though Father. Money makes the world go round. I mean, what else is there worth worrying about?"

"I could, of course, suggest several things. I will, however, ask you a question instead."

"Fire away."

"My question. What do you intend to do with any money that you make?"

"What do I intend to do Father?"

A pause.

"I don't intend to do anything. It's not about 'the doing'. It's all about the 'accumulating'. I want to be one of those few that are remembered for being successful in life. In fact, I want to be remembered for being the most successful in life. The richest of the rich."

"I see. You view success by the accumulation of wealth?"

"Of course, Father. What other quantifiable marker is there?"

"Hmmm." Father Thomas stroked his chin as he pondered this question. Then asked.

"Would you care to take a stroll with me young man? There is someone here that I would quite like you to meet."

The Richest Person In The Graveyard

Father Thomas led Mick up through the graveyard toward, then through, a small thicket of trees. The pair emerged from the trees into a beautifully kept open plot of land, at least an acre in size, surrounded by wild hedge rows, all buzzing with wildlife. Situated at the centre of this plot was a single solitary grave. Arriving at the grave, Father Thomas opened his arms out wide, the palms of his hands facing skyward. Gently he announced.

"Behold. The final resting place of Hetty Green*. Otherwise known as 'the richest person in the graveyard'."

The grave itself really wasn't much to look at. The headstone was fashioned from a good quality granite, in blue pearl, but was of very modest design. A typical two and a half feet in height, rounded at the top. Top centre of the stone face was a circled indent, containing the graphic image of a blue whale. Midway down the headstone was the engraved name, 'Hetty Green.' Underneath read the years, '1834-1916.' There was nothing else. Mick was unimpressed.

"The richest person in the graveyard you reckon. If this is the richest, then how poor were the rest of the sorry souls?"

Mick afforded himself a little chuckle in reward for his sharp wit.

"I do not lie to you Mr Fish. Hetty was, by today's standards, extremely wealthy indeed. By the time she shuffled off her mortal coil her estimated wealth was more than what would be many billions in today's money."

"Really! Wow, and this is the best memorial that she could afford. Was she tight or something? Not for me. I intend to have the most massive mausoleum you ever saw. It's gonna be made of marble and lined with gold. It's gonna have big pillars next to the door and statues of Lions guarding the entrance. It's also gonna have heating and cooling to make sure it always stays cosy inside. Yeah, they say you can't take it with you when you go but we will see about that."

Mick allowed himself another chuckle. He was on form today. Then suddenly he paused. Held his right hand in the air, with index finger extended, following which he vocalised his realisation.

"Wait a second. This field. This field is her mausoleum right. The whole thing is a memorial."

Nodding his head now in approval. "Smart." He reflected.

"No." Offered Father Thomas. "No. You were right the first time. Hetty was just 'tight', as you put it."

"Wha..."

"She chose to be buried in this field because at the time it was forgotten common land. She refused to pay for a plot in the actual cemetery itself."

"Ha, wow wee, you gotta give it to her. She was super successful but wanted to be remembered as a tight ass."

"Well Mr Mick, if you don't mind me saying so, I think you may be missing the point here."

"Which is?"

"Which is, success should not be measured by the amount of wealth that you accumulate. Rather what you use it for."

"Ha. Amen to that. Exactly what I said. She should have used it to buy a hossin great big monument so that everyone could see how successful she was."

Father Thomas put a hand to his head in despair.

"Mr Mick. What you are failing to see is that big flashy monuments do not matter. They won't define how you are remembered. Have you not noticed for example how immaculately kept this field is?"

"Ah. Okay. She left a load of money to ensure this place is well kept. That's pretty smart."

"No Mick. No, she did not."

"Oh. Well, do you guys keep on top of it then?"

"I have already told you she chose not to pay for a plot in the church graveyard."

"Yeah, you did. Okay, well, spare me the mystery. What's occurring here then. You got some well-trained rabbits or something?"

Another chuckle. 'On fire,' he thought to himself.

"This field is kept pristine by a small army of volunteers, made from direct descendants of the people that Hetty helped with her wealth when she was alive. In fact, the reason Hetty has been able to remain here is because the locals all chipped in after her death to purchase and protect this plot of land. So that she might rest in eternal peace."

"Eternal peace please. You mean until she gets dug up to make room for a car park. Or until an asteroid hit or the sun blows up the Earth. It'll be eternal pieces then instead, eh?"

Mick allowed himself a belly laugh for that one.

"Seriously though, padre. What you are saying is that she spent all her money on making other people happy, rather than herself?"

"Well Mr Mick. Certainly, something like that."

"Wow." Mick turned away and gazed contemplatively off at the horizon.

"I know." Said Father Thomas knowingly. "Quite something eh?"

"I would say." Mick agreed, quickly followed by.

"What a mug!"

xx lol xx

Conversation continued, circling their differing views towards the accumulation of wealth. Once that had run its course Mick turned attention to the graphic that was etched into the gravestone.

"So, why a whale? Was Hetty a large lass?"

Another chuckle.

"Why do you think that comment is funny Mr Mick?"

"Oh, come on. It's just a bit of light humour."

Mick said this, but having been called out he did feel a little bad about the pun.

"Sticks and stones some might say. Only those that do, have never experienced the true depth of pain that a hateful word can inflict. Even when said in jest. Bones can be healed, Mr Mick. But there are no stitches for the wounds inflicted by careless words."

"Okay. Point taken. You are right, I'm an idiot."

Acknowledging Mick's repentance, Father Thomas rewarded him with a warm smile

"Clearly, Mr Mick, you are not."

"Well, I am sorry. I don't know why I said that. Seriously though, why has Hetty got a picture of a whale on her headstone?"

"Hetty's family made their fortune in the whaling business. Hetty never forgot her debt to those glorious creatures."

"That is actually quite cool. It's a very good engraving, I think. Very impressive."

"Oh, it's much more impressive than that young man. It is said that if you stare long enough you will see the whale begin to move, in mysterious ways."

"What is it with you lot and your mysterious ways?"

'Back on form,' he thought to himself.

"Yes, quite. Genuinely though many people have witnessed the whale dance, and swim, and move about the headstone as if the headstone were the ocean itself."

"Yeah right. That'll just be shadows from the sun setting. Unless there's any mushrooms growing in this field, eh."

Chuckle.

"Maybe you should think about a career as a standup comedian young man. I'm sure you would make a billion there."

"Nice one, Father. Thanks."

"A billion terrible puns that is."

This time it was Father Thomas that allowed himself a chuckle. "Anyway Mr Mick." He continued. "Might I suggest that you spend some time here to contemplate the idea. You can watch the whale whilst you do so. Just to see for yourself."

"Well, I suppose I've got nothing better to do. You couldn't fetch me a chair though, could you? And maybe a nice cup of tea?"

Offering a look to the heavens Father Thomas sighed then made off to retrieve for his guest a chair and a cup of tea. In fact, he thought he might quite fancy a cup of tea himself. Though he would be adding a little sip of brandy into his.

xx lol xx

Mick finished his tea. He was now reclining in a deck chair, enjoying a perfectly warm evening, staring at a stone whale, waiting for it to move.

'How awesome,' he thought to himself. 'How awesome it must be to be the richest person in the graveyard.'

A sudden flicker of movement caught his eye. Mick sat up straight. Well, as straight as one can sit up in a deck chair. He stared harder at the whale carving in front of him. A gentle breeze followed. The whale fluctuated again. Mick took a backward glance to his right. As he had suspected there was a large patch of pampas grass growing there. The sun was currently set at just the right angle behind the pampas grass, facing onto the whale emblem. A gentle breeze was enough to sway the grass in front of the setting sun, which in turn interrupted the light on the headstone, which in turn created the visual illusion that the whale carved there was moving.

"Hah.' he thought smugly to himself. 'I knew that it would just be a trick of the light.' He stared back toward the gravestone and spoke aloud.

"Nice one Hetty. But I'm afraid you're not gonna make a mug out of me."

It was then that the whale in the gravestone turned to face him and replied.

"Good for you young man. No one likes to be made to look like a mug now do they?"

xx lol xx

All at once Mick scrambled, trying to get to his feet whilst at the same time trying to back away from the gravestone. Not easy to do when starting from a reclined position in a deck chair. Mick was soon scrabbling about on the floor, all tangled up in stripy wooden chair, pointing at the headstone and gibbering.

"You can't... be... be... wha... what the... I mean. You can't be real. What... wha... How are you doing that? Are you Hetty?"

The whale was swimming, merrily back and forth, about the headstone.

"You can call me Hetty if you like Mick. Yes, why not. Hetty is a rather nice name, I think. I shall be Hetty Blue, if that's alright with you. Is that alright with you Mick?"

"Oh my days. You are talking to me."

Mick had made it onto his knees and had regained a little of his composure.

"How do you know my name?"

"Well Mick, I know all about you. I have been sent here, you see, to ask for your assistance."

"Ask for my assistance?" Mick repeated, a little flabbergasted. "I'm not sure that I can be of any use to a stone whale I'm afraid."

"A stone whale is only how you are perceiving me right now. I'm not actually made of stone. And I don't live in someone's headstone. I come from a beautiful city. A city far out in the ocean, deep beneath the waves named Amortizon. The city is a multicultural haven, where different species cooperate rather than prey upon each other. It is a place where there are no super rich and wealth is evenly distributed. It is known as a place where funds are shared, with excellent and stable public facilities.

"Sounds positively utopic." Mick chipped in sarcastically, unimpressed by the fact that there were no 'super rich' in this city of which Hetty spoke.

"It is." Hetty agreed.

"Or rather, it was."

Hetty went on to explain how the city had become a victim of its own success. Rapid growth attracted many migrant workers. The population boomed and soon there was not enough housing.

There was still enough work though and with extra mouths to feed vast areas of land were given over to farming. Here new migrant workers were typically assigned. Humans eventually followed the migrants in their fishing boats. Those assigned to toiling the open farmland were the most vulnerable to being caught up in human nets.

Soon there was a shortage of workers willing to risk working in the fields. Eventually the lack of farming led to a lack of essentials. Prices started to increase. Landowners, keen to capitalise on higher market prices, now offered higher wages to attract workers and account for the increased risks. Other industries soon had to increase wages too, to retain their own workers and dissuade them from going off to work in the fields. With prices and wages increasing, both businesses and individuals began taking out loans, to cover extra costs.

Hetty explained that things in the city had gotten so bad that the pufferfish economists were threatening a hyper-inflation event.

"Once that happens." Hetty concluded. "I fear we may slip past the point of recovery forever."

"That sounds tough for sure. But what does this have to do with me?"

"Well Mick. You are a money man. You know how money works. You have built up a successful loans business and kept it stable for a good many years now. Our council has done well to a point, but now they are making a hash of things, and we need a capitalist mind, such as yours, with fresh ideas to help get us out of this hole. I have been sent by the council to request your help."

"Really? You must be craaa... Wait a minute."

Mick stopped speaking. He looked up at the sky to his right. Raising his right hand up, he anchored his thumb under his chin, his index finger horizontal, gently tapped against his lips. Mick was considering properly the opportunity that was being offered to him.

'This could be it', he thought.

This could be Mick's shot at finally becoming a billionaire. He looked back at Hetty.

"Alright then." He said. "Suppose I do agree to come and help you. First, how am I supposed to do that? I mean, I'm human, and you're a fish."

"A whale actually."

"Alright. A big fish. Whatever. The fact remains that I am not a fish, or a whale. So how am I supposed to come and help you in your city?"

"You just let me worry about that. All you have to do is agree."

"Hmmm. Okay. Suppose I say yes. There would have to be some conditions."

"Name them."

"You would have to put me in charge of your central bank."

"It was assumed you might demand as much. I already have authorisation to agree. In fact, we would very much like to put you in charge."

Mick was expecting an argument here. The fact he did not get one suggested he could maximise on his other conditions.

"Okay, good. On to my payment then. I propose I work on a commission basis. This will be set at 75% of any profit generated for the bank."

"75%!" Hetty exclaimed. "That seems very high."

"It may sound high. But from what you have explained, 75% of the bank's current profit would not be very much. If I can come in and turn things around, then I see no reason why a 75% share would not be seen as acceptable."

Hetty considered this.

"Well, we have already established that you have built up and maintained a successful loans business for some time. This does suggest you are to be trusted in that respect. Okay. Done. Anything else?"

"Yes. I want to be exempt from whatever tax laws your city has in place. If I am working to save your city, I don't expect to be paying out big chunks of my earnings in tax."

"Hmm. I guess only a real banker would avoid paying their fair share of tax."

Hetty then sighed, then agreed.

"Okay. Done. Right, let's get mov…"

"Ah, ah, ah." Mick cut in. "There is one more condition.".

"More? Really? Okay, go on then. What else is it you would like?"

"Well, if I am going to come and live amongst the fishes, I don't wanna be no cute little Nemo type fish. I want to be a shark."

"Of course you do, Mick. Of course you do. So be it. A shark you shall be."

"I mean like a Great White shark. I don't want a hammer for a head, or anything weird like that."

"A Great White shark Mick. Yes. Consider it done."

"Okay. In that case I'm in."

"Excellent news Mick. Excellent news. Let us not waste any more time. We really should get moving immediately."

"Right." Then remembering his human self Mick questioned.

"So how do we do this? Do I have to climb into your headstone somehow?"

Already a slight mist had begun to rise about Mick's feet.

"No Mick. Nothing like that."

A gentle twinkling sound floated in on a slight breeze.

"You just sit yourself back down and relax."

Doing as he was instructed, Mick sat back down in the chair. He noticed that the mist had risen to the level of his bended knees.

"Can you hear music?" He asked out loud. "Sounds like someone is playing a tune on windchimes."

As he said this, he noticed his voice slur a little. He had in fact become a little drowsy, suddenly catching his head as it nodded forwards.

The mist had become all consuming. A tall shadow formed in front of Mick, that looked something like a giant bird wearing a top hat. Its arms were outstretched forwards, at the end of these dangled the most grotesque looking hands that Mick had ever seen.

"Whar... whars dah..."

He struggled to speak. His arms had flopped to his sides and his head was bouncing around like a nodding dog.

"Just relax."

He could hear Hetty's voice over the music.

"Just relax and close your eyes. Sleep Mick. Sleep. Sleep now."

Mick let his head flop back to rest on the chair. He closed his eyes and felt himself begin to sink down. The sensation of sinking continued until eventually there was no sensation at all.

334

Shark Face

"Wake up!"

Dreamily, Mick began to open his eyes. The world around him slowly came into focus. The scene in front of him was beautiful, like a wonderful ornamental garden, created on the side of a cliff face. The landscape was filled with colour, including tiger orange, caramel peach, buttercup yellow, bright poppy red, light rose pink, sparkling grape purple and kiwi fruit green. All presented and framed within a deep ocean blue. Dashing amongst the plants in this garden were equally beautiful little creatures, sporting their own stunning set of colours in complement to their surroundings. A large shape swept in from behind him.

'Wow!'

He thought to himself.

'That looks like a sea turtle.'

It was a sea turtle.

All of a sudden Mick realised where he was, and blind panic kicked in.

'Help. Help. I can't breathe. I can...'

Mick thought he was saying this aloud and, in fairness, his mouth was moving. Nothing though was coming out. His panic level increased.

Mick began to sink.

The coral garden rose out of sight as Mick descended into the darkness beyond the shelf break.

'Oh my, oh my. I'm drowning... I... I'm... HELP! HELP ME!'

'Alright Mick. Relax. I've got you.'

'Wha... what was that? Who said that?'

'It's me, Hetty. Who else would it be.'

Hetty's presence was a surprise. Ironically, he had not spotted her because she was so massive. No longer a small carving in a headstone, Hetty now filled up the entire dark sky above Mick's sinking body.

'How are you talking to me?'

'Yeah, I probably could have prepared you better there. We use telepathy to speak to each other down here. We could try it your way but it's very hard to talk with a mouth full of water.'

'Oh. Makes sense I suppose. That's actually quite interes... Wait. Help me. I'm drowning. HELP ME!'

'Well, you are sinking, granted. But you're not drowning.'

'But I can't breathe. How do I breathe?'

'Have you not noticed yet that you are not out of breath. Despite the little scene you're making.'

'I'm not wha...'

Hetty was right. Mick checked himself, and despite not breathing through his mouth he was not lacking oxygen.

'You're a fish. From now on you will get the air that you need using your gills. We can discuss the science of those in detail later. More importantly, we need to get you swimming.'

All the while Mick had been panicking, he had been continuing his descent. It was already very dark. A little further and it would be pitch black.

'You may be a shark, but you do not wanna go any further down there. Trust me.'

Mick trusted her.

'Okay. What do I do?'

'It's easy. Just wiggle your bum.'

'Wiggle my bum?'

'Yes. That's what I said. Just wiggle your bum.'

'But I'm a fish.'

'And?'

'Since when did fish have bums?'

'Like that is it Mick? Well, put it this way. If you don't start wiggling that place where your bum used to be, pretty soon you are gonna end up with nothing left to wiggle. Instead, you are going to be dinner for those things that lurk beneath.'

Mick found his wiggle.

'Okay. That's the way.'

The more Mick wiggled the more natural it started to feel. Within a very short time, he was not wiggling but waving. Mick developed his awareness of the immense power pushing him forward. The harder he pushed, the more oxygen he received, the harder he could push. Make no mistake, Mick was a machine and the exhilaration he was feeling far outweighed that of any fast car he had ever driven. Mick felt truly alive.

He soared upwards. Back toward the shelf edge and the oriental garden. He burst into the sky above the coral reef like a rocket then roared back and forth above the coral like a jet fighter. The creatures below looked up in wonder and awe.

'Yes!'

He thought to himself.

'Make no bones about it. This is my time. This is where I become a billionaire. This is where I will be remembered as a true success.'

Mick the Fish had arrived.

Amortizon

The underwater city of Amortizon was founded many moons ago, in the gigantic rusting hulk of an unfortunate merchant naval vessel. As the hulk attracted more residents, it slowly divided up into the equivalent of municipal buildings and modern housing. It now sat proud as the centre of a city, surrounded by outcrops of reef and other rocky formations as well as large flatlands, used for farming.

Hetty explained to Mick how the society had become civilised. A council of representatives was formed, and it was agreed that the different species would stop preying upon each other. Instead, they turned to farming to produce their foods.

Most residents now happily ate a rich vegetarian diet of seaweed and underwater fungi. Some still enjoyed the occasional sea snail burger, but sea snails were regarded as unintelligent so thought of as fair game. To the sea snail farmers' credit, they were all reared and certified as free range. Being slow snails though meant that they didn't require an awful lot of range to be 'free' in.

Along with some of the city's residents, the snails also fed a spin-off industry, where farmers were able to sell their empty shells to local fashion houses, who in turn were able to satisfy the demands of the city's rising hermit crab population.

Fashion aside, everyone being well fed meant that everyone was happy. A fair system had been established that ensured little differences in personal wealth. The health service, and all other public services were second to none. If a resident was willing to work for the greater good, then a cleaner in this city could be just as prosperous as a doctor. As Hetty had summarised already, word of Amortizon spread throughout the ocean and soon record numbers of sea life began to migrate.

This quickly led to the city's first real growing pain of having to house all the newcomers. The council put their heads together and set up the Nautical Housing Scheme (NHS). They assigned subsidised high rise council housing in existing shipwrecks to newcomers. Available wrecks were very old, and all suffered from leaky roofs and damp issues. Still there were long waiting lists of new arrivals keen to live in them and have a home that they could call their own.

The second headache was more of a crisis. This occurred when the boats arrived. The city's popularity meant that larger and larger numbers of fish were migrating there. At first, other than accommodation, this was not a real problem. Every new resident was put to work and new infrastructure and farming was slowly developed in line with the population increase. The city plodded from strength to strength.

Inevitably, the increase in population led to decreases in populations elsewhere. Soon the humans abandoned previously favoured fishing grounds and eventually stumbled onto the rich bounty that Amortizon had become. At first it was just a single boat. Then it was two. Then it was four. Then it was many. The boats came at night and had been hauling away the residents of Amortizon in ever increasing numbers.

As the labour force available to toil the fields reduced, so too did some fields go unattended. Many crops started to fail meaning successful harvests increased in value. As farmers competed for labour to tend their crops, the price that workers demanded for their labour increased. As the price of labour increased the farmers turned to the bank for cheap loans to pay for the increased labour costs. Eventually the farmers increased their crop prices further, to service the loans that they had taken out. The workers themselves were then forced to take out their own cheap loans, to cover the increased costs of foods they needed to eat, that they themselves worked to produce on the farms. With food costing more there was less to spend on other things and the whole economy slipped into decline.

Prices increased.
Wages increased.
Debt was created.
Prices increased further.
Debt increased further.
Inflation was loose.

This was the big problem that Mick had been brought into address.

xx lol xx

It was a wet day in Amortizon. Mick was currently being shown around the bank whilst nursing a hangover.

Mick insisted on a night out before seeing the bank, so the previous evening Hetty had taken Mick to what was regarded as the hippest part of town, located on the outskirts of the city. Fortunately, Hetty was a whale so there was no need to wait at the Whale-Way Station for transport.

Upon arrival, the night kicked off with several shots of Squid Ink. A delicacy served only from the bar of a little-known backstreet sushi venue. Hetty then took them to Ed's Crab Shack for a bite to eat. Ed, or Edward, to give him his full name, was a bit of a hermit so being summoned by Hetty, to come out from the kitchen and meet Mick, made Ed a little crabby.

With Ed threatening to bring the mood down the pair moved on. They made their way past the local bathhouses to the sea horse racing track. There were literally thousands of sea horses to bet on and Mick was soon left feeling utterly discombobulated by it all.

Leaving the track, Hetty took Mick to the infamous Aquarium nightclub. Mick was shocked to see glowing jellyfish dancing naked on podiums dotted about the club venue. More shocking was that he seemed to be finding them quite attractive, which he decided to put down to the copious amounts of Squid Ink he had consumed.

After a few hours dancing they left the club and grabbed a pot of cheesy fish flakes from a takeout, to share on their way back to Hetty's.

Despite the hangover Mick woke up keen to see the bank. Hetty was happy to oblige. In Hetty's case there wasn't much room for manoeuvrability but, fortunately, the bank was the most cavernous area of the old merchant naval vessel that it was located in. This meant that Hetty could at least get in and out of the space to show Mick around. Mick was very satisfied with the bank and decided it would double up as his new residence.

xx lol xx

Amortizon traded in a currency called 'Tanks.' It was a simple currency to understand, in that there were a hundred 'Tinkies' to a 'Tank'. Tinkies and Tanks were forged from old oyster shells. These were usually bequeathed, upon an oyster's passing, to their remaining oyster relatives. A whole oyster shell could fetch a very good price on the open market and usually served as a fitting inheritance.

Multiples of Tanks could be converted into pearls, with different coloured and sized pearls accounting for different multiples of Tanks. For example, a typically sized white pearl could be traded for 10 Tanks. The equivalent sized pearl, in blue, was worth 100 Tanks.

Many oysters were gainfully employed in the production of pearls, and, on average, a hard-working oyster could expect to receive roughly three percent of the value of whatever colour pearls they managed to produce.

xx lol xx

Once settled at the bank, it was time for Mick to start putting his recovery plans for the city into action. He already knew that the best way to cool down an economy was to increase interest rates. People tended to better consider their spending when faced with higher amounts of interest to pay back on their loans.

The first part of Mick's plan then was simple. He would raise the interest rate on all existing and future loans, from 2% to 15%. This was quite an increase, but these were exceptional times. For the interest hike to be accepted Mick knew he first had to win the public's confidence. To do this he planned to tackle the major cause of the crisis, humans, head on.

'Okay Hetty, this is what I want. I need you to put out a call, to all your whale friends. In turn, I need them to do the same to all their whale friends. Basically, I want as many whales as possible to be here, in Amortizon, by midnight, seven days from now.'

'I am happy to put out a call Mick, but these whales will not just come here out of the goodness of their hearts.'

'Understood. I have already checked the vaults. Let them know that each whale that answers the call, and assists with my plan, will receive 10 BPs* (*blue pearls) as payment.'

'10 BPs!' Hetty exclaimed. '10 BPs is more than most of these guys earn in a year. Are you sure the bank can afford it?'

'You leave me to worry about that. I can't imagine too many whales will make it here in that time so I am confident we will be okay. So, what do you say? Are you happy to put the call out?'

'Consider it done.'

With that Hetty turned tail. Being a rather large tail, this took some considerable time to do. Hetty then swam off to begin a tour of the outskirts of Amortizon where she would put out her calls.

Fishy Campaigning

With Hetty gone, Mick turned his efforts to winning the residents of Amortizon over. He took to the streets with nothing but a conch shell and an old lobster pot. He used these to elevate himself and his voice above the crowds which, slowly but surely, started to grow in number each time he stopped to deliver his speech.

'I am your new Chief Banker.
I am here to save your precious city.
By focusing on our five top priorities.
Slashing inflation.
Inflating the economy.
Bringing down debts.
Eroding NHS waiting lists.
Stopping the boats.'

It was the oddest thing, but none of those listening in the crowds could remember agreeing on what were 'their' five top priorities. Also, who in sea was this shark, standing there, addressing them from an old lobster pot? Nobody could remember voting for him.

'Oh well, whatever, never mind,' they thought. He seemed to look like he knew what he was talking about. Come to think of it, the priorities he stated may indeed have been their top priorities, if only they would have taken the time to think of any for themselves. It was pleasing to know that their top priorities were now being focused upon.

Above all else this shark looked the business. Much more so than that last banker that had been in charge. And so it was, that after seven days and nights of campaigning, Mick the Fish had the population of Amortizon eating out the palm of his fin.

xx lol xx

The day had arrived for the next part of Mick's plan. Mick, having managed to procure a bottle from the undersea market, knocked back a stiff shot of squid ink for Dutch courage before setting off from the bank to rendezvous with Hetty.

Approaching the meeting point Mick was shocked to find so many whales had answered the call. There were Sperm Whales, Humpback Whales, Gray Whales, Minke Whales, Beluga Whales, Killer Whales and even a pod of unicorn horn Narwhal Whales. Then there was Hetty, surrounded by a clan of her own Blue Whales.

'Hetty. What the...?' Mick's tone was exasperated

'You said to put out the call for as many whales to come as possible.'

'I said to put a call out, yes. I didn't mean for you to bring all the whales in the ocean. We have to pay this lot somehow.'

'You said money was not a problem.'

'That's not what I said Hetty, and you know it.'

'I don't think I do know it. You said call up all the whales and I did. You have to pay them now.'

Mick might have sweated at this point, had he not been a fish in the sea. Regardless, it was almost midnight and he had only one option now, which was to press ahead. He had chosen midnight as this was the preferred time of the fishing boats to begin their sweeps. Right on cue the sounds of multiple boat engines could be heard approaching in the waters above. They were coming. It was time to begin.

Mick briefed Hetty and other representatives from the various whale clans. Once everyone knew what was expected of them the whales moved off into their allocated positions.

Assault at Amortizon

Marvin and Troy were on the bridge of their boat, surveying the chaos that was playing out in front of them. It had all started just after midnight, when they'd arrived at the fishing grounds. The crew had been preparing to feed out the nets when Captain Troy spotted a small pod of whales circling nearby. Whales had become notorious for interfering with a catch, so Troy gave the crew orders to hang fire whilst he directed the fishing boat to a different spot. The whales followed.

After a time, Marvin reported another pod of whales, on the starboard side. There were now two pods of whales, one either side of them. Troy's only option was to press straight ahead. As he did so he became aware of other fishing vessels in the area. Lights that were on the horizon started to grow brighter, meaning the other boats were heading in his direction. Feeling a little unsettled, Troy toyed with the idea of turning his boat around and heading back. It was then that a deckhand reported a third pod of whales had settled in behind them, at the stern. Something was not right. Troy started to panic. He dropped the boat's speed to a crawl, then attempted a turn to port.

'Bumph...'

The bow of the ship was nudged back into the direction of straight ahead.

Troy tried to turn starboard instead.

'Bumph...'

The boat was nudged again, back into the direction of straight ahead. Troy had never experienced anything like this. Panic morphing into terror.

'Were the whales attacking them?'

Troy killed the engine.

'Bumph. Bumph. Bumph.'

The boat was being pushed forwards from behind, steered by nudges at the front. Other fishing boats were being pushed in the same manner in the same direction. Troy realised that they were being rounded up.

Soon enough Troy's boat was surrounded by other boats and ships of various sizes. Like Troy all the other skippers had shut off their engines.

Members of the assorted crews could be heard shouting panicked questions back and forth. There must have been a hundred vessels all bunched together, surrounded by circling whales.

Then all the whales dropped, en masse, under the water. An eerie hush descended as the crewmen across all the boats fell silent. In the darkness all that could be heard was the sound of the ocean, lapping against the assembled boats.

Troy dared to hope.

The silence held for a full five minutes.

Then...

'BOOOOOOOM!'

Underneath the water Mick had given the order to charge. In a mass coordinated effort, the assembled whales all swam toward the surface as fast as they could, on a collision course with the assembled boats. When they broke the surface, they broke most of the boats as well. The scene quickly turned to carnage as the whales broke from formation, turning their attack into a free for all frenzy. Mick swam back and forth amongst the melee, issuing commands as he went. He had given very clear instructions before the assault began, that the humans themselves were not to be harmed. They had in fact predesignated one of the fishing boats to remain intact, ensuring that all the different crews were afforded rescue. This turned out to be the boat that Marvin & Troy were occupying. Some of the smaller whales had been given the task of ferrying stranded crew members to the rescue ship. These whales were no savages.

It took the whales less than an hour to crush the fleet of boats. The bow of the final broken ship gently slipped below the surface. Mick and the whales had retreated to the seafloor, where they were now watching the incoming vessels settle. Mick had planned the site of the ambush to perfection. The vessels had been targeted to ensure that they would land at the more affluent edge of the city. A city that now had many shiny new housing complexes, capable of housing an untold number of residents.

Mick of course already had the deeds to these new premises written up in his own name. He was now Chief Banker of the city, and Chief Landlord of the most desirable real estate in that city.

'Today...' He thought to himself.

'Today has been a good day.'

After stopping the boats Mick moved to resolve the NHS waiting lists using his new housing stock.

Initially he matched the subsidised rental fees of existing NHS homes. Because of this he had no trouble filling his new properties to capacity and freeing up the old homes for others on the waiting lists.

Mick was already revered as a hero in Amortizon, so the public did not bat an eyelid when he implemented his interest rate hike to 20% on existing loans. He did not, of course, apply the same rate to savings. The hike was larger than he had originally planned as more whales had shown up than were expected, thus costing more, and Mick had to replace the expended bank coffers.

With the humans gone, the city's labour force was no longer being pulled from the sea. It became easy for farmers to attract workers back to their fields. As a result, wages stalled. Residents began to feel lucky to have a job at all. Availability of essentials increased, prices stabilised or came down, the economy started to grow. The puffer fish relaxed.

Mick, who was pulling 75% of the bank's profits, as well as the rental income from all his new properties, was well on his way to making his billion.

xx lol xx

'Hey Hetty. What do you think of that then eh?'

Two months had passed since the boats had been stopped. Mick was in a triumphant mood.

He had just sold off the last of his boat homes to occupying tenants. In all cases he had engineered it so that the tenants would have to take out a mortgage with the bank if they wanted to buy. Now he had sealed the last of the deals he was able to increase interest rates again. This time they would be increased to 25%.

Mick's profit share from the bank meant that he would make more money this way than from the rental income. In addition, he would no longer be responsible for the maintenance of the boat homes.

'I'm sorry Mick. I just don't agree with what you are doing.'

Hetty had been working for Mick since the great assault. As it happened Hetty pretty much did everything that was needed to keep the bank running. Mick's job, it seemed, was to take all the glory for the city's success.

'Well then Hetty.' Mick replied. 'It's a good job then that I am the boss and that I am the one being paid to do the thinking. Since you put me in charge, I've turned around the fate of both this bank and this city.'

'Yes Mick, I agree. But the residents are starting to struggle again. The cost of living is still too high and now you are proposing to put the interest rates up further, when they should be coming down.'

'Nonsense Hetty. I'm not proposing to put the rates up. I am putting the rates up. Besides, residents have stopped taking out new loans and are focused on paying off their debts at last.'

'There are rumours though that some have had to revert to stealing to pay their debts.'

'Rumours indeed Hetty.'

'I'm just saying that now is the time we should be bringing interest rates down. Not putting them up further.'

'Hetty, you know full well that we are paying back the money we used to pay off your friends. Once that has been resolved I will drop the interest rates.'

'Once you've made your billion you mean?'

'You knew what my ambitions were when you offered me the job. Nothing has changed.'

'I at least think that we should increase the interest on savings.'

'Again Hetty, it's a good job that I am the one being paid to do the thinking.'

xx lol xx

Soon enough another two months had passed.

'Well Mick, I hope you are happy. The council has just closed the last public facility. They can't keep up with the interest rates on all their loans. Their income has been especially poor since you stole most of their tenants from the old NHS homes. They have had to drastically reduce the headcount of the civil service, so jobs have been lost too.'

'That's not my problem Hetty, if they can't manage their finances properly.'

'What is that supposed to mean?'

'Well, look at me for instance. I am doing very well and so is the bank.'

'That's because you are taking all their money Mick. We can't carry on like this. You must drop the interest rates. Now.'

'Sorry. No can do. It will be at least another six months until the bank has recovered the funds, we used to pay off the whales.'

'What about your own money Mick? You don't need all that wealth. You could use it to do some good for the city.'

'We can have that conversation after I have become the city's first billionaire, but not before.'

Mick took a moment to imagine Amortizon in the future. A statue of him erected in the city centre. The residents stopping to look up in admiration and talk about the success of his great wealth.

He let out a pleasurable sigh.

'Yes Hetty. We are working towards a glorious future indeed. But we will not get there without some pain.'

'Yes Mick. But whose pain are we talking about?'

xx lol xx

Two more months passed. All public services had ground to a halt. Schools and hospitals had been forced to close. The number of homeless had surged and large swathes of residents had by now upped sticks and left the city. Those that had once considered themselves better off were now on the front line of the struggles. Mick found himself very busy dealing with requests for remortgages or extensions on loans. Mick, having seen his own incomes start to reduce, decided instead to repossess the homes of any residents that could not keep up with repayments. If they could not afford to pay for them then Mick would just take them back and sit on them until someone showed up who could.

'Mick, this is madness. You have more than enough money to stop this and save the city.'

'You call it madness Hetty. I call it capitalism. This is why you head hunted me right? Because you know I am good at this.'

'Good at what Mick? You are getting rich and fat whilst the city starves.'

'I think you will find that you are doing pretty well for yourself too.'

Mick was not aware that Hetty had, for the last few weeks, been giving her money away to those in greater need.

'I'm just one more million away Hetty. One million Tanks then I will slash the interest rate, and everyone will be better off. It's called tough love Hetty, and the people will thank me for it. You'll see.'

xx lol xx

By the end of the following month residents were queuing up at the bank to withdraw what savings they had left. The funds that the bank had built up started to dwindle very quickly. Added to this were queues of homeowners, no longer begging for mortgage extensions or repayment holidays but instead coming to hand in their keys. The residents were cutting their losses, now leaving the city in droves.

Within the space of a single week Mick's income dried up completely. The bank had been run dry and only he and Hetty were left in the city of Amortizon. On the bright side he did now own every property in the city. He was however still ten thousand tanks away from his goal of making one billion.

'Hetty. How many tanks do you have saved up?'

'Ten thousand, one hundred.'

Mick's shark eyes lit up.

'How would you like to buy a business from me? You can have any business you want. In fact, you can have ten. A thousand tanks a piece.'

'I don't want to buy anything from you Mick. In fact, I am leaving Amortizon.'

'But you can't leave Hetty. Look around. We won. I won. With your ten thousand tanks I will be the first billionaire of Amortizon, and we will own the entire city.'

'Look around!' Hetty exclaimed. 'Look around for goodness' sake. There's nothing left. Here, you can have my money."

Hetty tossed Mick her bank card.

'Congratulations. You're the winner. Well bloody done.'

With that Hetty turned her rather large tail and swam off into the distance.

Falling Tree

Mick had done it. He had achieved his life goal. He was now, officially, a billionaire. Briefly buoyed up by his success he took himself off to the now empty sushi bar and cracked open an abandoned bottle of squid ink to celebrate. As he drank, he noticed hanging on the bar wall, a poster of a tree. On that poster was a quote he had seen many times but had never contemplated.

"If a tree falls in a forest,
and there is nobody there to witness it,
does the tree make any sound?"

Mick was not one for philosophy but for some reason those words hit him in a way that he was not prepared for.

The silence, from the dead city surrounding him, grew louder and louder, until it reached the point that it was deafening. Mick now knew what it felt like to be the richest person in the graveyard. He put down his glass and instead started to drink straight from the bottle.

Trying to quash a feeling of nausea Mick gulped, and gulped, and gulped, until eventually he found relief and was claimed by oblivion. His shiny shark eyes shimmered, then fell shut as he passed out.

The Awakening

'GASP!'

Mick rose from his bed like a drowning victim breaking the surface of the sea.

'Gasp! Gasp! Gasp!'

He couldn't get his breaths in quickly enough.

The sheets were damp.

Mick was soaking in sweat.

Sitting up in bed, his duvet cover fell to his waist.

Mick slapped a palm against his chest in a bid to help regulate his breathing.

The clapping sound activated the curtains which obediently began to retreat.

Bright sunlight burst into the room, momentarily blinding him.

His breathing began to slow.

His vision began to clear.

His sense of self started to return.

No, wait.

His sense of self had started.

His new self.

Mick was waking up in the same bed, in the same house, in the same street, in the same city, on the same planet.

But this was not the same Mick.

The Crooked Vulture

The Rt Hon Josh Robertson had returned home about an hour prior. The evening had been spent hosting a charity event at the local town hall. A fundraiser for ex MPs who had, throughout their careers, become accustomed to the finer things in life, then found it a struggle to maintain their high standards when drawing only from their final salary pensions.

All costs for the event had of course been drawn from the public purse. These were ex-public servants after all. Members of the public were able to attend, but only if they were willing to pay for a ticket. Ex-MPs, and any related entourage, were of course admitted for free.

The night had consisted of champagne and caviar on arrival, then a fine seven course dinner. This was followed by a charity auction, hosted by a minor celebrity comedian. Items for the auction were donated by local businesses, all in the hope of lobbying favour from the event organisers. Brandy, cigars and dancing followed until 11pm, when carriages arrived to ferry the guests back to their various residences.

The night had been a huge success. Well over fifty thousand pounds had been raised. No bother that, after costs, this would effectively result in a deficit of twenty grand. Josh didn't mind this in the slightest. He had given those retired MPs and the town a night to remember, and he could easily make up any shortfall from his budget.

That though was a problem for another day. Josh was exhausted and a little bit tipsy. Having already gotten into his nightgown, sleep was what Josh desired the most. Pulling back the curtain on his four-poster bed he proceeded to get cosy under the luxurious duvet.

Purchased from the dark web, the duvet was filled not with fibre, or duck, or goose feathers. No. Josh's quilt was rare, and it was vulture feathers that kept him warm at night. He sunk his fat head into his fat pillow. Pulled down a mask over his eyes and quickly drifted into sleep.

Meanwhile At Gangle Manor

"I'm not saying that I don't like it, Ella. It's just that I think it's not very good."

"How can you like something that you think is not very good?"

"Hmm. It's just that it doesn't really make any sense. It's kind've, all over the place and just... Well, just a bit noisy really."

"It's called 'improv'. It takes a high level of skill to change course on a whim. I should know."

The pair were having a vinyl day, making their way through and listening to some of the many hundreds of records that were stored in the Manor. Presently they were listening too and discussing the relative merits of jazz music.

"Look, all I'm saying is that if it goes all over the place then you can never copy it, and if you can't copy it then how will you ever know if you are even doing it right?"

"No, I get it. You prefer your music to be all verse, chorus, verse, chorus, bridge, chorus, chorus, chorus, repeat, repeat, repeat, repeat and on and on and on and on until the day you die. Like local radio."

"Local what?"

"It doesn't matter. The point is that you prefer listening to the same songs over and over and over again because it's safe. You end up calling them good and, of course, they can be copied by wannabes on weekend TV shows and you can get to judge them because you know what the original sounded like and if it sounds just a tiny bit different to what you are used to then you say that something is rubbish and feel all smug about it because you know what it should sound like because you have listened to it a million times and will probably listen to it a million times more."

Amari sat still, a record in her hands, head cocked to the left, staring at Ella. After a moment of quiet had passed Amari asked.

"Are you finished?"

"Hmm. Maybe. I think so. Yes. Yes, I have finished."

"Good. I know you love a high horse to sit on and all but gees, that was a little bit next level. Don't you think?"

"Maybe. Sorry."

"Apology accepted. Talking of improv though. I have been working on a new theme tune."

"Amari. Please. We've been ove.."

"Just listen."

Amari was away.

"If there's someone strange,
They ain't behaving good.
Who you gonna call?
Lord Gangles!
Da na na na, da na naa.
When you go to slee..."

"ENOUGH AMARI!"

Amari stopped mid-song, wounded by Ella's outburst.

"Look, Amari, I'm sorry. I really don't want a theme tune though. Especially not something that has been stolen from somewhere else."

Amari looked confused.

"Look. I'll tell you what. Why don't you try your hand at a poem for me instead."

Amari's face brightened.

"Really?"

"Yes." Ella confirmed. "Poems are much more poignant than novelty theme tunes. If you insist on doing something..."

"I do." Amari confirmed.

"Ahem. Yes. Okay. If you insist on doing something, then work on writing me a poem."

The sound of bird song broke out all around the manor. The bird song seemed to work in harmony with the current rolling brass melodies coming from the record player.

"Ooo. That'll be us then." Amari said. "Race ya to the Gangle cave?"

"It's not a cav..."

Too Late. Amari was already gone from the room.

xx lol xx

After taking the call, and sliding down the pole, the pair were sat together at the storyboard in the cav... Sorry. Cellar.

Thankfully, from Ella's perspective at least, most of the garish modernism from the cellar's previous incarnation had been removed and the original items restored. Ella had however conceded that several elements did require updating, so there now existed a Victorian, industrialised themed room updated with various mod cons, ensuring both maximum style and maximum comfort. Both were happy with the compromise. The only thing Ella still didn't like was the pole, which was not in the least bit practical. Amari though was like an overly enthusiastic child about the pole, so Ella had decided, for now, to let that one slide.

"Okay," Amari started.

"We've got an overweight, over privileged, under qualified politician type person to deal with. This one believes he should be Prime Minister and that he would make a better PM than any other minister that he serves with. He believes this not because he thinks he knows what's best for his people, but because he thinks he knows how best to fiddle the system to get what he wants, then sell the results back to the people, so that they think they have been given to them what's best."

"Clear as mud. What's his name?"

"This one goes by the name of the right 'dishonourable' Josh Robertson."

"I know that guy. He was the MP for my town. He condemned the foodbank if I remember rightly. Then told us all what an excellent thing he was doing as the excess food there was attracting rodents and that by closing the bank down, he would reduce the number of disease carrying rats in the area, thereby stopping the next big pandemic before it even had a chance to begin."

"Wow. Is this one really worth saving?"

"Ours is not to question why Amari."

"Why?"

This earned a look from Ella.

"Listen, we signed up to do the assignments we were given to the best of our ability. Without question. This one should be no different."

"Hmph. Okay. Well, what do you have in mind?"

"I'm just gonna play jazz here."

"Not again, please. It makes my ears want to bleed."

"Just go with me. So, I am thinking culture. A culture where the rules are sacred. Everybody works together in the best interests of each other, thus maintaining that culture."

"You said 'culture' quite a lot there."

"Indeed, I did Amari. And what animal rhymes with culture?"

"Rat."

"Really?"

"Scumbag."

"Come on Amari. Play the game."

"Okay. So, let me see. Culture... No."

"No, what?"

"No, I do not want to be a vulture."

"Ah ha. It's not about what you want to be though is it? It's about choosing the best fit for our subjects. With this one being a bit crooked I think a vulture is perfect. Besides, they are quite magnificent birds, and you should be honoured to be offered the chance to spend some time amongst them."

"If you say so, lady jingle jangle."

"We don't have time for you to have a strop. I am off to compose. You can start work on the narrative. After that I'll get changed and we can be on our wa..."

Amari looked away, obviously fighting to hold back a grin.

"What? What is it?" Ella asked.

"What is what?"

Amari was trying to sound innocent but failing miserably.

"What is it you are finding so funny? Do you think what we're doing is a joke?"

"Aww. No." Amari sounded pained. "It was meant to be a surprise."

"What was? Come on, out with it."

"Okay, okay. You were supposed to find it for yourself but now you've forced me I suppose..."

Amari was grinning ear to ear. She then patted her flat palms together in a little show of excitement and requested that Ella follow her over to the changing area.

The changing area was one part of the cellar where most of Amari's modernisations remained. Specifically, the cylindrical glass cabinet, containing the Gangle ensemble, still stood proud in the centre of the changing area. The uplighters were currently turned off meaning the contents of the cabinet were shrouded in darkness.

"Okay, are you ready?" Amari enquired.

"What have you done this time?" Ella groaned.

"You'll see. Okay, close your eyes. Ready? Three. Two. One."

Amari hit the button for the lights.

"Open your eyes!"

The cabinet lit up and its contents were fully revealed.

"Ta da!" Amari offered triumphantly.

It was no exaggeration to say that Ella's jaw instantly detached and landed on the floor.

"What do you think?"

Amari asked.

"Awesome eh."

On display, in the glass cabinet, was a new outfit that Amari had commissioned for Lord Gangles.

The top hat was sleeker, finished in a deep purple crushed velvet. The mask, previously of leather, now composed of a soft vulcanised rubber, a rich gloss black finish. The gloves were much more slender, the windchimes somehow giving the impression of excessively long fingernails, painted and sharpened to a claw. The boots were knee high, to be worn over the trouser, laced bottom to top and with purple silk bow decoration at their backs.

Finally came the body suit. Black in colour but shimmering deep purple when caught in the light. It was a full length, one-piece, figure-hugging Lycra bodysuit. Embroidered onto the left breast was a golden capital 'G'.

"What have you done?" Was all Ella could manage.

"What have I done? I've only gone and brought old Gangles into the 21t century."

"Wha…"

"Yes. That's right. You needed to get with the times. All the superheroes are wearing outfits like this nowadays."

"I… I'm noh… How many times. I'm not a superhero Amari!"

"Course you are. You just need a bit of help with your branding is all. Besides, you are gonna look well hot in this."

"Well wha... What are you talking about Amari? We're not in the business of eroticism. We are in the business of helping people. If you think I am wearing this then you are very much mistaken."

"How do you mean? Do you not like it?"

"No, I do not. Where is my other suit? I want to wear that."

"Umm..."

Amari was looking at the floor, seemingly trying to drill a hole with the big toe of her right foot.

"Yeah. About that. I umm..."

"What have you done Amari?"

Ella was becoming a little exasperated.

"Well... I thought you would love the new suit so I sent all your old suits to be cleaned then put into storage."

"YOU WHAT!"

The realisation dawned on Ella that she would have no choice but to wear this new suit.

"YOU... AMARI... YA, YOU. YOU JUST... GRRRRRRRR!"

Laissez-Faire

Josh opened his eyes. He was standing in the middle of a bustling marketplace. The onslaught combination of noise, energy and smell was tremendous. The hustle and bustle of trade, the promise of a good deal. This was all so instantly appealing that he didn't think to question how he had got here, and he couldn't wait to have a look around.

Josh turned on his heel and bumped straight into someone. That someone was a woman, with strikingly bright fire red hair. Thanks to Josh she had just spilt the vial of absinth held in her hand.

"QUEL IMBÉCILE!!"

Shouted the woman.

"Look what you have just made me do!"

"I'm terribly sorry." Offered Josh. "But you really should pay more attention to where you are going."

"Where I am going! Where I am going! Are you serious? You stupid English pig!"

"I say. I will not stand for that. Clearly you do not know who you are talking to."

"And just who is it that I am talking to? Please tell me bon ami, for I am all ears."

"I, young lady, am the Right Honourable Josh Robertson. An elected member of parliament. I am here in representation of my people."

"Elected member of parliament you say?"

With her right hand the stranger stroked at her chin.

"You mean like a politician? You are a politician, no?"

"Yes."

"Ah. In that case, please accept my apology. We may have gotten off on the wrong foot."

Josh offered a smug smile in acceptance of the apology.

"My name is Laissez-Faire. It is my pleasure to meet you."

Laissez-Faire knew that if Josh was into politics, then he was most likely corrupt. Laissez-Faire also knew that most politicians, like Josh, had access to a public purse. Finally Laissez-Faire knew all the places that she could empty it for him. Laissez-Faire who knew, gave a small curtsey, then offered up her hand to Josh.

"Well, that's much more like it. Very good."

Josh was being his patronising best as he closed his hot greasy pudgy little hand over hers.

"And what is it that you do, Lessy Fare?"

Laissez-Faire retrieved her hand and wiped it discreetly on her trousers.

"I sir? Well, I do everything. This..."

Laissez-Faire raised her arms into the air and rotated in a full circle.

"This is my marketplace."

"Your marketplace?"

Questioned Josh incredulously.

"But you're a woman."

"Indeed, I am bon ami. I will take that as confirmation that you have a good eye, no?"

"But I... I mean. How does a woman get to be the proprietor of such a busy marketplace? How do you find the time after all your domestic chores?"

"Wow. I see now you are a special kind of a man. You live in a cave maybe?"

"Sorry. A cave? What do you mea..."

"Never mind, never mind." Laissez-Faire wafted a hand about. "I now know that you have both a good eye and an outdated sense of what is acceptable. I know just the stall that you will be interested in. Follow me."

After weaving through several thin pathways, past just some of the many stalls, they arrived at a doorway draped with a thick musky smelling curtain. Once a deep rich burgundy, but now faded and worn. Laissez-Faire pulled back the curtain and ushered Josh inside.

The transition, from bright to dark, meant that Josh temporarily could not see, and the first thing that hit his senses was a strong smell of patchouli oil mixed with cooking spices. He wrinkled his nose in disgust. 'Bloody hippies,' he thought to himself.

Slowly his eyes adjusted to the gloom, and he found himself face-to-face with a stuffed Lion head. Josh's face lit up with joy. The Lion's face did not.

"Oh my!" Josh exclaimed. "What an incredible specimen. Where on Earth did you get this?"

"Actually, nowhere on Earth. Not your Earth at least."

Josh was not listening. He was already onto the next display item, a mounted deer head.

"Just remarkable." He said. "I mean, the workmanship on that is incred..."

He turned to gawp at the mounted head of a Bengal Tiger.

"Will you look at that. I mean, Lezzy. You have done well to bring me here. You must be so very proud to be the purveyor of such fine goods."

"Goods is one name, yes. Murdered animals is another. In fact, I prefer my animals to be alive, but I could sense you were the kind who gets excited by dead things."

"These are not dead things Lesley."

"I think you will find that they are."

"Of course they're not. All you need is a little imagination my dear and these beasts will come alive right in front of your very eyes."

"I sincerely doubt that monsieur, but whatever you say."

"Oh, this one takes me back."

He was now patting the head of a Springbok.

"I remember a two-week team build vacation. Me and a few other fellow MPs you know. We all expensed ourselves a safari so that we could hunt beasts just like this. Ah. The thrill of sneaking up on a beast. Lining up the gun, then... BOOM!"

Josh clapped his hands, then rubbed them together in delight.

"I have a head just like this one hanging in one of my reception rooms at home."

"You must be very proud."

"Indeed. Indeed I am…"

Josh's voice trailed off and he froze to the spot. His eyes had locked on to the most glorious specimen he had ever seen.

"Oh my." Said almost in a whisper. "Is that what I think it is?"

"Do you think?"

"As I live and breathe. Is that an Andean Condor?"

"You mean the vulture?"

"Yes, the vulture. Do you not know anything about birds?"

"Well, I know that this bird looks like a vulture."

"Oh Lizzie. This is no ordinary bird. This is a king amongst birds. The king of all birds in fact. This bird is the largest bird of prey that there is and can live for over seventy years."

"If you don't shoot it first."

The specimen was of a male Andean Condor, dispatched in its prime. He was fixed, by his massive talons, to a solid wooden plinth. His wings, that could span five feet either side, were tucked in by his sides. A white ruff of small fluffy feathers circled his neck. Contrasted against his black feathers these gave the impression of a grand Elizabethan rabato. The head, bereft of feathers, sported a punk style mohican, otherwise known as a caruncle. A whirlpool of tinted purple and pink skin led down towards burnt orange eyes, centred with dark black pupils. Finally, the beak, a masterclass in practical design, was shaped like a giant claw. This vulture, the Andean Condor, was indeed a creature to behold.

"It's beautiful." Josh said with reverence.
"It's dead." Offered Laissez-Faire in retort.
Josh responded with a look of disgust.
Not wanting to lose a sale Laissez-Faire quickly added, "...beautiful. It's dead beautiful."
This seemed enough to satisfy Josh. He smiled and turned his face back to the bird.
"I simply must have it." Josh stated. "How much?"
"Well, I do like a man who knows what he likes. For you I can offer the special price of ten thousand euro."
"Done."
Already reaching inside his jacket to retrieve his wallet, Josh agreed the price without hesitation. He opened the wallet to retrieve his MP expense credit card but found that it was missing.
"What the... Where has that gone?"

He placed his wallet on the side and started checking his other jacket pockets, retrieving their contents and placing them on the side as well.

In all he found some old chewing gum, a few tatty receipts, some loose change and a tired old looking pocket watch. This last item surprised him as he last recalled seeing the watch at the back of a junk drawer in his kitchen.

Next, he started on his trouser pockets. From these he retrieved some keys, a half-eaten meaty snack and a stale, slightly discoloured hanky.

Surveying the contents of his pockets Josh felt panic rise in his chest at the prospect of losing his purchase. Patting himself frantically he started to babble.

"I don't... I um, I have no idea what I... Where could my card... I, it's just, I never leave home without it you see. I don't understand. I must have it. I must."

"Ah, monsieur grosse tête. Calm yourself, please."

"But I... You don't understand. I must have that bird. I must."

"Of course you must. And you will."

Josh stopped patting and looked up.

"A fellow traveller came through this way not so long ago. He was looking for a cloud to buy. I mean, have you ever heard of anything so ridiculous?"

Josh, despite being a member of parliament, pulled an appropriate face to indicate that he had not. Laissez-Faire continued.

"He did though make an interesting observation about how we do things here. I have been open to changes since. Therefore, for you, I will accept a trade."

"A trade?" Questioned Josh.

"But I have nothing here to trade with you."

"Ah, but you do, monsieur. You have a beautiful timepiece that I would gladly accept in payment."

"What, that old ta..."

Josh stopped himself.

The pocket watch that Laissez-Faire was referring to had been handed down to Josh by his father, who had in turn received it from his own father. There was quite the fantasy story behind the watch.

Apparently, Josh's grandfather once visited a strange land in his dreams where time stood still and men could be transformed into animals, such as birds and fishes and donkeys, and had great adventures. He recounted walking the streets of a strange marketplace, where he happened upon a fellow rendered unconscious outside a tavern. In the fellow's open hand was a pocket watch.

As he was dreaming, and as the dream was his, his grandfather decided that there would be no harm in helping himself to the timepiece, so he simply took it from the sleeping man. He rounded a corner, intent on studying the timepiece in private. He clicked the button to flip the lid and awoke, to find himself back in his own bed. Inexplicably he found the pocket watch next to him on his nightstand.

Tragically Josh's grandfather died a few days afterwards and Josh's father inherited the watch.

The watch itself was pretty to look at but had never worked. Other than sentimental value Josh regarded the timepiece as worthless, supported by the numerous valuations Josh had sought when looking to get rid of the damned thing. What Josh had no way of knowing is that this timepiece had been designed and built in The Distance. The hands did move. Just not in a way that Josh would ever understand.

In The Distance there were only two times. The right time and the wrong time. The watch was here with him now because it always was here, and here, this particular timepiece was almost priceless. A fact that Laissez-Faire knew only too well.

"Done." Said Josh.

"Indeed, you have been mon ami." Laissez-Faire whispered to herself whilst shaking Josh's hand.

Josh handed over the watch.

Laissez-Faire handed over the bird.

Both then went their separate ways.

For The Birds

Josh happened upon a small Persian cafe, where he was able to trade his old chewing gum for a cup of tea and a session on a hookah pipe. After finding a suitable outside spot he placed the vulture on the table in front of him, then settled down to admire his new acquisition.

Josh took a sip of his tea, followed by a deep draw from the hookah pipe. Reclining on the exhale, he closed his eyes.

"May I congratulate you on such a fine purchase."

The complement came from a stranger's voice. Feeling smug, Josh allowed himself a smile at the comment before opening his eyes.

"You may indee…"

Josh stopped short when he realised that there was nobody there.

'Hmm. That's a little odd,' he thought to himself. 'I was sure I just heard someone spea...'

"Yes. You did well to get me in exchange for an old watch, I think."

"WHAT THE ...!"

The chair that Josh had been sitting in was pushed back against the wall behind him. Had he not been so overweight he would have been out of the chair and standing. As it was, he found himself with his back against the wall, staring at a talking stuffed bird.

"Please, allow me to introduce myself. My name is Vellere Carter. I am a vulture originally from the Sudanese region of Africa. Pleased to make your acquaintance."

Josh looked down at his left hand, where he found he still had a grip on the mouthpiece from the hookah pipe. He then looked toward Vellere, then back down at the pipe's mouthpiece.

"Oh, I know what you're thinking." Vellere offered. "You are thinking that someone has drugged you and that you are imagining that I am talking but really I am just a silly old stuffed bird."

Josh just stared.

"Well, is it what you're thinking? Conversations generally work better when there are at least two participants involved."

"I... I... It's... It's just that I... I don't understand. You say that you're from Africa, but everybody knows the Andean Condor is native to South America. Also, Vellere sounds like a girl's name, but your caruncle tells me that you are a boy."

"Oh."

"And how can you be talking to me? You're not even alive."

"Well, there at least you are wrong."

Vellere paused, looked up to the right, turned back to Josh and continued.

"Well, actually you are right. You are right that I am not alive here. In this bird. In this stuffed one I mean. But I am alive normally. I mean where I am. I am alive where I am. I am just using this old bird as a communication aid. A little like a mobile phone I suppose. Only without buttons."

"A communication aid? Where are you communicating from, and why with me?"

"The where is not as important as the why. You see, word has spread that the Rt Hon Josh Robertson is a man that gets things done. A man of great political skill. Also, a man that very much likes vultures."

"Word has spread you say?"

Most would feel pride at such a compliment. Josh however, being the self-entitled, over privileged excuse of a being that he was, felt nothing of the sort. Of course, word had spread. Why would it not have?

"Okay then bird."

"Vellere."

"Okay then Vellere bird. What is it you want and what's in it for me?"

xx lol xx

Vellere explained that she resided now in a land known as Vulcon. Vellere was part of a society made up of many community flocks, dispersed across the land. Society was run by electees to a Centralised Head Committee, or CHC for short. Vellere herself was a member of the CHC.

Each community was expected to harvest a rare dragon fruit, known only to Vulcon. Harvests were paid to the CHC as tax. The CHC then used the harvests as payment to the dragon monkeys, rulers of the neighbouring land, Dragonia, where the fruit was considered a delicacy. In return, the dragon monkeys of Dragonia patrolled the borders of Vulcon, stopping the dragons of Dragonia from crossing into Vulcon in pursuit of prey, thus ensuring there was always enough to feed the many vulture communities in Vulcon.

In Vulcon, every four years or so, each community flock member was given the chance to vote on who made up the CHC. Each was afforded two votes. One to elect a member of their community to the CHC, then later, another vote to determine which of the successful electees should be the Prime Vulture, or PV for short.

"Sounds familiar." Josh observed. "I'm assuming it is usually the same representatives being elected each time?"

"Barring some sort of tragedy, yes. It is typical that once elected always elected. Stability is what our society values most."

"Hmm."

"All of the rules that we abide by in Vulcon are founded on three sacred commandments of our religion, 'Vulconism'."

"Politics and religion. What could possibly go wrong." Josh mused out loud. "Go on then. What are the sacred rules?"

"One. honour life & never ever kill. Two, honour death & hold vigil for the dying. Three, honour thy community."

"Fascinating." Josh quipped.

"They may not sound exciting, but CHC stability and rule, based on these three commandments, has kept our society safe and in good stead for a great many cycles."

"Uh huh, sure it has. But, oh wait a minute. You vultures like eating dead things, don't you?"

"Vultures feed from the dead, yes. But vultures never ever kill. All creatures in Vulcon know and respect us for this. Vultures do not kill, so in turn, vultures are not prey."

"Hmm." Josh mused whilst stroking his chin.

"There is enough death already. We do not have to kill. We search the lands for sick or wounded souls. When we find a creature close to the end, we make it our business to stay close and keep them company. We will not let a fellow creature die alone. In their darkest moment we will be right there with them."

"So, when you circle prey you are keeping them company?"

"Indeed. It is the way of Vulconism. When an end is imminent, we will come together to encircle the dying body. We hold vigil for one full day and one full night after a passing. Only after this time will we hold the wake and begin our feast."

"What about, 'honour thy community.' How does that work??"

"Vulconism demands that we let our old, our young and our sick be the first to feed from a corpse. Once they have had their fill then the rest of the community can feed."

"Okay. The young I can understand. But why the old and sick.?"

"It is what Vulconism demands."

"Of course it is. Good for you. So, what does any of this have to do with me?"

"You will recall I spoke of the Prime Vulture?"

"The PV. Yes."

"Well, we recently lost our PV."

"Oh?"

"Yes. Tragically so."

"Tragically? How did he die?"

"She."

"She?"

"Yes. She. He was she. She was PV."

"Oh. I see."

Vellere shared the story of PV, Bewla Kasha. Bewla was an ingenious soul, the like of which is rarely seen. Pioneer, inventor, explorer, disrupter. Over many years Bewla garnered a reputation for innovation and creation, her popularity rising in unison. It was inevitable that Bewla would eventually be nominated for the CHC. It was said that she accepted the post under duress.

Other members of the CHC were instantly intimidated by her popularity and chose to make her feel unwelcome at the CHC. Catching a whiff of something off, which is saying something for a vulture, Bewla declared that whilst she was in post she would work to weed out any CHC corruption. It was this pledge that saw her voted as new PV. Bewla poured herself into the task.

Soon enough Bewla requested an all community gathering. She stated to her colleagues in the CHC that this was for a celebration, to reveal a new invention. A creation she had named the wind turbine. It would turn night into day and winter into spring. Only those closest, including Vellere, knew that she intended to use the event to publicly reveal corruption she had uncovered at the CHC."

"Oh, I see." Said Josh.

"No, CHC." Vellere corrected.

"No, I meant, I se... "

"Anyway." Vellere continued, cutting Josh off.

"On what was to be the grand opening, Bewla flew up to the turbine blades, to cut the ribbon, you see. To officially present her invention to the masses."

"Then what happened?"

"Then, what happened is that some bird brain pushed the start button before the ribbon was cut. Bewla was approaching the turbine with the sun in her eyes. She didn't notice that it was already in operation."

"Oh, I see." Josh said again.

"Sadly, she did not."

After the accident several CHC members put themselves forward for the PV role. The public though were not trusting of the CHC as rumours of foul play had emerged since.

"Understandable." Josh offered.

"Maybe. But without a PV in place our society is beginning to wobble. Communities have threatened to hold back harvests until the corruption that Bewla spoke of is exposed."

"Ah."

"I am intending to take a sabbatical. I need somebody to serve in my place whilst I am gone. The communities have demanded that any new member to the CHC must be impartial. An outsider. Someone new."

"Uh huh."

"Someone like you Josh Robertson."

"Like me?"

The penny dropped. Josh was genuinely surprised.

"Yes, like you. We require someone skilled and experienced. Your career speaks for itself. You could even be the next PV."

The vanity button was pushed. Josh was caught, hook, line and sinker. This was his chance to finally be top dog. Or rather top bird. For a man with his skill set this would be a walk in the park.

"Okay then bird."

"Vellere."

"Okay then Vellere bird. Say I am in. How does a man like me go about becoming a bird like you?"

"Are you saying you are in?"

"Indeed I am. I will come and join your CHC and help sort your mess out."

"That is great news."

"How do we do this then?"

"Okay. First take a long draw on the hookah and breathe out."

Josh did as he was asked. The exhale produced a thick cloud of vapour.

"Again." Instructed Vellere.

Josh did as he was told, producing an even thicker cloud.

"Now what?" He asked.

"Just sit back. Close those chubby little eyes of yours and listen for the music."

Josh closed his eyes. Soon enough he could hear melodic chiming sounds. Slowly the chimes became louder. Colour began to fill his usually dark mind. An odd feeling, that he could not name, began to swell at the pit of his stomach. He felt the world tilt then suddenly opened his eyes.

"Hold on a second. How dare you call my eyes chubb..."

He was stopped mid-sentence. Standing in front of him was a creature of divine beauty. A face, not too dissimilar to that of his beloved vulture. A hat made from crushed velvet that glistened in the light. Hands of the like he had never witnessed before. Outstretched arms crowned by weeping willow fingernails, all making the most beautiful melodies. Then the body, clad in a skintight Lycra, deep purple bodysuit. Little of what the suit concealed had been left to the imagination. Distracted by an unexpected lust, the insult from Vellere was forgotten.

"Beezus!"

Josh exclaimed out loud. His eyes now began a second, much slower crawl over the creature's body.

"You are certainly pleasing to the eye. My gosh you are."

He bit at his bottom lip, drooled a little and started to rub his hands up and down upon his own thighs.

"Do I get a night with you as a part of this deal th...?"

Lord Gangles suddenly whiplashed both arms.

A violent crashing sound was the last thing Josh heard before he passed out.

Try Not To Die

"Ouch. My head." Josh moaned as he came too.

"Ah yes. Bit of a rough transition that one. Ahem. Never mind. That will clear in just a jiffy."

Josh was blinking against the pain and the light. As both started to lift, his eyes began to focus. Revealed was his new feather laden body.

"Well, this is quite the get up." Josh said, after having a good look over himself.

"How marvellous."

"You are surprisingly calm I have to say. Most people suffer quite a shock when they first awake."

"Well, as we have already ascertained, I am better than most people. I have to say this form feels rather natural."

"Good. That is good. Then we can get cracking straightaway. You must be keen to try out flying."

"Keen to try out flying?" Josh questioned.

"Well yes. We have wings. Flying is how we get around."

"Poppycock." Was Josh's response. "In my world we have legs, but you'll rarely see me walking anywhere. We have transport for that."

"Well, here we fly. We are our own transport."

"Pah. If I had known that I may not have been so quick to sign up."

"But most people would be excited about the idea of flying."

"And as we have already established, I am better than, thus not like, 'most people'. Unless you're talking business class I'm not really interested."

"You are going to have to fly if you want to get anywhere, so I suggest you have a practice. There's nothing to it. Run and flap your wings to get airborne, then keep flapping. Once you feel high enough you can stop and let the thermals carry you."

Reluctantly Josh followed Vellere's instructions and soon found himself up in the air. After regaining his composure, following the exertions of take-off, he was surprised to find that he quite enjoyed being up there, in the sky, without a care in the world. Just flying.

xx lol xx

Vellere was all set to leave on her sabbatical but first she took Josh to meet the other elected CHC representatives. They included:

Ruppell: from old money, he held a general contempt for those he was meant to be serving.

Bearded: sycophantic, she seemed big on self-promotion but little else.

Whitehead: a good old-fashioned bully that liked to get his own way.

Slender-bill: a bird with vast ambition but very limited vision.

Palm-nut: a 'good time' yes bird, wanting to be liked by everybody.

Redhead: clearly carried an axe for grinding.

Lappet-face: smug, self-entitled, vile. A born liar. A little like Josh in fact.

Turkey: a general non-entity, truth be told.

Yellowhead: he seemed totally incompetent but could make a good fall guy if needed.

Griffon: nothing mythical but certainly fierce.

Hooded: managed the harvest revenue but clearly had ambitious beyond his current role.

It would be fair to say that the CHC felt like a very crooked bunch.

Josh would be right at home.

First Blood

Later that day news came in of a dying elephant. Spotted in the Eastern region of Vulcon. Josh was about to experience his first vigil.

Swiftly he, Vellere and all the other members of the CHC were airborne. After a relatively short flight Josh spotted a large gathering of vultures on the ground, already surrounding the fallen adult elephant. There was much chatter amongst the birds, growing louder as more vultures arrived. The beast at their centre was in the last throes of life. The CHC took up prime positions within the circle.

"SILENCE!" Shouted Whitehead.

He was clearly enjoying his moment.

Josh noticed Lappet-face smirk to himself as the surrounding thong fell quiet.

"Fellow vultures." This was Slender-bill.

"Show your respect."

It wasn't clear to Josh if she was referring to the dying elephant or to the CHC. A ripple of negative energy could be perceived in the crowd.

"Now, now, everyone." Palm-nut's turn.

"Slender-bill, of course, means respect for our fallen friend. We are here to honour a life that is ending. Let us not forget the commandments."

Palm-nut bowed his head. To Josh's amazement the gathered crowd all followed suit.

"Um, e, I, um, eer..."

This was Turkey now, clearly struggling to get his words out. This guy had the presence of a wet fish.

"Yes Turkey." Palm-nut stepped in.

"You are right. Let us join, together, and begin our vigil."

Holding vigil, it turned out, involved a lot of chanting. According to Vellere this induced both a sense of calm in the dying, and a rewarding meditative state for the flock.

Unfortunately, vulture vocal cords weren't really up to much. The resulting noise, to Josh's ears at least, was more 'Velociraptor Vs T-Rex' than 'Om Mani Pädme Hum.' However, after going at it for long enough, aside from a raging sore throat, Josh could not deny the trance-like state he found himself in.

Thankfully it didn't take long for the fallen elephant to give up the ghost.

"SILENCE!"

Whitehead was at it again.

Josh snapped out of his reverie as the chanting abruptly stopped. Palm-nut stood forward.

"All. Our friend here has passed. Let us begin the second stage of our vigil. Please bow your heads and show your respect through silence. Respect the silence."

A hush fell upon the gathered birds. Josh bowed his head and closed his beak. As the silence deepened, he became aware of his surroundings in a way he had never really been before. The sun would soon set. The colours were changing all about him.

The elephant at the centre of the circle had begun the process of decomposition. Putrid smells started to emit from the elephant. Josh felt his stomach start to rumble.

Once past the shock of finding such an unpleasant stench appetising, Josh found the rumbling in his belly worsening. The stronger the smell of rot, the more his new little vulture belly rumbled.

xx lol xx

As time rolled on the conflict in his mind grew. He knew that the smells should be making him feel sick. Instead, he was feeling ravenous. The restless energies surrounding him suggested that the other vultures gathered were feeling the same way. Regardless, the flock held vigil and maintained discipline.

As the vigil came to an end Josh could think of nothing other than diving onto the elephant corpse and filling his face with rotting elephant flesh.

Talking of faces, Lappet-face now took centre stage to address the gathered flock.

"Friends. Our vigil is over. Let us commence the wake. Can the sick, the old and the young please come forth."

Various breaks in the crowd appeared to let birds from the back come through. These included sprightly infants, frail elder birds, that could only hobble, and the sick. Some of whom had visible injuries whilst others carried their sickness on the inside. All the sick birds kept their heads down, clearly ashamed of the priority they were being afforded.

Each bird began to feed as soon as it reached the centre. The young pecked eagerly, the old picked slowly, the sick peeled deliberately. Clearly the elephant was enough to feed the whole flock, but as Josh watched those feeding, he started to become anxious that they might eat it all.

Aware of how much self-discipline it was taking to hold himself back he realised how it must be the same for all the other vultures in the crowd. It was not in Josh's habit to think of others but being aware now, as he was, of the restraint being shown here, he could not help but be impressed by the moral strength on display in this community.

Maybe there was something in this that he could learn from. Maybe putting the weakest members of a society first led to a stronger society overall. Maybe working in the interests of others rather than yourself is actua...

"I say. Quite the carry on eh?"

It was Ruppell, in his dulcet tone, that had just crashed Josh's train of thought. He was at Josh's shoulder, whispering conspiratorially into his ear.

"Ahem. Yes. Yes. Quite a carrion indeed. I can't wait to get my beak involved."

"Hah. My dear fellow. We don't need to sully our beaks by sharing dinner with the peasants."

"What do you mean?"

Josh was confused and a little anxious at the thought of not being able to get his fill.

"Once Vellere has skedaddled of on her holidays, I will show you what I mean."

Redhead now addressed the flock.

"Enough!"

She shouted this more with her face than with her voice.

"The old and the young... and the sick..." Redhead pronounced the word 'sick' with a tone of disgust. "...have had enough. I now formally pronounce this wake open to all."

Josh was jerked forward as a throng of hungry vultures all made to pile into the corpse. The previously disciplined, even touching scenes, descended into the chaos of a feeding frenzy. Josh desperately wanted to get involved but was curious to understand why the CHC members held back.

"Well done Josh."

Vellere was in his ear now.

"I am so pleased to see you have held back and let everyone else feed first."

"I. Well, I um... You know... I..."

"It's very humble of you. I know how much discipline it takes and for you to resist on your first wake shows some real character. You should be very proud."

"I um... Ahem."

Keen to move the conversation along Josh nodded at the carcass and asked.

"How long do you normally wait before you... You know?"

"Oh no. It's not for me Josh. I'm a vegetarian."

"Ha, ha, ha, haa! That's very funny."

"It's the truth. I am a vegetarian. I source my food from the trees and from the fields."

"But you're a vulture. Who's ever heard of a vegetarian vulture? It's not in your nature."

"What a ridiculous thing to say Josh. Everything I ever do will, by default, be in my nature."

"But I mean, you are meant to eat meat."

"Yet I choose not to. Choice is something that is in all our natures. You can choose to be or choose not to be."

"But I like eating meat."

"Then by all means choose to be a meat eater but understand I have simply made that same choice, in reverse."

'In reverse?' Josh questioned himself. 'What does that mean?'

"Anyway." Vellere continued. "Enough of this. It's about time I got off on my sabbatical. I will leave you in the trusted company of the CHC. Until I return may you choose well"

Vellere then took to the sky. As soon as she disappeared from view Ruppell tapped Josh on the wing.

"Right then old chap. Now that the old lefty stick in the mud has buzzed off, we can leave these peasants to it."

"But I haven't eaten yet. Where are we going?"

"You will see soon enough."

With all the other vultures on site distracted by their bellies, the CHC quietly made their exit from the scene, completely unnoticed, and flew back to their CHC headquarters.

The Club House

CHC headquarters were located way up high, in a sandstone mountain cave, on the border with Dragonia. The cave's mouth presented a ledge at its lip, used as a landing and take-off platform. On either side of the entrance were posted security vultures. Both Andean Condors, immaculately presented with sleek jet-black feathers and pristine white collars fitted snugly about their thick retracted necks. Clearly not birds to be messed with.

"Aristo & Phanes." Ruppell clarified. "The guardians of our little abode. They keep the riff raff out."

Past the cave mouth was a cavernous space, the heart of the CHC. At its centre was laid a large circle of stone, thick as a tabletop. With thirteen spaces marked out around its circumference it looked like the face of a clock. Clearly this was where the members of the CHC gathered to talk business.

Littered elsewhere about the cavern were groups of plump, feather lined nests, where members of the CHC could relax and unwind after a hard day of talking at each other. Along the back wall of the cavern were several exits. Josh assumed these would lead to sleeping quarters and the like.

"Who's hungry?" Griffon questioned the group in a high pitched, excited manner, softly clapping her feathers together.

"I could eat a horse." This was Lappet-face.

"In fact, I bet I could eat a horse no problem at all."

A grotesque smirk lifted the corners of his mouth as he spoke.

"I, I, I'm... Um, I could eat. I think."

Turkey chipped in, timed as a mouse.

"Well, I think it's only right that our new colleague takes the first sitting."

This was Bearded. She was clearly looking to carry favour with Josh, who was happy to play along since he was starving.

"So be it." Confirmed Ruppell.

"This way if you please fellow birds."

"I've told you before Ruppell."

Redhead piped up.

"I don't think it's appropriate for you to refer to us as 'birds'."

"Yes, quite."

Ruppell looked at Josh and rolled his eyes.

"Fellow Committee members, please would you follow me."

"Much better." Redhead said approvingly.

For Josh's part, at that moment, he couldn't care less how he was referred to. His stomach was rumbling so much he felt he might soon trigger an earthquake. Without further ado he hopped in line and pursued Ruppell out through one of the exits.

The exit fed into a corridor, which soon branched off into two.

The vultures veered to the right.

Then there came another branching, this time into four separate corridors.

The vultures veered to the far right.

Eventually they reached a dead end.

Hung on the wall was a picture of a glorious looking bird, haloed in bright light.

"Have you brought me here to show off your pretty picture?" Josh asked with impatience.

"Indeed."

Ruppell confirmed.

He then lined himself up with the wall and pecked at it three times.

'Doof, doof, doof.'

For a moment nothing happened. Then the wall shuddered, fell back into a recess and opened to reveal a hidden room. At the same time a breeze was released, carrying the stench of rotting flesh straight to Josh's beak, sending him positively giddy with excitement. There, laid out on a slab at the centre of the room was a large deer carcass.

Josh was unable to resist any longer. He did not wait to be asked but instead piled his body into the room then his face into the rotting mass and began to gulp down his fill. 'This is glorious!' Is all he could think to himself as he swallowed down chunks of foetid meat.

Gulp, followed gulp, followed gulp. He had never tasted anything like it. The rest of the CHC followed suit and piled their faces into the carcass. Soon there was nothing other than a pile of naked bones left lying on the slab.

xx lol xx

'Buuurrppp...'

"I say, excuse me. That one rather snuck up on me."

"Sign of appreciation Ruppell."

Josh then let out a massive belch all of his own. The committee cackled.

The CHC members were back in the main section of the cave, lounging around in the feathered nests, puffing on hookah pipes, letting their dinner go down.

Josh released some stale wind, after which he decided to broach the subject of where the corpse had come from and why they hadn't had to follow the three commandments.

Yellowhead piped up for the first time.

"The commandments don't apply to us. They are only there to keep society in check."

"But I thought... Vellere said..."

"Vellere. Ha." Whitehead had decided to chip in.

"All you need to know about Vellere is that she is pathetic."

"Come now." Palm-nut offered.

"She just thinks a little differently than the rest of us."

"A little differently?" Bearded questioned.

"I think you mean a lot differently. She is an idiot. Her lefty socialist behaviour and ideals threaten to undermine our whole way of being."

"She's so a-woke she's a-sleep. Snarf, snarf."

Lappet-face obviously thought he had just cracked a funny. He had however only amused himself. And what was that laugh all about?

"Seriously old chap." Ruppell chipped in. "You would do well to distance yourself from that one. Fortunately, it is clear, I think, that you, Josh Robertson, are one of us. Wouldn't you agree?"

For this first time in his life Josh felt a little torn. He had been genuinely impressed at the original feeding. At how the Vultures put community over the individual. Despite himself he had felt an alien warmth in his chest, watching the old and the young and the sick being put first. He had found that he quite liked Vellere and almost admired her choice of vegetarianism, confusing as that was.

All of that said, he had never, in his whole life, ever tasted anything quite so satisfying and delicious as the carcass from which he had just fed. Inevitably then, the old Josh won out.

"Of course I am one of you. I feel I have found my brethren in fact."

"Jolly good. In that case we can tell you all about our little setup here. I assume you know that we harvest dragon fruit in this land and offer it up to the dragon monkeys of Dragonia?"

"Yes. Vellere said that you offer them the fruit in return for their protection of the border."

"Yes, good. And yes, they do offer us some protections, in that they stop dragons from crossing into our territory. The truth of the matter though is that there has only been one attempted crossing in living memory."

"Oh. So why do you continue to hand over the fruit?"

"Me. Me. Me!"

Hooded decided that he would rather like to answer this question.

"Go on then Hooded. Tell this chap what we do."

"Hehehehehe."

His laugh was a little deranged Josh thought.

"There has always been a payment to the dragon monkeys to protect us against the dragons. But as there haven't been any dragons for ages I negotiated a new deal. We agreed to reduce border patrol to a minimum. This freed up funds to spend elsewhere. Now, for the dragon monkeys to keep receiving all the dragon fruit, they have to provide us with a fresh carcass at least once a month. Hehehehehe. I know. I am sooo clever. It's a total win, win."

"Quite. Thank you Hooded." Ruppell again now.

"So yes. We have had this going on for a little while. It had all been running swimmingly until Bewla got elected and started banging on about corruption. She was threatening to expose our little setup. It is most unfortunate, I think, that she had that little accident with that wind turbine"

Ruppell raised his eyebrows at Josh, communicating what was unsaid.

"Unfortunate, yes. Very unfortunate indeed."

Josh agreed with a knowing nod of the head.

"So here we are. With the PV gone but having started rumours of corruption before her departure. For some reason the public now seem reluctant to trust any of us. Communities have even started to hold back their payments of dragon fruit tax."

"The peasants are revolting." Hooded chipped in.

"Indeed, they are old chap. But Josh, we need to get them to start paying their full share in tax again. Otherwise, our payments to the dragon monkeys will decrease and they will stop providing us with ready meals."

"I see." Stated Josh.

Indeed, he could see. He could see his chance of becoming the next Prime Vulture that is.

"Well, in that case, I think it's time we moved on to talking about the elephant in the room."

"I wish there was an elephant in the room. I bet I could eat the whole thing myself. Snarf, snarf."

Josh stared at Lappet-face until Lappet-face shut up and looked down at his talons. Josh continued.

"Alright then. Let us discuss the issue of who, in this cave, should be nominated the next Prime Vulture."

The agenda had been set. Each vulture had taken up their respective position at the round stone slab. Vellere was still absent, though the group assured Josh that she had no interest in being PV, and that they would be best to continue without her. This suited Josh just fine who, having already taken the initiative to call the meeting, had managed to place himself as the meeting chair.

"I propose that we each pitch our ideas on how best to keep the dragon fruit tax coming in. Following this we can take a vote and, based on the best ideas, decide who should be the next PV. Whitehead, why don't you kick us off."

"Simple. Tell the communities that if they don't pay tax then bad things will happen to their loved ones."

"Bully them you mean?"

"Yes."

"Got it. Great. Okay, next. Palm-nut, how about you?"

"Oh, I don't know. You know I'm no PV. I am sure however that whatever the next PV decides is best will be best and that they will have my full support."

"Inspiring, well done. Griffon, do you have anything to bring to the table?"

"Well, I think we have a genuine problem in our lands with animals that come here without invitation. We need to tell the communities this, then raise the taxes to pay somewhere else to take them. Only we don't really send them anywhere. We just keep all the tax."

"Interesting. Good. At last, we may be onto something."

"Oh, oh, oh." Redhead was keen to get in on this action.

"Go on, Redhead."

"I don't know if you know but there are a lot of animals that like to sleep outside in the wild, and not in caves."

"Uh huh."

"Well, I think they make the place look untidy. I suggest we criminalise the practice. We can then raise extra taxes by issuing them fines."

"Wow. Ruthless, but inspired. Okay, who's next?"

Ruppell waved a wing around in the air.

"I say that either they pay their taxes, or we round them up and put them in a workhouse."

"Very Victorian of you Ruppell. Do you still have workhouses here?"

"How should I know? If we don't then we damn well should."

"Okay then. Slender-bill. You must have a good idea."

"I do, yes. We need to slash the taxes for the rich, thus increasing their power over workers. Then we make a rule forcing the rich to share a minimum with the workers, which the workers will eventually need to give to us to cover their taxes."

"Not sure I get it, but okay. Lappet-face?"

"I don't think I need any ideas. Everybody clearly loves me, and I am sure they would happily pay more taxes knowing I was in charge."

"Wow. You really are an idiot aren't you."

"I am n..."

"That wasn't a question."

Lappet-face shut up and looked down again.

"Bearded. Have you got anything? Or are you going to be like Palm-nut and stay perched on the fence?"

"As it happens, I believe that perching on the fence is a very difficult thing to do, but I will do this in support of whomever should become the next PV... boss."

Josh gave a sigh.

"Yellowhead?"

"I'm afraid I've not had time to prepare anything. Um, if you could give me some time maybe to..."

"Turkey?"

"I, um, yes, erm, I think, maybe..."

'Squeak', 'squeak', 'squeak', was all Josh could hear.

"Okay. Hooded, that just leaves you."

"Hehehehe. I don't care what you do. I will end up as PV eventually."

"Well, I can't say that I don't admire your confidence."

"What about you old chap?"

Ruppell turned the question onto Josh.

"What, pray tell, is your idea?"

"Ideas, Ruppell. Ideas. It's all very simple. If you want the masses to do something you just have to make them scared. Redhead and Griffon are both on the right track, though their ideas need refining."

"Go on."

"So, first, we make a big deal of how migrant bird numbers are increasing. Swallows for instance. We introduce a rumour that they are developing a taste for rotten meat and are a threat to our food security. We then communicate how we need to sure-up taxes to pay for increased border patrol. There will be some resistance so next we will tell them how migrants from the Far East have started spreading bird flu and that we are on the verge of a pandemic. When everyone starts to panic, we will introduce a short flockdown. Only dragon fruit workers will be allowed out. This will encourage more vultures to start labouring for dragon fruit. Again, we will require more taxes to increase border patrols to now stop the nasty migrants and disease."

"Inspired old chap."

"I also like Redhead's idea of persecuting those that sleep outside. We can do this one just for fun though. It's clearly a lifestyle choice so if they want to continue enjoying a view of the stars each night then they should be willing to pay for it. Am I right?"

The committee members all started to thump their wings down on the table. 'Here, here,' they all said out loud, talking over each like a bunch of five-year-old children.

"That does it then." Announced Ruppell.

"I say Joshy here is installed as the next PV. All in agreement raise a wing."

Everyone raised a wing, though Josh noted that Hooded was a little slower to do so than the others.

"Right then Josh old chap. Congratulations. You are now our new PV."

Although pleased, Josh had to ask the question.

"Do we not need to put this to the public first? So that they can have a say?"

"Hah, you mean like democracy? Oh no. We only like them to think that they have a say. We will tell them these are exceptional circumstances, so we have chosen on their behalf. I mean, if they don't like it what can they do about it anyway?"

"Absolutely nothing!" Lappet-face shouted in delight, followed by a... "...snarf, snarf, snarf."

This time the rest of the vultures joined in with the laughter.

Victory In Vulcon

The following day word was sent out to all the communities that a new PV had been selected. Josh visited communities based in the South to introduce himself. To the North he sent a representative. Josh wasted no time in kicking off his campaign of disinformation.

First the gentle rumour of an expected increase in migrant swallow numbers this season. Then some gossip as to how the increase would add pressure to local services. Next the rumour that swallows had developed a taste for rotten meat and may be in direct competition with the vultures. By the time Josh's campaign had finished, the average bird in the street believed swallows were now a threat to their very existence. The pending migrant crisis was the worst thing to be facing them in a generation.

When the first swallows began to arrive, tired and hungry from their long journeys, instead of receiving the usual untroubled welcome they found instead that the local vulture communities were all out hostile. As the swallows began arriving in larger numbers, tempers bubbled over, and the vulture communities soon turned to violence. Migrant swallows were hunted down and physically evicted from all vulture territories.

After the swallows had been evicted Josh presented himself in public, standing under a new flag he had commissioned, waxing lyrical about the great vulture victory and how a great crisis had been diverted. His next victims would be the swifts.

There was news, he said, of a deadly bird flu pandemic sweeping toward the land, being spread by the swifts. Rather fortuitously for Josh, someone in the crowd sneezed as he said this.

A mild panic rippled through the crowd. The offending vulture was instantly given a wide berth, making him very easy to spot. Josh seized on the opportunity and sent Aristo and Phanes into the crowd to apprehend the offending bird and place him in quarantine. The sight of this action taking place increased the panic level significantly. It was then very easy for Josh to declare a national flock down, that would last two cycles, whereby only essential dragon fruit workers would be permitted to leave their homes.

'We are all in this together!' Josh valiantly declared as he left the stage.

The communities, unified in their newfound hatred of migrant birds, felt a sense of togetherness throughout flockdown. They were only too happy to act in the national interests and stay isolated.

As predicted the number of volunteer dragon fruit workers increased significantly, as did the yields produced. Josh and the rest of the CHC publicly flocked down with the rest of society. However, in private, away from the public gaze, the CHC partied their time away. Thanks to the increased yield in dragon fruit, they were able to increase the number of carcasses ordered from the dragon monkeys.

By the time that two cycles had passed all the swifts had been evicted and the flockdown was able to be lifted. The population did rejoice at the wisdom of their new unelected leader.

Josh then kicked of the campaign against outside sleepers. He decreed it a criminal offence to choose to sleep under the stars. Anybody wishing to sleep in this land must do so only under a roof. Not all the creatures in the land could afford a roof and soon all the wild sleeping animals were going the same way as the swallows and the swifts.

Eventually the streets were free from rough sleepers and again the population did rejoice at the wisdom of their new unelected leader.

Under Josh's rule the CHC had reduced spending on border patrol to an absolute minimum, using the funds instead to buy even more corpses for themselves.

Day and night they now feasted. The size of their greed, overshadowed only by the size of their fat bellies. Josh had achieved his ambition. He was sitting pretty, loved by the masses and by the CHC. It was agreed that Josh was the most successful PV this land ever did see.

Then things started to fall apart.

xx lol xx

The first issue that became apparent was a lack of labour in the land. The vultures would usually be benefiting from a mass of cheap, willing labour, made up from the migrating birds whom they had recently evicted. Yield reduced as a result.

As yield went down the CHC eventually stopped spending anything on border protection. Instead, they diverted all income to fund their increased appetites.

The next big issue was a marked reduction in the number of available corpses in the land. The vultures, it seemed, had unwittingly evicted most of their future food source when clearing the streets of outside sleepers. Unbeknown to the residents of Vulcon, albeit for different reasons, Dragonia was suffering from a similar issue.

Increased spending on corpses by the CHC meant food was being taken away that would otherwise have fed the dragons of Dragonia. It was inevitable then that the dragons of Dragonia would soon start crossing the now unprotected borders into Vulcon in search of food.

Dragons were happy to hunt live prey. This swiftly led to a real food crisis for the vultures and workers soon became too weak to work. There followed a complete collapse in the production of dragon fruit. In turn this meant that the CHC had to stop their feeding parties as their funding for the procurement of rotten corpses shrivelled and dried and turned to dust.

With the whole population of Vulcon, including the CHC, facing starvation, opinions of the Rt Hon Josh Robertson rapidly changed.

Hooded saw a chance to publicly throw his boss under a bus. He told the vulture communities how Josh had created the recent crises to serve his own selfish ambitions to be a PV. He declared that the corruption that Bewla Kasha sought out had finally been exposed in Josh. To put things right he would immediately install himself as PV.

The communities were so relieved that they completely forgot about any corruption before Josh had come to power.

Hilarious Nefarious

Vellere Carter had arrived back at the CHC and was currently perched with Josh, encouraging him to reflect on his recent experiences.

"I thought I was doing the right thing." Josh insisted.

"Right for who?" Vellere challenged.

"For the communities. For everybody. I saw how you treated the young and the old and the sick on that first day and I felt inspired. I really did."

"So, what happened?"

"When I returned to the CHC it occurred to me that the best way to ensure your traditions continued was to ensure that the status quo remained in place. I needed to get the public past their concerns regarding corruption so that they would start trusting the CHC again."

"I see." Vellere nodded.

"And you thought that the best way to do that was to introduce more corruption."

"Yes. No. Well, maybe. I don't know. What I do know is that I have only ever acted in the best interests of those that I represent."

Josh said this was such conviction that Vellere concluded he believed it.

"Josh. This, right here, right now. This is your opportunity to finally stop lying to yourself. To face who you are and decide that now is the time to do better."

Josh was offended.

"I'm sorry. But who do you think you are to talk to me like that?"

"Josh, I am only trying to hel..."

"No, no, no. No. I simply won't have it. I am a good and honourable man. I have a title that says as much. I will not have the likes of you, who has only known me for five minutes, suggest to me that I am anything but."

"But..."

"Stop!" Josh raised a wing tip into the air.

"I wish to hear no more."

Josh was more irritable than usual as he had not eaten for some time. He was, by his own reckoning, starving to death. He turned his back

on Vellere and took off to search the planes for
food.

xx lol xx

After a time cruising the thermals, Josh happened
upon a single lone lion cub. The cub had gotten
itself tangled up in some mountain scrub. It had
disabled its limbs and somehow managed to tie its
own mouth shut, meaning the cub was unable to
cry out for help. Having clearly been trapped for
some time, the cub had since stopped fighting to
free itself and seemed resigned to accepting its
fate.

Josh began to circle, as was vulture custom,
satisfied for now with the promise of a meal to
come. Several hours had passed when, to Josh's
absolute dismay, the cub's mother roamed into
the area, clearly looking for her lost baby.

'Damn it!'

Josh was consumed by his hunger. If he allowed
the mother to find the cub, then the cub would be
saved, and he would not get to eat. In a sudden
desperate move Josh swooped down toward the
lion, landing directly in front of her. The lioness
roared but knew not to attack a vulture.

"Lady lioness. Forgive the intrusion. My name is the Rt Hon Josh Robertson. May I ask, are you seeking a lion cub?"

"Yes. Yes, I am. One of my babies is missing. I am desperately worried. Mr Robertson, can you help me? My Robertson, have you seen my baby?"

"Fear not lady lioness for I have seen your cub. The cub is safe but appears to be stuck in some mountain scrub. I have seen the cub on my travels, not twenty kilometres from here, in that direction."

Josh then extended a wing in the opposite direction to where the cub was currently stuck. The lioness was overcome with relief and joy.

"Oh, Mr Robertson. You are a fine and honourable bird indeed. Thank Beezus for the vultures."

The lioness then bounded off in the direction that Josh had sent her. Josh was a little surprised by how fast she moved, suddenly realising that twenty kilometres may not have been enough.

He then took back to the sky to assess the situation. The cub was still stuck. Very weak, but still very much alive. Josh would have to move quickly if he was to get his meal.

Commandment 1
Honour life & never ever kill

Josh circled the air until he spotted a suitably sized rock. He picked the rock up into his talons. He flew then hovered over the cub. He dropped the rock in line with the cub's head.

Commandment 2
Honour death & hold vigil for the dying

Josh preferred his meat to be on the rotten side. Beggars though cannot be choosers.
He repeated this to himself as he feverishly picked at the warm flesh from the lion cub's still twitching body.

Commandment 3
Honour thy community

Josh was making good progress on the carcass when he heard a vulture in the near distance squawking hysterically. Looking up, he spotted a wing pointed in his direction. The bird then took off and flew in the direction of the CHC.

To be fair Josh did experience a minor pang of guilt, though he quickly swallowed it down, then went at what remained of the cub with fresh gusto.

xx lol xx

Next a vulture shaped shadow passed over Josh's head, followed shortly by a 'thud.' It was Vellere landing.

"Josh. What are you doing? What have you done?"

Vellere was beside herself. Josh lifted his face from his meal to look Vellere in the eye.

"The commandments you live by are your commandments, not mine. I am not a scavenger. I am an apex predator!"

Just as Josh finished talking a large roar came forth. Josh straightened his back triumphantly in response. Vellere, seeing, then pointing over his shoulder declared.

"No Josh. That is an apex predator."

Josh turned to look over his shoulder and was horrified to find the cub's mother bounding toward him. Vellere had taken to the air already. Josh turned to do the same but found he was now too heavy to take off. Panic took hold so he started to run.

It quickly became apparent that a fat, unfit, and full of food vulture was no match in speed to an angry lioness.

"Fly Josh, fly."

Came the cries of Vellere from the sky above him. Josh was in no state to reply. The lioness was rapidly gaining on him.

Looking around for options Josh spied a crack in a rock wall just ahead of him. It would be too small for the large lioness to squeeze through but for a vulture...? Yes, for a vulture it was just the right size.

He turned to assess the situation. The lioness was almost upon him. Vellere had spotted where Josh was heading and had landed herself on the other side of the crack in the wall. She extended her wing through the crack towards the ailing Josh, encouraging him on.

"Come on Josh. You can do it. Just a little further. Run Josh, run."

"Josh's little legs were on fire. The recently consumed cub sloshed violently about in his belly. Sweat poured from his head. The lioness, so close now he could feel her exhaled breath tickle at the base of his neck. He had nothing left. He wasn't going to make it.

Vellere, from the other side of the rock wall, stretched her wing as far as it would go. Josh, in turn, reached out to the safety that she promised. The tips of their wings met. Josh's wing slipping into a full embrace. Their eyes met. Vellere's look of anguish was replaced with hope. Josh's look of sheer panic, replaced with confidence. They both believed that Josh could make it.

Behind them the lioness roared with frustration. Pushing herself to her absolute limit she leaped in a final pursuit of her quarry. At that same moment Josh used the last of his strength to yank Vellere's wing as hard as he could. Unprepared for this Vellere was pulled from the safety of the rock wall, then swung, by Josh's wing, into the path of the incoming lioness. Josh let go and Vellere was lost.

Josh's callous action afforded him time to slip through the crack in the rock wall. Having reached safety, he doubled over then proceeded to throw up his dinner. After fully ejecting the cub's remains, he was light enough to fly again.

The lioness was at the crack in the wall, trying to work her way through to the other side. Josh did not wish to hang around longer than he had to, so took to the sky. The lioness watched him rise with a roar full of anguish and pain and frustration. After reaching a safe distance, Josh turned around to face her, flying backwards.

"Ha. Stupid lioness. Call yourself an apex. Who's the apex predator now? Me, not you. I am a vulture. I am a prime animal. I, the Right Honourable Josh Robertson, am a right..."

'ᵦbbbbbbbbbbbrrrrrrruuUUUAAAHHHHHH!!'

'WHOMP!'

Josh had been too busy taunting the lioness to notice the aeroplane approaching from behind. He was sucked into one of the jet engines, leaving only a gentle shower of black feather and red drizzle in his wake.

The Unawakening

Josh woke up.

Screaming!

"Arghhh! Arghhh! Arghhh!"

"Sir. Sir. Are you alright sir?"

Josh's butler had burst into the pitch-black room. He dashed to the curtains and yanked them open. The sun burst violently into the room. Josh held his right forearm up to cover his eyes.

"Blast it man. Close the damn curtains. That light is too bright."

Jeeves did as he was told.

Josh then moved to turn on a bedside lamp. He found that he was covered in sweat and black feathers that had burst from his bedding.

"What the..."

He looked up to survey the room, before letting out another, though this time much louder scream.

"Arghhh!"

There, standing on top of the dresser, at the end of his bed, was a large stuffed Andean Condor staring back at him.

The Lonely Cloud

"What the actual...!"

Amari burst through the Everywhere Door, into the cellar, in a very bad mood indeed.

Ella trailed behind her.

"Some we win, some we lose." Ella offered.

Amari spun on her heel to face Ella.

"Lose!" Said emphatically.

"Lose!" Said again, for emphasis.

"That piece of trash threw me under an angry lion to save his own skin. Who would do a thing like that? I was trying to help him."

"He did throw you under a lion, yes. And then I threw an aeroplane at him."

"That was a nice touch, I agree. Only I didn't really get to enjoy the moment, on account of the fact that an angry lion had ate my face."

"Fair."

"I mean, why do we even bother trying to help people like him?"

"Everybody deserves at least one chance, Amari."

"Do they though? Do they really?"

"It is what we signed up for whether we like it or not. We offered him a chance to change. He turned it down. Ivy will pick it up from here."

Both took a second to contemplate this.

"Anyway, first things first. I need to get out of this ridiculous costume."

Amari brightened a little.

"I could help you with that if you like?" A knowing smile was offered, which Ella reflected in kind.

'Ding Dong. Ding Dong. Ding Dong.'

Somebody was at the front door.

"Typical. Hold that thought. It sounds like we have a visitor."

The Everywhere Door swung open to let them upstairs.

xx lol xx

The door opened into the kitchen area where the pair found Sid, supping already from a cup of tea that one of the staff had made for him.

450

"Sid!" Ella exclaimed. "This is a nice surprise. Do we have a new job? Why didn't you just phone?"

Sid glanced at Ella, then back to his cherry blossom tea.

"Interesting costume you have on there." Sid commented.

"I, um, err... No. This. Ahem... I..."

Amari chuckled in the background.

"It matters not what you wear Ella."

"It's temporary Sid, I promise. I, um. Anyway, why are you here?"

"I am here Ella as I have a rather special assignment for you, and it felt only proper to deliver the details in person."

"Oh, okay. Well, I'm sure me and Amari can handle it, whatever it is."

"Amari will need to sit this one out."

"What do you mean? I can't do an assignment on my own. It's just not pos..."

"You won't be on your own Ella. It's just that Amari is not yet qualified. Your next assignment is going to be a transition and that requires the assistance of a fully qualified Angel."

"A transition. What, you mean like somebody dying?"

"Yes Ella. I mean like somebody dying."

"Oh." Was all that Ella could manage in reply.

"I wouldn't normally present you with such a case so early on in your career. But, well, this is a special case and... Needs must."

"I understand." Confirmed Ella. "Okay then. Please, tell us all about it."

Ella and Amari both settled into a seat and Sid began to tell them about Ella's next subject. A lonely old man named Charlie Thatcher.

xx lol xx

After Ella had gotten over hearing Charlie's name again her first thought was to challenge the logic. Charlie had passed several years ago. In fact, as Ella had been living in The Distance, the number of years in her previous realm would be much higher. How could it be that Sid was presenting Charlie as Ella's next case, in the here and now in The Distance.

Sid was at pains to remind Ella, again, that time worked very differently in The Distance. Here, again, there was only ever the right time and the wrong time. As it so happened, now was the right time for Ella, as Lord Gangles, to return to her realm and to assist Charlie with his transition.

Ella then picked up on Sid's reference to 'her realm,' surprised to learn that Lord Gangles could operate in other realms outside of The Distance. Sid explained how, specifically, in cases like Charlie's, the subject's grip was so tight that it was necessary to lead them through a waking dream within their own realm, as it was there that they needed to let go. The subject would be completely consumed in any world that Gangles created but would continue to move within their own realm as if awake. Any passerby would simply assume the subject's behaviour was related to a mental health issue.

Ella then questioned what people might think about witnessing a Lord Gangles walking about within their realm. Sid explained how the HoT-wire worked on additional levels when operating in realms outside of The Distance. The HoT-wire not only worked on the subject's brain waves but could also work on all other subjects in the vicinity, to block them from seeing Lord Gangles.

Next Ella asked about the Angel she would be working with. His name was Jacob La'dor, though he often used a different surname whilst on assignment. Apparently, Jacob was a very famous Angel. His speciality was assisting with reluctant transitions. If there were a book on this subject, Jacob would have been the one to have written it. It appeared that Ella and Charlie Thatcher were both very honoured indeed. Ella questioned how the Angel would be hidden from view within the realm. Sid told her that Angels never hide themselves, in any realm. Beings simply chose not to see them.

With all concerns addressed Sid laid out what would be the necessary narrative theme. Usually this would be down to Ella and Amari, but in transitions it was the subject themself who set the scene.

Charlie's theme was to be a journey with the clouds. To transition he needed to let go of his past by reconciling a memory and the associated guilt that he harboured. Ella pressed for more detail, but this was all that Sid would offer. Ella already knew of course how the narrative would end. She just had to construct the journey in a way that would harbour Charlie from the physical realities of what would be happening to him.

When Ella had been preparing for previous assignments, she had felt a certain excitement. A rush of adrenaline, that she had the power to create something that someone else could participate in. A world in which she, Dr Ella Songg, was effectively a God. For this assignment though everything felt different.

Ella was to accompany a soul on their final journey within their realm. Ella would be witnessing and participating in their final moments. There were no real choices for the subject to make. All that was needed was patience and encouragement, steering the subject toward the necessary realisations that would lead them to their eventual transition. The feeling that this job elicited was not one of excitement, but rather one of privilege.

xx lol xx

Following Sid's departure Ella and Amari got to work on the narrative and composition for Charlie's transition. Jacob dropped by the following day to introduce himself and review what narrative had been put together.

Ella thought he was a little cliche for an Angel. Tall, muscular, youthful looking, full of kindness and charm. When Jacob arrived it was Amari who let him in. On her way to answering the door she announced that she would send Jacob in alone, leaving the pair space to bond and get to know each other.

Jacob praised Ella for her work, which he said was 'exceptional,' especially as this was her first transition case. Over a glass of wine, the pair reviewed and rehearsed how the scenes might play out. Ella knew that Jacob was doing this to humour her. Being so experienced he didn't really need to rehearse.

The next morning, Amari was in the cellar, helping Ella get into costume.

"I still think, if you would have given the other suit a chance."

Ella had gotten rid of that skintight monstrosity as soon as possible. She had, though, taken Amari's general point on board about the outfit needing an uptick in style.

Ella then was adorned with a long dark brown leather dress coat, reaching just below the knee. The coat was buttoned lined but open, revealing a smart Victorian style waistcoat, made from the finest deep blue wool, on top of a stiff collared white floral-patterned shirt, highlighted by a gloriously flared silken silver cravat. The trousers fitted well against Ella's strong legs, pinstriped in style and cut loose at their bottoms. The new boots were of the finest quality leather, finished with a strong wooden heel.

Ella had stayed true to the original Gangle's outfit but now the materials were fresher, the cuts were cleaner, sharper. The new mask and hat were both light as a feather and the windchimes incorporated wrist supports.

As a final touch Ella had dyed her hair silver grey and allowed it to flow soft and long, down to her shoulders. The overall feeling was of strength, kindness and presence.

'Now this suit,' Ella thought to herself, 'feels good'.

"Okay." Started Amari. "You remember, Josh will be there already, on the other side of the door. As soon as you enter the realm, start with your transmissions. This will make sure that nobody sees you."

"Yes, I know."

"Do you remember where you are going, what the street name is?"

"Well, the Everywhere Door should drop me in the right place, so I don't see why it mat..."

"Amuse me. Please."

Amari was clearly worried for her companion.

"Okay, yes. Fine. Doughty Street. That is where Charlie is."

"Good. Very good. Okay then. Final check. Have you got everything? Keys, phone, purse."

"I'm not going to the pub Amari."

Amari looked a little put out but conceded.

"Fair. I am just worried about you."

Ella cupped Amari's face in her palms and looked her in the eye.

"I will be fine. I will be back here before you can even notice I have gone."

Amari let her face lean into the warmth of Ella's palm. She gave the palm a kiss, then reached up to pull Ella's hands down.

"Yes. You're right. I am just being silly. Come on. Let's get your gloves on. Jacob will be waiting for you."

Amari helped Ella with her new gloves then gave her hands a little squeeze.

"Wait a minute." Ella said. "Did you compose that poem? I would love to hear it."

The Everywhere Door creaked open behind them.

"It can wait. Until you get back."

Amari offered a gentle smile.

Ella smiled back then stepped into the doorway.

Rising

Fortunately, the Everywhere Door opened to a terraced house on Doughty Street, that was opposite Charlie's house. Ella had agreed to meet Jacob out on the street itself. Looking up and down the street it was clear that he must still be inside with Charlie.

'Good,' thought Ella. 'This gives me time to create a bit of ambiance.'

The day was bright and sunny, so Ella started to generate fog from the nostrils of her mask. Soon the fog had built to a level where it was blocking out the sun, creating a perfect atmospheric haze. Ella then heard Charlie's door open. Jacob and Charlie were coming out.

'Showtime.'

Ella waited until Charlie had navigated the steps and made it through the rusted front gate. She left it a minute, so that Charlie could catch his breath, before slowly making her approach. Ella had chosen her approach angle so that the sun would be behind her, knowing that this would cast her shadow large in the surrounding fog. Charlie had noticed her. He looked a little panicked, asking Jacob, who was currently presenting to Charlie as a cloud, who she was.

Ella drew closer.

The fog had become so dense that all other sights, including Jacob, were hidden from view. It was just Charlie and Lord Gangles, one on one.

Charlie was frozen.

Ella raised her arms slowly.

"Oh my God!" Charlie said out loud.

"What is... I mean... What are... They can't be..."

"Oh, but they can." Confirmed Jacob from the background.

"But it... It looks like... I mean... It looks like..."

"That's right Charlie. Behold Lord Gangles. Lord Gangles who have wind chimes for fingers."

Ella smiled behind her mask. A little perverse maybe, but she had come to love the part when her subjects freaked out. With Charlie's attention fully captured Ella increased the wind from her nostrils, setting the wind chimes, and Charlie's special composition, in motion.

Charlie fell into a trance.

Ella increased the breeze, increased the volume and increased the fog.

Charlie's transition narrative had begun.

461

First Reveal

At first Ella found being out in public, in her old realm, most disconcerting. However, as Sid had promised, the HoT-wire seemed to be doing its thing, keeping her concealed from view. One person, a young child, did a double take, as if they had seen her. For everybody else though Ella was passing through their realm as if she were a ghost unseen.

It was amusing to watch Jacob in this realm. He was completely visible, but Ella observed people actively looking the other way whenever he passed.

The same could not be said for Charlie. Nobody would usually notice an old man. However, this old man had clearly seen better days and as the trio entered the park Charlie's appearance brought wary or disapproving looks from members of the public. It didn't help that to everyone else he appeared to be talking to himself.

Eventually Charlie was engaged by a beautiful young woman named Leia. She seemed to see Charlie. She also appeared to see Jacob but made nothing of it.

The narrative played out so far was calm, warm, gentle and relaxed. So much so that Charlie went on that afternoon to engage with several people in the park. It was heartwarming to witness the kindness in those strangers that were not scared off by his appearance. Those who were happy to make a little time to talk, to acknowledge his existence.

The afternoon wore on and Charlie, weary from his adventures so far, dozed on one of the park benches. Jacob, without consulting Ella, had disappeared somewhere. This was frustrating as Ella could not do anything to wake Charlie by herself. Soon night descended.

A gang of youths appeared on the scene. They surrounded Charlie's bench before eventually deciding to wake him from his slumber. Charlie awoke with a shock. Ella needed to quickly change gear on the narrative.

The group seemed to be involving Charlie in some back-and-forth banter and all appeared to be going well, for a while. Then Charlie became agitated and started rambling.

Ella had only been half listening but zoned in as Charlie was saying:

"...how the hell was I supposed to walk down the street again, after they all knew that I lost you? After they all knew that you both left me."

'Wait,' Ella thought. 'Did he just say 'both?'

Ella had been briefed about Ebony, but who else might Charlie be talking about. Intrigued, Ella decided to use the HoT-wire to see into Charlie's mind's eye.

Her timing could not have been worse.

Charlie had started shouting and stomping, *sort of*, all over the place. He was stabbing his fingers toward the ground, shouting, 'Boom!', 'Boom!', 'Boom!'

Ella knew that Charlie was currently immersed in the narrative as a thundercloud. However, the gang of youths who had, until now, been egging him on, suddenly saw him as completely unhinged.

Charlie reached a crescendo.

Pointing - BBBOOOOOMMMM!
Shouting - BBBOOOOOOOMMMM!
Stomping, *sort of* - BBBOOOOOOOOOMMMM!
The youths all backed off.

By using the HoT-wire when she did, Ella had unwittingly dived into a sea of fire, rage and destruction. Charlie's mind's eye was a blur of anger, sorrow and pain. Ella felt it all. Everything that Charlie was gripping onto so tightly, that had been destroying him for all those years.

Whilst in Charlie's mind Ella had briefly managed to make out two images, one big one small, but both were blurred and out of focus.

Back on the outside Ella was regaining her bearings as Charlie stopped, mid action, and fell limp. One of the youths rushed to his side. Collectively the gang then started to lead Charlie away, through the park. It was time for Ella to shift gears again.

xx lol xx

The youths took Charlie to a homeless shelter that was close by. Ella followed Charlie into the shelter, then followed him as he was led to a bed by the shelter manager. Ella was surprised to find that Jacob was already there, lying in a bed right next to Charlie's.

"Where the hell have you been? What are you doing here?"

"First of all." Jacob started. "We don't use the 'H' word."

Ella looked less than impressed at this.

"Second, I've not 'been' anywhere. Had you been paying more attention you would have seen me blended in with the youths that just accompanied Charlie here."

"Wha…"

"Don't be too hard on yourself. You are only human after all. You are just as likely to not see me for that reason."

"Bu… I… I'm… Okay." Ella doubtfully conceded. "But what are you doing here? Lying on a bed?"

"I often come here. It's one of those places I can be of use. Besides, tonight is a special night. I didn't want our Charlie to be in here all alone. I mean, look at him."

Charlie was led on a bed, doubled up, holding his stomach. He was babbling and whimpering and calling out to Ebony in muffled shouts.

"He's almost there." Confirmed Jacob. "A final push and we will have him over the line."

"Sounds a bit business-like when you say it like that." Ella reflected, then asked. "Do you know if there was anyone else in his life? Charlie's, I mean."

"Why do you ask?"

"It was just that earlier, he was angry. I mean really angry. He was ranting and he mentioned the word 'both'. 'After they all knew that you both left me,' he said."

"I don't know. Why didn't you just jump into his mind?"

"Oh, I did."

"And?"

"And it nearly broke me."

"Ah."

"I mean, there was so much anger and pain there. Much more than I expected. All I managed to make out were the blurred images of two shapes. One large, one small. Lying on a bed, I think. But it was too painful to stay there. I had to get out."

"Well..." Jacob pondered the word out loud.

"Well, what?" Ebony questioned.

"Well. I would say the man is a lot calmer now. Why don't you try again. Whilst you still can."

Ella was not keen on the idea of entering Charlie's mind for a second time. It was clear however that his anger had since abated. They were far enough into the transition that it should be relatively safe.

Ella drew a deep breath, re-tuned the HoT-wire and stepped into Charlie's story, ready to re-enter his mind.

xx lol xx

Charlie was sitting with Ebony in their old living room. It was raining outside. The rain was 'tip, tip tapping' against the window pain. The pair were talking calmly then Charlie grabbed at his waist. Ebony was then telling him to stop fighting.

'Stop fighting what?' Ella thought to herself.

Charlie then fell to the floor, crippled by whatever agony was in his stomach.

Ebony knelt gently beside him and started to stroke his hair.

Charlie began to calm down.

In contrast, the rain started to increase.

Ella decided this was the moment to find out who the 'other person' had been. She quickly flicked open the channel to his mind's eye and re-entered his memories.

Ella was immediately hit with a massive sensation of guilt that crashed over her head like a feral wave caught up within an ocean of pain.

'There it was again,' Ella thought to herself.

Charlie's living room began to dissolve. The floor opened up and Ella was dropped, falling like a stone into the abyss of Charlie's darkest memories. Down she went, falling through space and time. First toward the Earth. Then toward the ground. Then into the ground. They just kept on falling.

Deeper and deeper and deeper and deeper and deeper.

Together on a journey taking them toward the guilt that Charlie had buried long, long ago.

Then suddenly it was there.

Revelation

Ella finds herself sitting in a chair, in a room. In a hospital room, looking upon a hospital bed positioned in front of her. Two previously blurred images are now in focus. Ebony is sleeping, never to awaken again. The child, a newborn baby girl, is crying out for her mother. A mother who can no longer help her.

Charlie sits in a chair next to the bed and stares into the distance. A nurse lifts the baby and gently lays the tiny bundle onto Charlie's lap. Charlie appears not to notice. He does not move. He shows no reaction. Time has stopped for Charlie.

A second nurse, to the right of Charlie, leans in to retrieve the bundle. From an awkward angle the baby is lifted into the air. The swaddling that the baby is wrapped in slips to reveal the baby's neck and Ella sees it. As clear as day Ella can see.

On the baby's neck is a distinct birthmark. A birthmark in the shape of a musical note. In an instant Ella knows the truth and her understanding of the universe is transformed. This baby's name is Mary. This baby is Ella's mother. Charlie is Ella's grandfather. Ebony is Ella's grandmother. Ella has found her family.

Before she can take another breath Charlie's memory whizzes forward. Weeks later, Charlie is still sitting, still stock still. He is sitting in a comfortable chair in a psychiatric hospital. A psychiatrist is talking at Charlie.

Ebony suffered a complicated birth. As a couple they were both already in their late forties. Having given up long ago, a child had not been planned. When it came to the birth blood was lost. A lot of blood was lost. The baby could be saved but Ebony could not.

Charlie was crushed. His psyche snapped, like a brittle twig, into two separate pieces. His initial reaction was not uncommon. His inability to recover from it was.

Time started moving forward at speed. Blurred images whizzing around in front of Ella's eyes. The sun was rising and falling, quicker and quicker.

Light then dark, light then dark. All that time he was sitting still, still still, still sitting in that chair. Those that knew best eventually arranged for the baby to be placed temporarily into care. Only until Charlie was recovered of course.

Time leapt forward again. Charlie was very much older and had come some way back to Earth. He never, however, managed a proper recovery. Cut loose from reality by the grief of losing his soulmate,

Charlie could not see past Ebony and eventually the baby fell from his thoughts as if it were never there. In all the years that followed Charlie never questioned after the baby. Instead, he had spent every waking hour in mourning for his lost beloved.

Mary Songg. She was the other person in Charlie's life. It was his guilt of letting her go that was truly stopping him from moving on. Ella felt the sensation of a warm tear trickle down her cheek. She then decided it was time for her to leave. It was time for her to let Charlie go.

xx lol xx

Having composed Charlie's narrative Ella already knew what came next. She decided then to leave Charlie in Jacob's safe hands and set up the final scenes of his story to run on without her.

Ella made her way back into the park. Looking around she eventually found an old red storage shed. The Everywhere Door creaked open obligingly.

Before entering Ella took one last look around. She said 'goodbye' out loud, then stepped through the doorway, back into The Distance.

Epilogue One

'I'll show them!' Angel thought to herself.

She was outdoors, hunched over, focused on trying to start a fire.

'I will teach them to laugh at me.'

Angel was working frantically, a little out of breath.

'I will show them who is the real leader around here.'

At that moment a spark took. The embers started to glow. 'Ha!' She thought triumphantly whilst blowing gently into her cupped hands. There it was, a tiny flame. Gently she committed the flame to the tiny pile of wood shavings she had prepared for kindling.

"What time did I get?" Angel asked aloud.

"Eighteen minutes, seventeen seconds. Not bad but, unfortunately for you, not as good as my time."

"Damn it, Bea! How is it you're always beating me?"

"Well Angel, you either got it or you don't."

The statement was followed with a laugh.

"Fair enough." Angel conceded, adding a laugh of her own.

Angel then turned to address the small crowd of young teenagers that were gathered around the pair.

"Red team. I'm afraid I was a little slower than Beatrice. Points for this round go to the blues."

The announcement was met with an equal measure of cheering and groaning from the group.

"But the good news..." Angel continued, "...is that we now have two fires, which means double the amount of barbeque tonight."

This time the crowd cheered in unison.

"Okay then. Who wants burgers?"

A wave of hands appeared in the air.

A good number of years had passed, since Angel's experience as a wasp. Following that experience Angel made a vow, to herself, to be a better person. She vowed to become a real leader. To only lead those that chose to follow, that wanted to follow. Those who were inspired by opportunities to grow and learn, not inspired by fear. Angel wanted to be the example, not the rule.

The very first thing she did though was seek out and apologise to Beatrice. After making up Angel shared her desires to change, and Beatrice agreed that she would help.

Beatrice sought out volunteer opportunities for Angel, where she could start getting more involved in the community and learn new skills. Eventually Angel volunteered at the local youth club.

Funding had been cut so the club was desperate for volunteers to assist with activities for the young attendees. The club gave these kids somewhere to go other than the streets. Angel soon found she was a natural fit and quickly became an essential member of the team.

Then one day, out of nowhere, a private benefactor appeared and started putting funds into the youth centre. Said benefactor set up several scholarship funds, one of which was offered to Angel.

Angel went on to study and qualify as an Outdoor Educator. As part of this process, Angel, with her friend Beatrice, established an outward-bound group at the youth centre and, thanks to the continued funding of the beneficiary, the pair were able to take the kids on regular excursions.

Angel was now teaching and inspiring children from backgrounds just like hers. Instilling values, confidence and kindness. Looking ahead, Angel and Beatrice were working on a plan to roll their programme out nationwide. Angel had found a place in the world and the world had welcomed her with open arms.

xx lol xx

Mick the Fish, following his time under the sea, also awoke as a new person. He had realised how completely and utterly pointless it was to be hoarding his wealth and instantly got to work on distributing his monies, to the people and places where it could do the most good.

One project he had taken particular pleasure in was the funding of the local youth centre. The scholarship scheme he put in place had already helped change the lives of many within the local community. The knock-on effect would help change and inspire the lives of many more. Mick had also stepped in with help to reopen the local food bank. By tapping up several business associates Mick had been able to set up a charity that would ensure the bank's long-term survival.

With regards to his existing loans business, after waking up the first thing that Mick did was to go into the office and give all his staff an immediate pay increase. He then set to work slashing interest rates on all existing loans. He still needed to turn a profit, but this would now be in line with what the business needed, as opposed to all the trappings of wealth that he had previously believed were desirable.

On Mick's books were several loans that had been running for excessively long terms. So, the next thing that Mick did was make personal visits to all of those affected. He compared the interest that had been charged over the term against what the interest rate would be had the loan been offered today. He then wrote a cheque for the difference and presented this back to the individuals in question.

Winston was one of those to benefit. After recovering from shock Winston was able to clear his other debts outright, with money left to spare. He used the excess to start up a new mechanic business, ensuring this time that everything was above board.

For Madi, Angel's mum, the situation was more complicated. A little dangerous even. So, Mick went further. First, he secured her a new two bed flat by the docks. Then he employed Madi to train and work in his shop. As for Madi's ex, well... Mick still knew a few people from his dad's old days and that situation was quickly resolved.

Mick's heart was broken when he learnt that Bob's heart had, literally, broken. Mick stepped in to arrange a funeral, and personally covered all associated expenses. Bob was given a beautiful service at the local church and Mick was genuinely surprised to see so many people turn out for the service. It was a shame, he thought, that these people did not come when Bob was still here. Bob was allocated a prime spot in the graveyard. A headstone, in the finest quality blue marble, was ordered to mark the spot.

After the funeral Mick came to visit the grave at least once a month, so that Bob would not feel alone. Today Mick was accompanied by someone special. A cherry tree, overhead, was shedding its bloom, rose-pink petals settling on the ground like confetti.

"Well Bob." Mick said aloud. "We finally did it. We finally got married."

Mick gently squeezed Mary's hand, triggering a rush of warmth to surge from her heart, as her heart forged the moment into a memory. A moment that would now remain as part of the cosmos for eternity.

xx lol xx

Unlike the others the Rt Hon Josh Robertson had chosen to remain putrid following his time in The Distance. If anything, he had become even more disgusting, his sense of entitlement increased. Time, however, was not to be as rewarding to Josh as it had been to the others.

Josh was found dead in his kitchen, discovered by his butler, not more than four weeks after he had returned. Investigating officers, Orwell & Huxley, found that Josh had died following a night out.

Another fundraiser for retired MPs, meals and drinks covered by the taxpayer. Apparently, Josh ate very little at the event. This was because he had developed a penchant for eating raw meat, following his experience in The Distance. Not just raw. Josh preferred his meat on the turn and had taken to leaving produce on the side, rather than in the refrigerator.

Being at a meal all night, but not wanting to eat any courses, had been torturous for Josh. When he finally arrived home, he was ravenous. Josh tore open a large packet of mincemeat and dived in face first. He attacked his meal with such gusto that he had soon shoved too much meat into his mouth to chew. The condensed meat lodged in his throat.

Josh could not get a breath. A Violent panic rose up within him, sweat dripping from his forehead, unable to call out for help. It was then that he turned and found Ivy, standing there, scythe in hand, facing him, a huge smile spread out upon her bony face.

Soiling himself was Josh's last physical act within this realm, which he did, right before Ivy swung her scythe and decapitated him.

Meanwhile At Gangle Manor

"So, you are saying that the old man..."
"Charlie."
"Yes. The old man Charlie. You are saying he was in fact your grandfather?"
"Yes."
"And you didn't know that until you helped him transition?"

"Yes."

"Because you saw your mum as a baby?"

"Yes."

"But you met the old man..."

"Charlie."

"Yes. You met Charlie, like years ago in your chip shop?"

"It wasn't my chip shop but yes. Sort of. He gave me a special 50 pence piece. Sort of."

"But then you said he died. Before you came to live in The Distance."

"Well, he was murdered. At least that's what I thought at the time. I'm not so sure now."

"Wow. And then you came to The Distance and that's when you met your grandmother, Ebony?"

"Yes. I met her right before I met Sid for the first time."

"But she didn't tell you anything?"

"Well how could she? I would never have believed her anyway. Besides, I wasn't sure then if I was dreaming or not."

"This is so mad. So, like the old man..."

"Charlie."

"Yes. The old man Charlie thought he was all on his own in the world and all the time his own granddaughter was there, serving him his chips."

"Yes."

"Whoa. That is so cosmic, 'cus he's what inspired you to come here, and you would never have found out about him otherwise right?"

"Maybe."

"Wow. It's all just blowing my mind right now."

The conversation went on like this into the early hours. One of a million similar conversations that the pair could eventually have over the coming one thousand years or so.

Epilogue Two

The Everywhere Door slowly creaked open.

A tall man, wearing a dark hoodie, steps through the door.

He turns to look at the door.

He finds he has emerged from an old wooden storage shed.

The shed is red.

'This is it.' The man thinks to himself.

'This is the last thing I will do for him.' He thinks to himself again.

'After I have done this, I am done. I am going to tell him, no more.'

The tall man, wearing a dark hoodie, is angry.

If it were daytime, if you could see his face, you would see that the tall man, wearing a dark hoodie looked tired.

Very tired.

The man had been under the employ of his current boss for many years.

The man was working, wanting to buy something back. Something he had given away.

The man had done terrible things.

The man decided he had just one more terrible thing to do.

He moved away from the shed, out into the park.

Finding a suitable spot to linger he fell back into the shadows.

Moments passed.

His target shuffled into view.

The tall man, wearing a dark hoodie, waited a moment. He ensured the coast was clear.

The tall man, wearing a dark hoodie, crossed over a section of the park.

The tall man, wearing a dark hoodie, emerged into the children's area.

The tall man, wearing a dark hoodie, was now in front of his target.

Ensuring again that the coast was clear, the man made his move.

The tall man, wearing a dark hoodie, appeared suddenly on the path, in front of the old man, shuffling his way through the park.

The old man, shuffling his way through the park, did not notice the tall man, wearing a dark hoodie, blocking the path in front of him.

The old man, shuffling his way through the park, did not notice the glint of serrated blade that the tall man, wearing a dark hoodie, held tightly in his left hand.

The tall man, wearing a dark hoodie, blocked the old man from further shuffling.

The tall man put his arm around the old man, placing his tall palm firmly onto the old back.

The tall man, wearing a dark hoodie, drew back his left arm, releasing it toward the old man that had been shuffling his way through the park.

The old man would shuffle no more.

The tall man, wearing a dark hoodie, sheathed the knife.

He grabbed the legs that had shuffled and dragged them into a copse of trees.

'Be sure to check the old man's pockets,' he had been told

He checked the old man's pockets.

The old man wheezed.

His last, maybe.

The tall man, wearing a dark hoodie, left the old man.

Alone.

The tall man, wearing a dark hoodie, made his way back to the shed.

He made his way back to the Everywhere Door that would take him back to him.

He approached the door.

He was overcome by a flush of heat.

The tall man wearing a dark hoodie, pulled down his dark hood so that his hot head might cool down.

Ella's father, a tall man, wearing a dark hoodie, took one last look around.

Bruce then pulled open the door and stepped through, back into The Distance

Final word

The Ballad of ~~Lord,~~ ~~Super,~~ Lady Gangles

When you lay to sleep at night
Eyelids closed, devoid of light
Dreamworld is the realm you seek
But through The Distance you must sneak
As you pass through unawares
The sound of chimes you may hear there
If all around your dreams come true
It means that she has come for you
A journey now that must take place
Of dark and light and sin and grace
Then when a choice is offered you
Don't miss your chance to start anew
It's not a trick. No deals. No angles
A chance to change is Lady Gangles
To choose to live your life anew
Don't waste the choice been offered you
When eyes reopen to the light
See this, a chance, to do things right

Amari Animate

Acknowledgements & Final Thought

Formal acknowledgement to Andrea Cook/Watts (my better half) - for naming the Equidistante and effectively handing me the key that unlocked everything else.

Random thanks to Neil DeGrasse Tyson (& Chuck) for helping me understand that I shouldn't worry about the fact that I don't understand Quantum physics. Just know that they are there, role with it, and all is good - I think.

Special thank you to Mr S J Smith for your review on Charlie. Self-doubt is crippling. I have no team & little idea what I am doing. Your review lifted me at a time in the writing of this book that I needed lifting & I am very grateful.

Finally thank you to everyone else for everything else.

& please forgive any spilleng, grammer or, mistackes

*

Writing Charlie, I was motivated by the idea of how people can be forgotten whilst they are still alive. Ella's Songg has at its heart the idea of being remembered after life.

After publishing Charlie my mum commented how it must be nice to leave something behind that people would remember you for. This got me thinking about who remembers who and for what etc. As I write, Google tells me the current global population stands at 8,123,115,050. No demographic data exists for 99% of all human existence but using the 1% we do have, experts propose a guestimate of 117 billion humans - so far born to this realm.

Based on sales of Charlie, of the 8.1 billion people alive today less than <0.000001% of them will have seen the book. Chances of being remembered - zero.

Considering a slightly more successful author, who wrote about a wizard, they can claim a global percentage of >6% having read their work. Very impressive, and will definitely be remembered - but for how long?

To the most successful book of stories we all know about then. Bit of a cheat as he didn't write it but, with estimated sales of over 5billion (Wiki) the central character will likely be remembered for some while to come. However, even this figure accounts for only 4.3% of all humans ever.

In the distant future, when we have integrated with AI & worked everything out, no longer tied to fragile bodies, the Earth obliterated by its own sun etc., chances are even he will have been forgotten. (at best regarded an historical curiosity by scholarly minds of that time).

The point I am looking to make is that it does not matter whether you are remembered or not. Apart from you and your closest, there's not a single entity anywhere in existence that really cares. Acceptance is liberating.

What matters is being here now. Right here, right now. The moments we share. Me writing these words. You, one of the few, reading them. The moments happened; they are happening. We will all be forgotten about in the end but this moment, and every moment you and I ever have, has no option but to last for eternity, simply because they happened. As time stretches lazily into the future, the moments will always exist. As we are now, we will always be. Not remembered but alive. Always being, always there, somewhere, in The Distance. Thank you to you then, the reader, for sharing this moment, and for ensuring our eternal existence.

References:
The Assassination of Bon Lemon *(p.275)* Loosely inspired by conspiracy theories (*emphasis on the word theories*) following John Lennon's murder on 08/12/1980.
An Angels Ascent *(p.281-282)*. Angel's Rally adapted from Winston Churchill speech, 13/05/1940
Hetty Green *(p.320)* a real person (please refer to Wiki). Died 03/07/1916.
Fishy Campaigning – Mick's 'top 5' *(p.349)* inspired by PM priorities delivered 04/01/2023
Everything else – completely made up :-)

Keep in touch and stay up to date by following us on our
Facebook page.

See here for a link:
https://sites.google.com/view/rosellahousepublishing/home